Routledge Studies in South Asian Politics

Poverty and Governance in South Asia

Syeda Naushin Parnini

Routledge
Taylor & Francis Group

LONDON AND NEW YORK

First published 2015
by Routledge
2 Park Square, Milton Park, Abingdon, Oxon OX14 4RN

and by Routledge
711 Third Avenue, New York, NY 10017

Routledge is an imprint of the Taylor & Francis Group, an informa business

British Library Cataloguing in Publication Data
A catalogue record for this book is available from the British Library

Library of Congress Cataloging in Publication Data
    Parnini, Syeda Naushin.
Poverty and governance in South Asia / Syeda Naushin Parnini.
      pages cm. – (Routledge studies in South Asian politics ; 5)
    Includes bibliographical references and index.
    1. Poverty–South Asia. 2. Poverty–Government policy–South Asia. 3.
South Asia–Economic policy. 4. South Asia–Politics and government–21st
century. I. Title.
    HC430.6.Z9P63452 2015
    339.4'60954–dc23
                    2014023311

ISBN: 978-0-415-73604-6 (hbk)
ISBN: 978-1-315-74193-2 (ebk)

Typeset in Times New Roman
by Taylor & Francis Books

MIX
Paper from
responsible sources
FSC
www.fsc.org   FSC® C013604

Printed and bound by CPI Group (UK) Ltd, Croydon, CR0 4YY

Contents

List of illustrations

Figures

Tables

Abbreviations

ACD	Asia Cooperation Dialogue
ADB	Asian Development Bank
ADP	Annual Development Plan
BCIM	Bangladesh, China, India, Myanmar Forum
BIMST-EC	Bay of Bengal Initiative for Multi-Sectoral Technical and Economic Cooperation
BRICS	Brazil, Russia, India, China and South Africa
CAS	Country Assistance Strategy
CBO	Community Building Organization
CIDA	Canadian International Development Agency
CPI	Corruption Perception Index
CPIA	Country Policy and Institutional Assessment
CSF	Coalition Support Fund
CSO	civil society organization
CSR	corporate social responsibility
DFID	Department for International Development
DP	development partner
DPT	Druk Phuensum Tshogpa (Bhutan Harmony Party)
DSC	Development Support Credit
EBRD	European Bank for Reconstruction and Development
ERD	External Relations Division
FDI	foreign direct investment
FPTP	first-past-the-post
FY	fiscal year
GDP	gross domestic product
GNI	gross national income
GST	Goods and Services Tax
HDI	Human Development Index
HDR	Human Development Report
HGI	Humane Governance Index
HNPSP	Health and Nutrition Population Sector Programme
HPSP	Health and Population Sector Programme
IBRD	International Bank for Reconstruction and Development

ICDB	Investment Climate and Doing Business
ICPD	International Conference on Population and Development
IDA	International Development Association
IFAD	International Fund for Agricultural Development
IFI	international financial institution
IMF	International Monetary Fund
IMR	infant mortality rates
JSA	joint staff assessment
LDC	less-developed country
MDG	Millennium Development Goal
MIC	middle-income country
MIRA	Maldives Inland Revenue Authority
MMA	Maldives Monetary Authority
MMR	maternal mortality rate
MNC	multinational corporation
MPND	Ministry of Planning and National Development
MTBF	Medium-Term Budgetary Framework
NGO	non-governmental organization
NSS	National Sample Survey
OD	Organizational development
ODA	official development assistance
PBSC	Palli Bidyut Sangram Committee
PDS	public distribution system
PESF-II	public expenditure support facilities
PFM	Public financial management
PFP	Policy Framework Paper
PIFM	PRSP Implementation Forum
PIU	project implementation unit
PoA	Plan of Action
PPP	Public Private Partnership
PRGF	Poverty Reduction and Growth Facility
PRS	Poverty Reduction Strategies
PRSC	Poverty Reduction Support Credit
PRSP	Poverty Reduction Strategy Paper
RCSC	Royal Civil Service Commission
REB	Rural Electrification Board
RMG	ready-made garments
SAARC	South Asian Association for Regional Cooperation
SAFTA	South Asian Free Trade Area
SAP	Structural Adjustment Program
SAPRIN	Structural Adjustment Participatory Review International Network
SAPTA	South Asian Preferential Trade Agreement
SBL	single borrower limit
SBO	social business organization

SIDA	Swedish International Development Cooperation Agency
SLFP	Sri Lanka Freedom Party
SOE	state-owned enterprise
SWAP	sector-wide approach
TGST	Tourism Goods and Services Tax
TNC	transnational corporation
UNDP	United Nations Development Programme
UNP	United National Party
USAID	US Agency for International Development
WGA	World Governance Assessment
WGI	World Bank Governance Indicators
WTO	World Trade Organization

1 Introduction

Introduction

In order to examine the connection between governance and poverty, this work provides case studies of governance reforms and poverty reduction strategies of seven countries in South Asia: Bangladesh, Bhutan, India, the Maldives, Nepal, Pakistan, and Sri Lanka. This study shows that South Asia can be an excellent comparative study, given the widespread emphasis on governance reforms in the region over the past two decades while highlighting significant inter-country diversity in terms of comprehensiveness of reforms and heavy concentration of poverty.

The concept of good governance was first introduced by the World Bank in the development discourse when they published a report in 1989 about Africa. At that time the World Bank argued that "Underlying the litany of Africa's development problem is a crisis of governance."[1] Thus, it can be argued that after the end of the cold war, "good governance" emerged as a fashionable buzzword in the development discourse.[2] The concept of governance makes explicit a paradigm shift from a traditional development economics approach towards a development politics approach. Since 1989, the "good governance" concept has become prominent on the international aid front. The World Bank defines governance as "the exercise of political power to manage a nation's affairs." The officials of the World Bank and the International Monetary Fund (IMF) argue that providing foreign aid to developing countries remains necessary but that good governance plays a crucial role in adapting to the process of globalization.

A number of significant criticisms, however, have contested the free-market fundamentalism and globalization discourse typical of the 1990s and the Washington Consensus.[3] This gave rise to a period of more socially aware governance. Of course, globalization has numerous facets. One particular version of interest here focuses on the way in which state functions seem to be being gradually subsumed under broader institutional constructs.[4] Surprisingly, in this new century, the major threats to the global financial system have come not only from the periphery but from the core.[5]

There has been a complex worldwide expansion, driven by the diffusion of power and influence through international financial institutions (IFIs) such as the World Bank or the IMF as well as the growing salience of private, civil society organizations and other non-state actors. These twin forces have had a profound effect upon the role and capacity of states to pursue national welfare options and have also posed a challenge to development, particularly in South Asian countries. However, states still remain significant actors in world politics, by contesting globalization and the market orthodoxies of the earlier "Washington Consensus" era through active public engagement that has brought to the public sphere a meta-politics of institutional legitimacy in which the procedures of the global governance are subjected to greater public scrutiny. The question is whether or not this process itself is legitimate. After all, the efficiency models of governance are popular among the policy communities that inhabit the corridors of the IMF, the World Bank and World Trade Organization (WTO), but these models can easily be contested.[6]

In the era of globalization, intense intellectual debate about development has been embodied in an ideological choice between either the state or the economic forces of the market as the source of a country's overall progress. Since the early 1990s, modernization theorists, neo-Marxists and neo-liberal thinkers have contributed to the debate. The post-cold war era has witnessed a reorientation of the development discourse; the novelty of this trend has been attributed, by the donor agencies, to the good governance agenda. The impetus of this change came from the experience of the failed postcolonial "development states" of the Third World, the demise of the communist bloc and the desire to identify the social forces which had arisen to challenge or overthrow authoritarian states in socialist countries, such as in Central and Eastern Europe.[7]

The recent changes in development discourse lie in the triumph of neo-liberalism over communism after the end of the cold war; it is primarily this triumph that produced the good governance perspective in the early 1990s. At that time, the notion pushed forward the "culture" of "the market," of deregulation, privatization and supply-side economics. This "culture" carried, along with its economic theory, strong normative views on the role of the state.[8] Although it promotes initiatives that enable citizens to claim and exercise their rights, neo-liberalism also advocates institutional changes that seek to make governance more responsive and accountable.[9] However, making real the rights, policies and processes that can deliver the promise of better governance remains a challenge and a far cry from current reality, hindered by entrenched power relations, persistent prejudices and inequalities.

Key arguments

This study explains the dynamics of poverty and governance including neo-liberal reforms, poverty reduction strategies and civil society participation viewed as the criteria of overall development. We also try to explore those aspects of governance problems that have challenged the local development and governance systems in South Asia. In particular, this book pays special attention to the neo-liberal development agenda[10] intertwined with governance reforms.

This has emerged from development theories influenced by historical colonialism in the developing countries of South Asia.

The central argument of this study warrants the claim that the end of the cold war and the rising concern to sustain US hegemony have led to the notion of creating a new "empire" in the era of globalization. The international development agencies, i.e. the World Bank, the IMF and other international organizations, are largely dominated by the US hegemonic power. The present conditions of political and economic failure that are peculiar to South Asian society have made their impact much more evident in recent decades. In this work, we argue that discussions of the poverty dynamics and governance problems in the context of South Asia have not attended adequately to the ways in which the discourses and consequences are properly understood. Our research uses evidence from South Asia to question current approaches to development learning and to consider the viability of the frequent introduction of new development agenda and poverty reduction strategies in recent years.

We build on the discussion by showing its relevance to the question of globalization. We argue that an increasingly multilateral aid agencies' concept of "good governance" today poses new challenges to weak governance and mixed developmental outcomes in South Asia. After developing the hypothesis of a state with both weak and competent governance (see Figure 1.2 on p. 15), we paint a vicious cycle of governance weaknesses to show how countries in South Asia remain weak in ensuring good governance to reduce poverty. We suggest that attention to the indigenous systems of governance and genuine democracy might be the guide to becoming a country with competent governance.

The most crucial section of our study, however, concerns the reasons for weak governance and poverty along with the governance agenda as it is set by the development partners and governments of individual countries in South Asia. The arguments are based on insights from various case studies in South Asia. In recent years, solid supportive evidence has begun to emerge that witnesses the results of the Poverty Reduction Strategies (PRS), the public sector reforms, the Millennium Development Goals (MDGs) as well as an increasing focus on "civil society" to accelerate development in the countries of South Asia.

Some scholars emphasize the negative effects of weak governments on rent seeking and, ultimately, economic growth. Weak governments that constantly are in fear of losing office are likely to be vulnerable to the pressure of lobby groups, which bias economic policies in favor of some groups at the expense of economic growth (Shleifer and Vishny 1993). An extensive literature supports the links between strong governance institutions and economic growth. The uncertainty associated with an unstable political context reduces investment and the rate of economic growth, which further contributes to political instability (Barro and Lee 1994). The high likelihood of a change of government is associated with uncertainty about the economic policies of a new government. Risk-averse economic elites and foreign investors hesitate to invest in economies which show uncertainty about policies and property rights (e.g., Alesina *et al.* 1996). Furthermore, foreign and domestic economic elites will shy away from investing in economies where bureaucrats have high levels of discretion, and they are subject neither to the oversight of state agencies nor to the scrutiny that is intrinsic to competitive elections (Beazer 2012).

Due to the individual countries' particular political settlement, most South Asian countries show rampant government corruption, fierce political competition, relatively inefficient bureaucracies, and weak political leadership. Moving from periods of military rule and strong one-party rule, the dynamics of political contestation in most South Asian countries have settled on a system of competitive clientelism, dominated by rival political parties, which compete on divergent views of nationalism rather than on economic ideology and policies. In recent years, successive governments in South Asian countries have pursued policies emphasizing privatization and export-led growth.

Conceptualizing poverty and governance

Poverty can be defined as a multifaceted crisis and a state of want or utter deprivation, caused by ignorance, unfair exploitation as well as natural disaster. Generally, a person is said to be poor when his inability to cope affects him both internally psychologically and externally. Poverty is sometimes not viewed as being closely connected to a person's system and will result in impatience, irritability, stress, anxiety, an inferiority complex, general fears and worries. Poverty can be viewed as having a physical effect on a person, such as family problems, poor nutrition, poor health, illiteracy, shabby appearance and lack of shelter and clothing.

Poverty is currently viewed in both an absolute and a relative sense. In the absolute sense, it is referred to as a condition of acute physical wants, starvation, malnutrition, disease, and lack of clothing, lack of shelter and almost total lack of medical care. Relative poverty, unlike absolute poverty, is more a matter of a subjective definition than the objective condition. Poverty, being a relative concept, is not confined to poor nations alone. Absolute poverty is understood as the condition of falling below the minimum standards of subsistence appropriate to each society. Absolute poverty is a growing phenomenon in both developing and industrialized countries.

The meaning and dimensions of poverty vary from situation to situation. There is no universally applicable measure or yardstick to describe poverty. However, efforts have been made by economists and other social scientists to define the term poverty. Gillin, for instance, defines poverty as:

> That condition in which a person, either because of inadequate income or unwise expenditures does not maintain a scale of living high enough to provide for his physical and mental efficiency and to enable his natural dependents to function usefully according to the standard of society of which he is a member.[11]

Thus, with a view to making individuals meaningful, functioning members of the society, every society has certain standards of living regarding minimum food, clothing, shelter, education and other amenities. Those who fall below this culturally prescribed standard, popularly known as the poverty line, are classified as poor.[12] According to the definition of the Canadian International Development Agency (CIDA), income-related poverty is defined by the following characteristics:[13] basic needs cannot be satisfied due to a lack of income and means; the prerequisites for acquiring an income and means are lacking. The ability to overcome this situation is absent. Especially in the poorest countries, which are subject to general conditions that impede development and can usually not be addressed by "good governance," present development approaches are increasingly directed towards self-help. However, the above definition of income-related poverty suggests that, due to the absence of resources, the poor have no self-help potential, and that the inability to extricate oneself from the poverty trap is the typical mark of the very state of poverty.

In ancient India, poverty was generally explained in terms of sin. The doctrine of Karma, which developed in India in the pre-Christian era, attributed poverty to the personal misdeeds of the individual in past lives. Buddhism shared with Hinduism this doctrine of Karma and the explanation of poverty. Original Christianity visualized poverty as a part of the general calamity resulting from original sin. This tradition continued throughout the Middle Ages. Also wealth was considered to be an ultimate obstacle to spiritual progress.

A variant of the sin theory of poverty appeared in Europe with the development of capitalism and of individualism, the ideology of the political economy of capitalism. Poverty was attributed to indolence, laziness, and the unwillingness to work hard, a general lack of personal responsibility towards oneself, one's family and society. Montesquieu observed that "a man is poor not because he has nothing, but because he does not work."[14] Poverty was 'rediscovered' in the United States, in Britain[15] and somewhat later in Europe. After a period it was widely assumed that poverty should have been banished by the welfare state. In Britain, the whole debate was dominated by Peter Townsend's major study, based on research that started in the late 1960s. He aimed to break out of the liberal tradition by arguing that poverty should be defined in terms of 'relative' deprivation.[16] Sen, addressing poverty in countries with very different standards of living, argued that there was an irreducible element of absolute need in any viable conception of poverty.[17]

One of the theories which emerged in the early 1950s as an explanation of the general poverty of the new states was that of the 'vicious circle' of poverty, popularized among others by Ragnar Nurkse.[18] This theory had been formulated earlier by Gunnar Myrdal with reference to the poverty of the Negroes in the USA.[19] Nurkse and others merely extended and applied it to the countries of South Asia. Tropical climate changes, socio-historical and quasi-structural factors, such as the high rate of population growth in the Third World, are the major factors responsible for the mass poverty of this region. A detailed explanation of mass poverty in the Third World was given through cultural anthropology in Gunnar Myrdal's work, *Asian Drama*. He explained why most Global South and Southeast Asian societies have been unable to break out of the vicious circle of poverty. He argued that the institutions and attitudes there have remained pre-modern and virtually unchanged since ancient times. It is the rigidity of the institutions and attitudes which explains the inability of the countries of South Asia to break out of the vicious circle of poverty.[20]

Poverty has grown as a core problem of development and spread to such an extent that it now threatens social and political stability and is a serious obstacle to the attainment of sustainable development in South Asia.[21] Fortunately, with the world-wide recognition of the extent and depth of the problem, have come the knowledge, skill and capital to eradicate this blight on human insensitivity. There is mounting evidence that the general breakdown of human security and hopes for the future have much to do with poverty and injustice.[22]

Dismantling government controls to expand the private sector has accompanied domestic and foreign demands for more public scrutiny and popular participation to make state regimes more accountable and transparent to citizens and investors at home and abroad. A vast reinterpretation and reorientation of national government are occurring. States are officially intact, and nations remain the basis of development, but nation-states no longer control development. No wonder governance is now such a prominent concern in development discourse. No coherent set of institutions has the power and authority to establish norms and enforce rules that govern development.

The question is, how can development be governed today? The question is more than contentious, which can be analysed historically and spatially. As we have seen, imperialism established modern development regimes, which redesigned regional economies to serve the world of markets managed by imperial nations. The British Empire designed territories of development in South Asia, which nationalists captured and redesigned by disciplining markets inside independent states. Thus, the spatial framework of development shifted from empire to nation, in the middle decades of the twentieth century. In the past twenty years, another shift has occurred. States have lost much of their disciplining power over markets and thus their leadership role in development. As that has occurred, national territory has lost its definitive role as the spatial framework that determines who is authorized to govern development and which people development must serve. Territorial boundaries had previously defined the participants, populations, and priorities in the development process. Now the links between development and territory are ambiguous. The leaders of development have diversified, they are now scattered all over the world, and their border crossings are ubiquitous. Nation-states still define official territories of development, but national powers to govern development vary tremendously. In general, these powers decline as national wealth does, until they reach virtually zero in the world's poorest countries. Growing inequalities of wealth and power among nations are an increasingly visible feature of the development process, but also increasingly invisible in the-mainstream development discourse, which treats all countries as equally sovereign territories in the world of globalization.

The disproportionate influence of rich countries is pervasive globally, in government circles, business, finance, technology, international agencies, consumerism, education, media, fashion, language, and other realms. A new imperial formation is emerging and globalization today has much in common with globalization a century ago. Then there was the British Empire, now there is the US Empire. Even India, the most powerful economy and state in South Asia, has now succumbed under its current leadership to pragmatically strategic subordination to the USA. Yet imperial authority is a thing of the past. In a world of nations, it no longer provides legitimate governance. But most states cannot provide effective governance for development. So who then will govern development? Balanced precariously between the real power of contemporary imperialism and the real authority of nation-states, in the shifting sands of globalization, leadership in development today has no clear organizational guidelines. Leaders have disparate loyalties and priorities. Their institutions pursue disparate goals. Their relationships with one another are messy, filled with competition, conflict, resistance, and negotiation among old, new, emerging, and aspiring leaders. Television images of protesters at World Bank and WTO meetings, or G8 meetings, represent only the most visible surface of the disorderly contestation under way in development regimes today.

Globalization has caused a profound shift in global dynamics, driven by the fast-rising new powers of the developing world like BRICS (Brazil, Russia, India, China and South Africa), and its long-term implications for human development. On the other hand, globalization has reflected on a process of growing inequality and social disparity between the rich and the poor. The UN Human Development Report (HDR) in 2013 pointed out that, in spite of real global economic growth, worldwide, human suffering is growing, particularly in developing countries.[23] More than one-third of developing countries have seen their average per capita income fall, leaving 1.2 billion people in poverty, living on less than US$1 per day. Nearly 60 countries are well off track from achieving the MDGs. In 2013, more than 40 countries in the developing world did better than had been expected in human development terms in recent decades, with their progress accelerating markedly over the past ten years.

The countries in the Asia Pacific region have performed relatively well and some of them have even achieved the largest decreases in poverty in human history. But sharp contrasts in the performance of individual countries remain and huge challenges still exist regarding the achievement of specific MDGs, in particular in South Asia.[24] For more than three decades now, these countries have continued their struggle for survival. Rather than pursuing rapid growth, the main focus is now on achieving equitable and pro-poor economic growth.

Since the UN Millennium Summit in September 2000, human poverty in its multi-dimensional aspects has become the prime focus of development, calling on the international community to give special attention to the less-developed countries (LDCs), including South Asian countries. In light of this, the Brussels Plan of Action (PoA) 2001–2010, adopted in June 2001 at the 3rd UN Conference on LDCs, singles out a number of cross-cutting priority issues and demands an increased focus on good governance at the national and international levels.

This work analyses the specific challenges that South Asian countries are currently facing and addresses the complex and context-specific nature of governance in its various dimensions. The aim of this work is to explore the magnitude and complexity of the problem of poverty and underdevelopment in South Asia. The poverty reduction strategy of any government in South Asia should be based on competent governance processes, aiming to adopt a pro-poor perspective where the poor can contribute to growth and human development. The scenario of poverty in South Asia will be discussed in detail and several programs of the governments and the international donors in South Asia to ensure good governance and reduce poverty will be evaluated. An important aim is to delineate the group which needs relatively specified targeting of free services such as health and education, access to the public distribution system, the benefits of employment generation and resource-building programs, that are in need of organizational assistance and empowerment on a priority basis.

Political underdevelopment

The studies of progressive realism conducted by Mick Moore and the analysis of quasi-states by Robert Jackson are interesting in the context of South Asia; when combined with a country's weak governance; they may also help explain the causes of underdevelopment. Moore's progressive realist approach is shaped by political underdevelopment in the developing countries while Jackson's concept of "quasi-states" is characterized by positive or negative sovereignty. Both theories have received a great deal of attention in recent times and are also relevant to the current study. Hirst states that sovereignty consists of both states' ability to make decisions independent of external authorities and their capacity actually to govern and also to have an effect at least on a respectable percentage of intended outcomes[25] This latter dimension of sovereignty, the capacity to govern, has long been lacking in many countries that attained independence in the great wave of decolonization from 1945–1975. In the case of the Indian subcontinent, India and Pakistan gained independence from the British colonial power in 1947 after having split into two parts, i.e. India and Pakistan. Bangladesh became East Pakistan, which gained independence from Pakistan in 1971 through a bloody liberation war.

Bhutan is a unique country which has been independent throughout its history and, like Nepal, has never been colonized by an outside power. A monarchy had ruled the country throughout most of its history and this country was never colonized. The elections for the assembly on 28 May 2008 overwhelmingly favored the abolition of the monarchy, paving the way for the establishment of a federal multiparty representative democratic republic. In the early twentieth century, Bhutan came into contact with the British Empire and Bhutan made the transition from absolute monarchy to constitutional monarchy in 2008 and its first general election was held in the same year. Ceylon was granted independence as the Dominion of Ceylon in February 1948. The Dominion status within the British Commonwealth was retained for the next 24 years until May 22, 1972, when it became a republic and was renamed the Republic of Sri Lanka.

The process of decolonization and the situation of the newly independent countries have been analyzed by Robert H. Jackson.[26] His work introduced a new term into the study of development, namely that of "quasi-states" (1991). The term "quasi-states" is now routinely associated with the limitations on independent action on the part of postcolonial states due to foreign economic intervention in the form of aid conditionality as set by the World Bank and the IMF. In this respect, Robert Jackson refers to positive and negative sovereignty and adopts the concept of "quasi-states."[27] This means that, even though states are recognized as equal through their membership of the United Nations, the developing countries lack the capacity to support themselves without outside assistance, let alone contribute to the international order. Stephen Krasner argues that the Westphalian model of sovereignty has never been an accurate description of many of the entities called "states," since breaches of the model have been an enduring characteristic of the international environment.[28] The Westphalian sovereign state model is based on the principles of autonomy, territory, mutual recognition and control. It is the central concept of the major theoretical approaches to international relations, where it is either an analytical assumption or a constitutive norm, and, as such, it provides a benchmark for analyzing variations to sovereignty.[29] Sovereignty is deeply embedded in world affairs as it provides an arrangement that is conducive to upholding certain values, which are considered to be of fundamental importance. Jackson created the term "quasi-state" to describe postcolonial states that had been internationally franchised and thus possessed the same external rights and responsibilities as all other sovereign states, that is, juridical statehood derived from the right of self-determination or negative sovereignty.

"Negative sovereignty" is defined as the freedom from outside interference, which is a formal-legal condition. However, at the same time, many countries lacked the institutional features of sovereign states as defined by classical international law and they had limited empirical statehood or positive sovereignty.[30] Positive sovereignty is where established states exercise effective dominion over their peoples and territories.[31] Jackson's negative sovereignty, as applied to quasi-states, was primarily involved in decolonization: it was the distinctive liberty acquired by the former colonies.[32] However, it is principally those ex-colonial states that are now likely candidates for failure. Therefore, Jackson's term "quasi-states" remains valid for many developing countries of Africa, though South Asian countries are neither failed states nor in the process of failure. Small countries in South Asia sometimes lack full autonomy in making economic decisions due to the fact that their development processes are more or less dependent on external assistance.

Robert H. Jackson's theories concur with the classical realist approach of Hans J. Morgenthau. Morgenthau's theory of "power politics" and Martin Wight's definition of classical international theory as the theory of survival in a historical reality are both relevant.[33] Quasi-states and their external support structures constitute a doctrine of negative sovereignty. Jackson argues that empirical differences and variations among states are greater today than ever before, owing to the globalization of international society.[34] The ways that inequality and underdevelopment spread and intensify as well as the ways they are addressed by international society have changed radically. Decolonization has added to the inequality by bringing into existence a large number of sovereign governments, that are in fact very limited in their capacity to govern. However, they wish to provide civil and socioeconomic goods for their populations and are supported by international society. Moreover, the Third World states have had the experience of colonialism. Both represent victims of past institutionalized discrimination and merit special consideration, compensation and assistance.[35]

Mick Moore[36] borrows many of Robert H. Jackson's insights,[37] especially when Moore argues that the political underdevelopment of much of the Global South largely results from the ways in which southern states have been created and political authority has been shaped through economic and political interactions with the Global North. The theories of both Jackson and Moore in international relations are in agreement with Morgenthau's classical realist thinking.[38] The policy goals and interests of most South Asian countries, as less powerful entities where state survival serves the prime concern, can be well understood in terms of the realist approach. This depicts a more 'realistic' notion of world politics while also allowing us to integrate domestic politics into the analysis in a conceptually consistent manner.

The realist view of nation-states as independent political communities is one that accords with much real-world dynamics notwithstanding their interdependent relations with other states, international donors, and with non-state actors. Another central tenet of realism is that the states are unitary, rational actors characterized by a decision-making process, leading to choices based on maximizing the national interest (Morgenthau [1948] 1985).[39] At a minimum, all political entities seek security; at most, they may have a more extensive agenda.[40] In realist terms, peace, justice and harmony are not simply achievable objectives. Classical realists recognize the existence of national organizations, international organizations, international donors and transnational financial institutions but take the view that the national organizations are the main instruments of states while the influence of the other agents on world politics is marginal.[41] This implies that governments are likely to marshal 'power' in an attempt to interfere in national and global markets to attain national interests in competition with other states, or in response to international donors, development aid agencies and non-state actors such as multinational corporations (MNCs), transnational corporations (TNCs) and international civil society in the global system (see Figure 1.1 on p. 15).

The progressive realist approach adopted by Mick Moore would require donors to be hard-headed about both the components and causes of good governance as well as about the political limits of Western intervention.[42] Moore pointed out four components of progressive realism: (1) balancing liberal projects and statist objects; (2) reducing the adverse effects of donors' presence and activities; (3) acting on evidence, such as the reason for misrule in the countries of the Global South and sources of income other than taxes levied on their citizens; and (4) a focus on encouraging better use of public money by Global South governments. Moore has supported a statement made by the British Department for International Development that Northern governments, which took a lead in strengthening international action, could enjoy more credibility if they invited the governments that receive their aid to reform themselves.[43]

Weak governance

Mick Moore argues that the states of the "South," though diverse, tend to be underdeveloped in the political sense: neither effective nor accountable to citizens.[44] The conventional response of aid donors is institutional transfer: trying to align the institutional configurations of Southern states even more closely with those of Northern polities. Moore warns that this may not be the best approach, however. The political underdevelopment of much of the Global South largely results, as he argues confidently, from the ways in which Southern states have been created and their political authority has been shaped through economic and political interactions with the wealthier countries of the Global North.

"Political underdevelopment" is claimed by Moore to be the result of uneven economic development. Moore further argues that a better appreciation of the nature of these processes of underdevelopment may lead to more appropriate policy. Our study echoes what Moore says about donor–recipient relations in the context of North–South discourse in world politics,[45] i.e. more attention should be paid to the ways in which Northern states currently help sustain development through local elites in the Global South, where the conditions under which state elites in the Global South rule can remain too independent of their own citizens.[46]

Actually, it is the poorer developing countries of the world that suffer from weak or bad governance. It is hard to challenge this claim because the empirical evidence is overwhelming. Even so, there is no consensus as to what actually constitutes good governance; and for most countries, few reliable (quantitative) indicators of the quality of governance are available. Nor can we realistically expect much consensus on the question of how closely poor governance and national poverty are connected. The Western donor agencies have the perception, inherited from colonial practice, that the governments of Third World countries, as Moore argues, are both: (1) ineffective, i.e. are unable to rule many of their nominal citizens or to pursue any kind of collective interest in an authoritative fashion; and (2) arbitrary, despotic and unaccountable. This kind of political underdevelopment is said by Moore to be a major cause of poverty and ills for many of the world's poorer people.[47] This can be said to be largely relevant in the context of the developing countries in South Asia.

The set of international factors, in different combinations, and in interaction with one another, has a strong influence on the current configurations of states in the Global South. The essence of these factors is simple: the states of the Global South are different from those of the Global North because they emerged into an international environment already dominated by the relatively rich and powerful Northern states. Politically, these Northern states have directly and indirectly created, shaped and controlled the states of the Global South. Economically, the wealth of the Northern states has created lucrative markets for many products from the Global South and provided strong incentives for groups within Southern states to control the marketing of these products.[48] Our analysis of South Asia supports Moore's general explanation of the causes of political underdevelopment. His central argument is that bad governance is neither inherent in the culture or traditions of the people of poor countries, nor a product of poverty.[49] It is rather the result of the ways in which state authority in the Global South has been constructed and is being maintained through economic and political interactions with the rest of the world.

International aid and development agencies have identified bad governance as a major obstacle to economic growth and improved welfare in poor countries. They are putting significant resources into trying to change that situation. Increasingly, aid is being made conditional upon performance and recipients' intentions in relation to governance issues, whether labeled corruption, institutional development, democracy, capacity building, transparency, rule of law, human rights or something else. It is striking that the inefficiency of the individual governments and the degree of intervention in politically sensitive issues have been noticed without giving much emphasis to a vigorous search for an explanation of the underlying reasons for the problem.

It can be asked why poor governance should be concentrated in poorer countries. The aid agencies and national governments appear not to have asked this question in any sustained way.[50] Yet, their answer to the question is implicit in their behavior. The reason appears to be some notion of institutional deficit. It is argued that poor countries lack the appropriate governance institutions, whereas those institutions are found in rich countries: they come in the shape of auditor-generals, police academies, independent central banks, legislative committees, responsible municipal governments, freedom of information laws, judicial autonomy, public policy research institutes, and many other things. Both the donor agencies and national governments in South Asia and elsewhere have largely different perceptions to address the major reasons for governance problems.[51]

The current study accepts Moore's arguments regarding the roots of political underdevelopment which shows the donors and national governments better ways of dealing with the Global South. It is ironic that aid donors and national governments focus on institutional transfer when the institutional configurations of poor states are in most cases already very similar to those of the developed states. From an historical perspective, the states of the world have never appeared more similar to one another than they do at present.[52] This emphasis on institutional transfer, of course, in part reflects the absence of alternative ideas about how aid money can be spent efficiently to improve governance.[53]

Our study reflects the view that weak governance and underdevelopment in the poor Third World result from the ways in which Southern states have been created and political authorities have been shaped through interactions with the wealthier Northern countries in the context of global economic and political systems. Moore is probably correct when he claims that political underdevelopment stems to a large degree from what might be termed a disconnect between states and citizens. Compared with the states of the advanced world, those of the poor world tend to be relatively independent of their citizens: they have sources of finance and other critical resources through which they are able to use international connections and resources to rule over their citizens in a relatively unrestrained fashion.

In poorer countries, public authority has been constructed in a context in which there was less bargaining between states and (organized) citizens than was the norm during the process of state construction in the Global North. In the Global South, state elites have more often either ignored their citizens or related to them more coercively. The governments have been able to do so because of the resources and support they (as state elites) could garner from their relations with other states, the international state system and international markets. We cannot say that the poor states are basically similar. It is true that they appear relatively homogeneous in their formal organizational characteristics, but in fact they are very diverse in their actual functioning.[54]

Analytical framework: paradigm of weak and competent governance

It is now widely acknowledged that institutions matter (e.g., protection of property rights, rule of law) in economic development (North 1991). Arrangements and rules are implemented in widely different ways across countries. At the core of the problem is an under-appreciation of how the relative power of organizations in a given society (what North *et al.* 2007 call the "social order") affects the understanding and enforceability of institutional rules (Khan 2011; North *et al.* 2009).

In particular, our analysis recognizes the importance of a society's macro-political equilibrium or what we call the "political settlement" in shaping a country's particular institutional arrangement, organizations and policies. Following Khan (2011), we define the political settlement as a combination of institutions and a distribution of power between organizations (e.g., political parties, the military, and bureaucracy) that is reproducible over time. Once a particular political settlement emerges, the relative power of different organizations is relatively stable and evolves along predictable paths. Empirically, these paths differ across countries. Unlike advanced economies, the distribution of power between organizations in developing countries typically does not allow the enforcement of many formal institutions such as property rights. Rather, these institutions are informally modified or partially enforced to ensure that the distribution of benefits is in line with the actual distribution of power, and many organizations informally operate to ensure these outcomes. This understanding sheds light on why institutions and organizations that appear to be very similar in their formal descriptions actually operate very differently in various countries.

Governance problems in South Asian countries are identified as a major cause of poverty and underdevelopment. In addition, the paradoxes also arise from a notion of a state–civil society debate for creating self-managed governance by making grassroots democracy work for the overall development of South Asia. Progressive realism and classical realist approaches are important in order to address the survival of small states in South Asia by figuring out the proper causes of underdevelopment and the crisis of governance, such an analysis may help locate appropriate development goals for the countries in South Asia.

The increased emphasis on market-based solutions naturally had its influence on the full range of ideas about governance. As a result, the recent neo-liberal bias has influenced many useful insights on the nature of institutions in structuring dissent and, under many circumstances, in promoting accountability.[55]

The good governance agenda can be described in terms of correcting perverse organizational incentives, unblocking institutional bottlenecks, diversifying civil society and reorienting its interface with state agencies, and other such 'technical' solutions. By adopting this agenda and its concomitant terminology, external agencies and national elites were able to disavow any interference in the domestic politics of the states in which they operated.

This study has proposed ensuring an autonomous role for all national actors within the competent governance of a state where international actors can act as facilitators (see Figure 1.1). Starting out from theories by the classical realists Robert Jackson and Mick Moore, this study develops a paradigm of weak and strong governance of a state. As can be seen in Figure 1.2, the weak and competent governance paradigms refer to competent governance under a sovereign and an autonomous state. In the context of South Asian countries, this involves the identification and analysis of various critical issues such as the limitations of the current governance programs and their implementation process. Understanding the root causes of weak governance and inventing tools to overcome these weaknesses to create competent governance are a crucial challenge facing South Asian countries. Ensuring an autonomous and indigenous governance system as well as attaining governability is critically important to reduce poverty and accelerate development in South Asia (Figure 1.2).

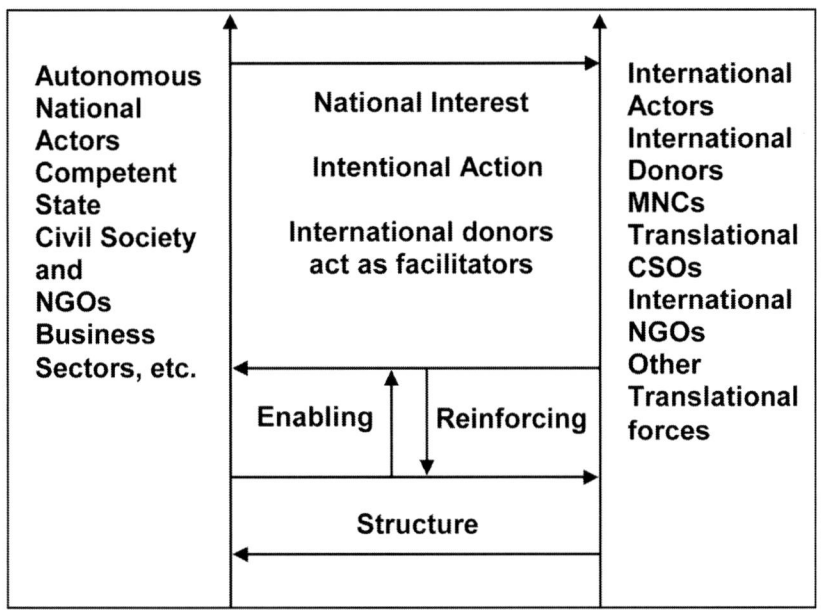

Figure 1.1 Autonomous national actors and international actors as facilitators

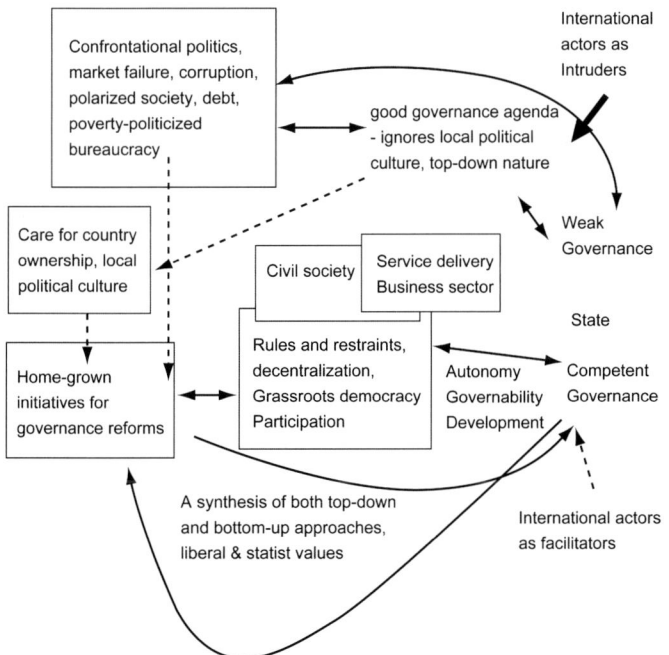

Figure 1.2 Weak and competent governance nexus

In Figure 1.2, we see states in South Asia that are continuously weak with weak governance due to domestic problems intertwined with a fragile democratic regime. This is believed to be causing a vicious circle of ever weaker governance and worsening underdevelopment to some extent.[56] Weak governance and underdevelopment can coincide with the paradigm of weak governance of states in South Asia. We can thus formulate the hypothesis that the current neo-liberal development programs intertwined with the "governance" agenda and poverty reduction strategies are hardly producing the best result to improve governance in South Asia. However, it is also possible for the donors to act as facilitators (see Figure 1.1) and to care for country-specific conditions on the basis of the indigenous governance process, allowing the recipients to run their own affairs autonomously. Political will and homegrown initiatives based on the local political culture can help create competent governance in South Asia. This has the potential to give rise to an indigenous process of democracy and governance in South Asian countries, and to the establishment of political norms that can reduce poverty and foster socio-economic development catering to local needs and demands. The countries in South Asia obviously have the potential to become states with "competent governance" on the basis of their own indigenous process of governance.

In a state of competent governance (see Figure 1.2), there will be a synthesis of both the top-down and bottom-up approaches as well as a cross-fertilization of statist and liberal values through decentralization, endogenous grassroots democracy and a set of credible state–society relations under a competent state-run governance system. All these homegrown processes can help initiate a competent governance system with autonomy and governability and can promote genuine development in the context of South Asia and elsewhere in the developing world. Moore's definition of political development can be applied to the paradigm of weak and competent governance. The paradigm of the state with a competent governance echoes Moore's definition of political development as the extent to which: (1) states exercise legitimate authority within their territorial borders and in interactions with other states, non-state actors and extra-territorial authorities; and (2) legitimate authority stems from the binding consultation with citizens and is exercised with regard for the preferences of citizens.[57]

The hypothesis is that there is a need to introduce more competitive and competent economic and political systems in the countries of South Asia, and also there is a need to ensure the presence and strength of the domestic forces committed to institutional change and sustainable development. To facilitate this process, it would be appropriate to use the elements of the weak and competent state paradigm shown in Figure 1.2 as a template to define the economic, political and legal institutions necessary to address predation, poverty and development in general. Local history and political culture can be expected to influence the exact nature of the institutions that will emerge in South Asia. Our line of reasoning also indicates, however, that fundamental scope remains for international donor agencies to facilitate the reduction of global inequality. To do so efficiently and effectively, they need to respect the sovereignty of South Asian countries in supporting the establishment of their own institutions, i.e. institutions that are more favorably disposed to productive activities and behavior on the basis of the indigenous process. Moore's progressive realist approach and Jackson's concepts as well as Henri Lefebvre's work[58] on state–society relations mesh well with the new interpretation of a state with weak or competent governance (see Figure 1.2). This is particularly important when we try and account for South Asia's current situation in the context of donor–recipient relationships and the "governance" agenda.

The governance structure, as argued in this study, is explicitly designed to produce a competent governance system (see Figure 1.2) with full state autonomy and autonomous national actors free from non-coercive external interventions (see Figure 1.1). Liberals view state power primarily as a (potential) threat to the well-being of citizens, and define "good governance" primarily in terms of legal, constitutional and other arrangements that protect against this threat. They include terms like responsiveness, accountability, democracy and participation.

By contrast, statists see the state primarily as a means of aggregating power and resources that may be used for the collective good. In their view, the weakness of government manifests itself as disorder, vulnerability to external threat, or failure to provide public services. Statists therefore tend to interpret "good governance" in terms of arrangements that promote the coherence and effectiveness of the state. They warn against loss of authority, order, capability and autonomy.[59] Despite occasional proclamations of a revival since its heyday in the arms of modernization theory in the 1950s and 1960s, the concept has largely dropped out of academic usage. Evidently, for 'diplomatic' reasons, the term 'political development' does not enter into the contemporary vocabulary of international organizations concerned about issues they label as "governance."

Moore uses the concept of 'political development' in a targeted way, to address a specific set of issues. Moore says that there are many countries in the world that signally fail to meet either the liberal or the statist criteria for reasonable governance. These states are both (1) relatively ineffective, i.e. are unable to rule many of their nominal citizens or to pursue any kind of collective interest in an authoritative way; and (2) relatively arbitrary, despotic and unaccountable. The two kinds of failure tend to go together most of the time. Correspondingly, states that score high on liberal values (responsiveness, accountability, democracy, etc.) also tend to score high on statist values (authority, order, ability, etc.).

The notion of a trade-off and conflict between liberal and statist values,[60] which animates so much political thought and routine political debate, does not appear relevant at this level of broad cross-national comparisons. At the cross-national level, the two sets of values are complementary rather than contradictory. Weak governance in those countries that score low on both sets involves governments that exercise little authority and, insofar as they rule, do so in an arbitrary and unaccountable manner. Understanding a state with weak and strong governance is the object of the current study. A state with weak governance in South Asia needs to balance the neo-liberal and statist values and components in order to become a state with competent governance and thus to achieve, as suggested by Moore and Jackson, the country's main development goals.

A competent governance system (see Figure 1.2) should have strong authority and a form of legitimacy that is neither exerted in a visible manner nor manifested in day-to-day administrative relations. Instead, the system should be seen as an organizing grid within which the local bodies must help improve efficiency, provide quality service delivery, preserve macroeconomic stability, and not least of all, ensure strong governance and indigenous democracy. The reorganization of relations between the state and local bodies is to occur through a set of legislative rules that will provide an almost, if not wholly, constitutional framework that will regulate the decisions of local bodies, and accord the central government powers to discipline local bodies if they do not sufficiently regulate themselves. Within the logic of management reorganization, decentralization can be understood as a social space "produced" (in a literal sense) in which social relations are rationalized within an abstract and objectified grid of a competent state.

Significance

The research methodology in this book is based on both primary and secondary data. A field survey was conducted both at the central and local levels in South Asia. At the central level, 122 persons were interviewed: government officials, donor agency officials, academics, journalists and civil society activists. At the local level, we studied 456 people in two urban and rural towns in South Asia.

A qualitative research approach is adopted here in this study. Such a method is noted by scholars as particularly apt for explanatory research in areas where little prior research has been conducted and where the aim is to gain familiarity with a problem or to generate new insights for future research.[61] The author of this study spent six months in the selected development project areas in urban and rural areas in South Asian countries. Mostly, the source of data was through conducting several unstructured and open-ended interviews. These interviews were followed up with a set of semi-structured interviews where the author focused on specific issues that were discovered from the unstructured interviews. Each interview ranged from a minimum of 30 minutes to a maximum of two hours. The author interviewed 578 respondents in total. The aim was to select representatives from various levels and various organizations in order to reduce specific biases. To achieve that neutrality, the author selected and interviewed government officials, donor agency officials, academics, journalists and civil society activists as well as field-level representatives and people in the villages where the development projects are in operation. The author was able to obtain information from government officials in charge of the World Bank section and also officials of the donor agencies in charge of the sections of governance and Poverty Reduction Strategies (PRS) in different South Asian countries. The author also managed to interview members of civil society, think tanks and other civil society groups, representatives of Transparency International, stakeholders and village people in New Delhi, Kerala, Dhaka, Kathmandu, Colombo, Thimphu, Islamabad and Male.

When the first round of unstructured interviews began, the author asked the informants to describe their views on and experience with democratization and governance reforms through public sector reforms, MDGs, the Poverty Reduction Strategy Paper (PRSP) as well as sector-wide approaches run by different projects under the Poverty Reduction Strategies in different South Asian countries. For that reason, the author conducted another set of interviews with the concerned villagers and asked them about the activities of the Health and Population Sector Programs and the Health, Nutrition and Population Sector Program, as well as sector-wide projects on health and education. The author conducted many interviews with several informants and compared comments given by various people, both at the central and local levels, on a particular issue to increase consistency and validity of the data (Yin 1984). We also collected data through direct observation: we observed several meetings between the World Bank officials and government officials in South Asia as well as attending a number of field-level meetings between project participants and the accompanying project personnel on site visits, this was mainly to understand the project dynamics. By asking respondents from various organizations and also from the sample areas open-ended questions, and by comparing different opinions and comments made by them, the author was able to arrive at an understanding of the effects of democratization and the governance agenda, public sector reforms and PRS on South Asian countries.

The aims of this study are to examine the following two questions. First, can South Asian countries achieve their development goals to reduce poverty in this region? Second, to what extent can the development agenda be appropriate to strengthen the quality of governance in South Asian countries and what should be done to improve genuine good governance by reducing poverty? In this work, several empirical issues and case studies in the context of South Asia are examined.

The move towards promoting good governance, both as an objective and as a precondition for economic development in South Asian countries, is, however, underway. It is hard to measure countries in terms of either good or bad governance. In reality, most of the poor and developing countries in South Asia are situated somewhere in-between. Some South Asian countries such as India, Pakistan and Bangladesh have not been able to reduce poverty despite having democratic institutions.[62] On the other hand, rapid economic growth and massive reduction in poverty levels have occurred in several Asian countries that did have poor governance structures and authoritarian regimes.[63]

The question is whether the flows of aid to South Asian countries have had the desired impact on growth and poverty, and if not, what modifications need to be introduced so that the development objectives can be achieved. A related concern of this book is to investigate the impact of the spread of markets on patterns of social organizations and state–society relations under the framework of governance reforms. Consequently, we will also address in our study the empirical issues and impacts of governance agenda on economic development and poverty reduction in South Asia. Other chapters will propose different approaches to overcome chronic poverty through governance reforms, which involves building grassroots institutions through endogenous governance and restructuring macroeconomic policies.

Notes

1 World Bank, *Sub-Saharan Africa: From crisis to sustainable growth* (Washington, DC: The World Bank, 1989).
2 Smith, B., *Good Governance and Development* (Basingstoke: Palgrave Macmillan, 2007), pp. 34–6.
3 We are concerned about and aware of the contentious status of the terms "Washington and post-Washington Consensus" and we use them to capture the changing international mood at the end of the twentieth century.
4 Doornbos, M., *Global Forces and State Restructuring: Dynamics of state formation and collapse* (Basingstoke: Palgrave Macmillan, 2006).
5 Ferguson, N., *The Ascent of Money: A financial history of the world* (New York: Penguin Books Ltd, 2009), p. 284.
6 Braset, J. and Higgott, R., "Building the Normative Dimensions of a Global Polity," in Armstrong, D. *et al.* (eds) *Governance and Resistance in World Politics* (Cambridge: Cambridge University Press, 2003), pp. 29–55.
7 White, G., Howell, J. and Xiaoyuan, S., *In Search for Civil Society* (Oxford: Clarendon Press, 1996).
8 Jean, J.B.,"The End of the Nation State: The rise of regional economies," *Journal of Marketing*, vol. 60, issue 1, (January 1996), pp. 120–122.
9 Mitchell, D., *Governmentality: Power and Rule in Modern Society* (London: Sage, 1999), pp. 4–14.
10 Svennson, J., "Why Conditional Aid Does Not Work and What Can Be Done About It?" *Journal of Development Economics*, vol. 70, issue 1, (2003), pp. 381–402.
11 Gillin J.K., *Social Problems* (Bombay: Bombay Publisher, 1965), p. 388.
12 Punit, A F. *Profile of Poverty in India* (Delhi: B.R. Publishing Corporation, 1982), p. 33.
13 Sussanne, N., "Poverty and Self-help among Small Farmers in Chad," *Applied Geography and Development*, vol. 54, (1999), p. 56.
14 Montesquieu, Baron de, *The Spirit of Laws*, trans. T. Nugent, vol. 1 (New York: The Colonial Press, 1900), p. 317.
15 Townsend, P. and Abel Smith, B., *The Poor and the Poorest* (London: Bell, 1965), p. 82.
16 Townsend, P., *Poverty in the United Kingdom* (Harmondsworth: Penguin, 1979).
17 Sen, A., "Poor Relatively Speaking," *Oxford Economic Papers*, 35, (1983), pp. 153–69.
18 Nurkse, R., *The Problem of Capital Formation in Underdeveloped Countries* (Oxford: Basil Blackwell, 1953), p. 4.

19 Myrdal, G., *An American Dilemma: The negro problem and modern democracy* (New York: Harper & Row, 1944), p. 30.

20 Myrdal, G., *Asian Drama: An enquiry into the poverty of nations* (New York: Pantheon, 1968), vol. 1, p. 26.

21 Deepa, N.P. and Elena, E.G., *Ending Poverty in South Asia* (Washington, DC: World Bank Publications, 2007).

22 United Nations Commission on Science and Technology for Development, *An Assault on Poverty* (Ottawa: International Development Research Centre, 1997), p. xi.

23 Available at: www.undp.org/content/undp/en/home/librarypage/hdr/human-develo pment-report-2013/.

24 Available at: www.unescap.org/pdd/publications/survey2013/.

25 Hirst, P., "Democracy and Governance," in Pierre, J. (ed.) *Debating Governance* (Oxford: Oxford University Press, 2000), pp. 13–35.

26 Jackson, R.H., *Quasi-States: Sovereignty, international relations and the third world* (Cambridge: Cambridge University Press, 1991), pp. 5–9.

27 Ibid., pp. 1–12.

28 Krasner, S.D., "Compromising Westphalia," *International Security*, vol. 20, issue 1, no. 3, (1995), pp. 115–51.

29 Krasner, S.D., "Rethinking the Sovereign State Model," *Review of International Studies*, vol. 27, issue 1, (2001), pp. 17–42.

30 Jackson, R.H., "Quasi-States, Dual Regimes, and Neo-classical Theory: International jurisprudence and the third world," *International Organization*, vol. 41, issue 4, (1987), pp. 519–49.

31 Christopher, C., "Degrees of Statehood," *Review of International Studies*, vol. 24, issue 1, (1998), pp. 143–57.

32 Jackson (1991), op. cit., pp. 13–15.

33 Morgenthau, H.J., *Scientific Man versus Power Politics* (Chicago, IL: University of Chicago Press, 1946), pp. 19–26, and Wight, M., "Why Is There No International Theory?" in Butterfield, H. and Wight, M. (eds) *Diplomatic Investigations* (Oxford: Oxford University Press, 1966), pp. 17–34.

34 Jackson (1991), op. cit., pp. 22–3.

35 Ibid., pp. 132–3.

36 Moore, M., "Progressive Realism: Improving governance in the global south," *The Institute of Development Studies*, October 2002, available at: www.ids.ac.uk/gdr/ position%20papers/paper-03.pdf.

37 Jackson (1991), op. cit., pp. 133–4.

38 Morgenthau, H.J., *Politics among Nations: The struggle for power and peace*, 6th edn, rev. Thompson, K.W. (New York: McGraw-Hill, [1948] 1985).

39 Ibid., p. 165.

40 Dougherty, J.E. and Pfaltzgraff, R.L. Jr., *Contending Theories of International Relations: A comprehensive survey*, 5th edn (New York: Longman, 2001).

41 Gilpin refers to this perspective as economic nationalism. See Gilpin, R., *The Political Economy of International Relations* (Princeton, NJ: Princeton University Press, 1987), pp. 47–9.

42 Moore, M., *Progressive Realism: Improving governance in the global south*, Position Papers (Sussex: Institute of Development Studies, October 2000).

43 Ibid., pp. 2–14.

44 Moore, M., "Political Underdevelopment: What causes bad governance?", *Public Management Review*, vol. 1, issue 3, (2001), pp. 387–9.

45 Moore, M. (1998), "Death without Taxes: Democracy, state capacity and aid dependence in the fourth world," in Robinson, M. and White, G. (eds) *The Democratic Developmental State: Politics and institutional design* (Oxford: Oxford University Press, 1998), pp. 1–20.

46 Moore (2001), op. cit. pp. 387–9.

47 Moore, M., "Is Democracy Rooted in Material Prosperity?" in Luckman, R. and White, G. (eds) *Democratization in the South: The jagged wave* (Manchester: Manchester University Press, 1996), pp. 37–68.

48 Jackson (1991), op. cit., pp. 124–7.

49 It is easy to find reasonable measures of formal education and literacy, mortality and longevity. But how far should an index of social development include measures of gender equality, crime, social exclusion, drug use, mental illness or social harmony? How would we measure these variables? And how would we weight them?

50 Moore (2000), op. cit., pp. 127–30.

51 In "The Browning of Latin America," Guillermo O'Donnell suggests coloring the map blue to indicate the effective presence of the legal state; green to represent intermediate. O'Donnell, G., "The Browning of Latin America," *New Perspectives Quarterly*, (October 1993), pp. 50–3.

52 Tilly, C., *Coercion, Capital, and European States, A.D. 990–1990* (Malden, MA: Blackwell, 1992), p. 195.

53 Olson, G.R., "Promotion of Democracy as a Foreign Policy Instrument of Europe: Limits to international idealism," *Democratization*, vol. 7, issue 2, (2000), pp. 142–67.

54 Tilly (1992), op. cit., p. 195.

55 Kaufman, D., Kraay, A. and Pablo, Z.L., "Governance Matters," World Bank Policy Research, Working Paper no. 2196 (Washington, DC: The World Bank, 1999).

56 See Julius, O.I.,"Surviving at the Margins: Africa and the new global order," *Current World Leaders*, vol. 35, issue 6, (1992), pp. 1053–72, and Olufemi, V., "The Politics of Global Marginalization," *Journal of African and Asian Studies*, vol. 29, issue 3, (1994), pp. 186–204.

57 Moore (2000), op. cit., pp. 127–30.

58 Though Henri Lefebvre's theories are Marxist-oriented, they adopt a state-based approach and a concept of national interest that have much in common with the classical realist approach. Henri Lefebvre's main body of work was published in French in the 1970s; his texts have only recently been translated into English. *The Production of Space*, on which much of Neil Brenner's article is based, was translated in 1991, and has generated a great deal of interest among North American social theorists; Lefebvre, H., *The Production of Space* (Oxford: Blackwell, 1991). Brenner's article provides us with an excellent introduction to Lefebvre's theory of state and serves our purpose here very well since it is one of the first ones to relate Lefebvre's analysis to globalization. See Brenner, N., "Global, Fragmented, Hierarchical: Henri Lefebvre's geographies of globalization," *Public Culture*, vol. 10, issue 1, (1997), pp. 135–67.

59 For a summary presentation of these two perspectives, see Poggi, G., *The Development of the Modern State: A sociological introduction* (London: Hutchison, 1978), Chapter 1.

60 The best-known statement of the statist case in relation to developing countries is Huntington, S.P., *Political Order in Changing Societies* (New Haven, CT: Yale University Press, 1968).

61 Scott, W., "Field Methods in the Study of Organizations," in March, J. (ed.) *Handbook of Organizations* (Chicago, IL: Rand McNally, 1965, pp. 261–304), and Eisenhardt, K.M., "Building Theories from Case Study Research," *Academy of Management Review*, vol. 1, issue 4, (1989), pp. 532–50.

62 Monem, M., "Good Governance in Bangladesh: The unheard voices," paper presented at the international conference "Towards a New Political Economy of Development: Globalization and governance," University of Sheffield, July 4–6, 2002.

63 Neumayer, E., *The Pattern of Aid Giving: The impact of good governance on development assistance* (New York: Routledge, 2003), pp. 8–11.

2   The political economy of South Asia

Traditional power dynamics and development

This chapter reflects on the political economy of South Asia and explores the relationship between macroeconomic policy and the pattern of governance in South Asia. To this end, the current chapter examines governance issues and the poverty situation in South Asian countries. It can be argued that due to the British colonial inheritance in South Asian countries, while the countries have developed sophisticated formal state rules and institutions, at the same time they are characterized by an immature political environment, which has successfully adapted the patronage system to a modern state structures. That led to the key contradiction on which contemporary South Asian countries are based, namely the gap between the formal institutions and regulations that apparently define the rules of the game, and the informal rules of the actors who manage those institutions and actually shape the country and society. Those actors are the main political parties who indifferently have ruled the post-independent structure most of the time, and have used the formal rules of the game to replicate an extended patronage system from top to bottom of society. That has created an apparently ineradicable patron–client web, based on personal identity politics, which exends down from the top decision-making levels of the state to the grassroots of society.

At the time of the independence of the Indian subcontinent from the British colonial rule in 1947, the power of the elites in independent India and Pakistan was based on landed property and these elites controlling the bureaucracy, education, trade and manufacturing roles at the local level in their respective countries. At the time of partition, India and Pakistan were essentially agrarian and pre-capitalist in their mode of production and trade, and immature due to colonization and occupation, in their political organization and administration. Within that framework, power among elites was exercised basically through family and patron–client relations and forms of economic exchange.

Furthermore, the colonial process set up a strong local bureaucracy in most of the South Asian countries which aimed at serving the rulers' exploitation system, not the people's needs. The bureaucratic system of exploitation was based on the relationship between occupiers and occupied, and also between the local power elites and the local masses, and grew stronger during centuries of existence. Politics and political participation, as we understand them today from a liberal democracy perspective, appeared relatively late in South Asian society and history. Following the milestones of the independence from the British Empire, instead of becoming drivers for political change and progress, they adapted rapidly to the respective country's socio-political traditional setting. Political parties became the means through which the ancient power structures, the patron–client relations, disguised themselves to operate in a modern "democratic" political setting.

With that framework in mind, today the main political parties should not be understood as different political ideologies confronting each other in terms of which political program better suits the country's development and the people's well-being. But they should be seen as factional groups made up of patron–clients favorites and with their loyalties based on widespread corruption and immediate rent-seeking aspirations. That is achieved through the capture of formal systems and institutions (i.e. public administration, ministries, oversight bodies, etc.), and by informal practices, which are by definition difficult to identify and are unaccountable, and point at redirecting public resources and assets towards private/factional interests. At the same time, the scope of action of these factions goes well beyond the political and public spheres. The political elites have close connections with the elites in the private sector, blurring the line between and often mixing public and private interests. The relations between politics and business is becoming stronger, with the threshold moving from lobbying, to having businessmen pursuing their own interests directly at the top policy-making level of the polity.

Systematic inequalities in wealth and power among social groups and regions remained starkly visible in development thinking. The Bangladesh freedom struggle dramatized inequalities, which in other ways also became prominent in India, Sri Lanka and Pakistan. Planning regimes tackled inequalities with administrative and legal action, supported by the burgeoning academic field of development studies, endowed in these decades with policy-oriented research centers focused on nations emerging from imperial regimes. In postcolonial countries, the political character of development—and the necessity of changing power relations in order to redesign development regimes, to serve national citizens—pervaded mainstream development thought. In that historic context, development theory and practice converged on planning, whose central goal was to reorient development around national priorities. Imperial regimes had turned the resources of subordinate regions into objects for *laissez-faire* allocation by markets in the world economy. National planning separated national and global market priorities, enclosing national economies and instituting state redistributive systems to make national markets serve national citizens (Myrdal 1968).

In South Asia, as elsewhere, national plans focused on national markets. Planners devised priorities for allocating public and private resources, acquired internally and externally. External funding came in the form of grants and loans directly from countries that sought to wield influence in former imperial dependencies, and indirectly also from the richest countries, for the same reason, through Bretton Woods institutions, the World Bank and the International Monetary Fund (IMF). Of the rich capitalist countries, the USA became most aggressively expansive. Following the basic working principles of their imperial predecessor, national planning regimes in South Asia strove to enhance and supplement private investment. They were not anti-market, but rather, pro-national market. Planning instituted a combined public–private apparatus for monitoring and managing national economies. Planning agencies organized initiatives like cooperative societies and community development programs. Governments set up public food procurement and distribution systems. They expanded national health and education. They added to large inherited portfolios of state-owned assets heavy industries, public utilities, banks and insurance (Bagchi 1989; Bardhan 1984; Chaudhuri 1979; Frankel 1978; Kothari 1971).

Bureaucratic controls on imports and exports, and business generally, spawned corruption as well as black and gray markets. Foreign exchange shortages put private and public sector companies into financial competition, driving profit-seekers underground. One estimate put the value of India's black market at nearly half its GDP in recent years. In addition, political pragmatism mixed development administration with political patronage. This sparked opposition from groups left out of the patronage circuit, deprived of development benefits. In the 1970s, this opposition became volatile in Pakistan, Bangladesh, India and Sri Lanka. Charges of corruption, inefficient, domineering and discriminatory state development practices became effective weapons in competitive politics. By the 1970s, leading and aspiring participants in national regimes were clashing openly over control of development. Bureaucrats, politicians, the military, domestic investors, and international financiers were tearing at the fabric of national planning regimes.

The transitional phase and the developmental phase

The ideas of what development means and what a development agenda hopes to accomplish have changed over the years. Recently these have shifted to new areas because of "changing aid faddism,"[1] and also in response to genuine concerns regarding the effectiveness of the development agenda to reduce poverty to improve governance in South Asia. The empirical findings suggest that the existing approach either has inherent flaws or has been implemented in a manner that largely contributes to development paradoxes.[2] Collier and Dehn argue that the instruments of development agenda are fundamentally flawed in many respects.[3] In the 1980s, the experience of stabilization and structural adjustment raised concerns about their critical impacts on the poor, which led to a reassessment of the role of the states and donors. The new conceptualization of aid has given a "human face" to the market-oriented economic reforms. As a result, a broad consensus has emerged that emphasizes the quality of development assistance rather than purely its quantity. This new concern arose from the donors' belief that much aid in the past has been wasted. It fits in well with the modified version of the Washington Consensus that now incorporates institution-building and good governance as essential ingredients of the reform agenda. A consensus on goals for poverty alleviation and social development through strengthening governance also emerged in the 1990s in the form of Millennium Development Goals (MDGs) and Poverty Reduction Strategies (PRS), which have been incorporated by South Asian countries into their development agendas.

The flow of foreign aid into South Asia has been affected by the new shift in aid ideas in recent years. The donors' perception is that the weaknesses of the institutions of economic and political governance reduce the aid-absorptive capacity in South Asian countries and keep economic performance below their full potential. Before discussing all these issues in detail, it is important to analyze the political economy of major South Asian countries.

We can see a transformation in national regimes beginning in the late 1960s that yielded new development regimes by 1990. The transition began slowly, soon after Nehru's death in 1964, when the famines struck India in 1967. Bangladesh independence gained political force at the same time, and then in 1974, famine hit Bangladesh. In both famine periods, foreign aid became critical, and in response, national regimes put new energy into the Green Revolution. Planners concentrated on investing state funds in sites of intensive cultivation, where well-endowed landowners controlled local labor, finance, and political institutions. Critics called this strategy "betting on the rich." Defenders called it the only road to national food security. This strategic blueprint led states to adopt development plans that called for increasingly expensive investments, which demanded more external finance, more in the form of debt. At the same time, the World Bank dramatically increased its lending under Robert McNamara, who led the charge to increase development loans and aid from rich countries and private banks. However, these new loans came with new conditions, collectively called Structural Adjustment Programmes, which began in the 1970s, and gained force and reach in the 1980s and 1990s. Under these programs, the World Bank and the IMF demanded that borrowing governments drastically reduce their regulatory and provisioning role in their economies, to assume the role of supporter and facilitator for private investors, who would, according to emerging mainstream economic thought under the so-called Washington Consensus, engage rationally in market activity to allocate resources most efficiently for the increase of national wealth.

There have been distinct development regimes in the South Asian countries in 1980s and 1990s. In Nepal, electoral democracy was established in 1991, opening development to wide public debate, as foreign investments grew, and as did a Maoist insurgency, carving the nation into regions of war and allowing the king to stage a royal coup in February 2005, purportedly to secure Kathmandu against revolution. Sri Lanka has endured civil war since 1981, and the nation that existed in 1970 has effectively disappeared. In Bangladesh, struggles over development brought military coups and a popular movement that established democracy in 1991, amidst a deep dependency on international finance and trade. In Pakistan, a government wracked by struggles for regional autonomy has experienced disruptions from two decades of war in Afghanistan, leading to more stringent authoritarian dependence on the USA. In the present contemporary development, regimes are currently in flux.

Freeing markets from state control became the feature of the international development mainstream (Leys 1996; SAPRIN 2004). Planning regimes unraveled under structural adjustment. Sri Lanka, Bangladesh and Nepal led the way in South Asia, starting slowly in the 1970s and accelerating in the 1980s. With declining relative prices for primary product exports, the burden of external debt grew heavier, while raising funds for large development projects (epitomized by the Mahaveli scheme in Sri Lanka, then the largest irrigation project in the world) became more pressing. At the same time, rising oil prices brought Europe and North America recession, inflation, and petro-dollars in need of circulation, while they brought South Asia higher costs for industrial growth, middle-class consumption, and the Green Revolution. The smaller countries first began borrowing on a much larger scale and succumbed quickly and decisively to structural adjustment. In 1981, India began to rely on foreign debt, and by 1991, internal and external pressures had forced economic liberalization. In the 1980s, neo-liberal free-market orthodoxy conquered the economic mainstream, where harsh critics of state planning, provisioning, and regulation become most influential. Development strategies emphasized private sector leadership in market-driven economic growth, emphasized imports and exports, and shifted the balance of power in national state-and-market asset allocation towards national and international business interests.

Development regimes in South Asia operate today inside the same national states that managed them in 1975. But today's regimes are fundamentally different, and their transformation has accompanied—if not caused—major shifts in national politics. In India, private capital and state governments have both gained increasing independence from New Delhi. The Congress Party lost its old hegemony, national government came to be composed of shifting coalitions of regionally-based parties, and state chief ministers now compete fiercely to attract foreign direct investments (FDI) to their individual states, all of whom have effectively made efforts to turn each Indian state into an economic hub.

South Asia is still widely known as a unique region with a high poverty rate. At the same time, due to bilateral conflicts between India and Pakistan over Kashmir since 1947, the recent nuclear arms race between these two countries has increased the probability of an accidental nuclear war in South Asia. Despite a high level of poverty, governments in South Asia have primarily pursued "national security" through increasing military capability taking its toll on human security. South Asia currently spends US$14 billion annually on defense, symbolizing a huge military expenditure, to promote their strategic interests in this region. India and Pakistan have been increasing their military expenditure at an average annual rate (in nominal terms) of about 12 percent. Therefore, the human opportunity cost of this expenditure can be calculated by the fact that half of the military expenditure in South Asia for one year could have provided primary school education to 119 million deprived children in a year and safe drinking water for two years to about 200 million people.[4] Even after six decades of economic development, we are still witnessing increasing numbers of people in South Asia suffering from hunger, illiteracy and diseases. Children are the worst victims of the chronic poverty in South Asia, who suffer from malnutrition, waterborne diseases and lack of primary education.

Governance and politics

In South Asia, particularly in Pakistan and Bangladesh, democracy as an institution is new and still fragile. Democracy is vibrant in India compared to other countries in the region. The Union Government in India was established by the Constitution of India. It is the governing authority of the union of 28 states and seven union territories, collectively called the Republic of India. The head of the executive branch is the President in India, who is the Head of State and exercises his or her power directly or through officers subordinate to the president. In India, the legislative branch or the Parliament consists of the lower house, the Lok Sabha, and the upper house, the Rajya Sabha, as well as the President. Ethnic heterogeneity of the Indian population seems to have supported the democratic competition for power and democracy.[5] Since the 1990s, India has been governed by coalition governments, in which, in addition to a major national party, many regional and ethnic parties are represented. Sumit Ganguly (2002: 50) argued that in the face of myriad challenges, "democracy in India has endured and has grown deep roots in Indian soil."[6] Gram panchayat is local self-government at the village or small town level in India and the *Sarpanch* is in charge of it.

   In Bhutan, the peaceful march to democracy has been a smooth one and it is a constitutional democracy. The King of Bhutan is the head of state. However, Bhutan was an absolute monarchy between 1907 and the 1950s. Bhutan adopted its first modern Constitution in 2008, codifying the institutions of government and the legal framework for a democratic multi-party system to commence constitutional democracy. Bhutan continues to consolidate its newly established constitutional democracy. Bhutan's parliament consists of an upper and lower house, the latter based on political party affiliations. The first elections for the upper house (the National Council) were held on 31 December 2007, while elections for the lower house, the 47-seat National Assembly, were held on March 24, 2008. Two political parties, the People's Democratic Party and Druk Phuensum Tshogpa (Bhutan Harmony Party, DPT), contested the country's first elections. Voters delivered a landslide victory to the DPT, which took 45 out of the 47 seats in the National

Assembly. On April 23, 2013, the second parliamentary elections for the National Council were held.

The Maldives is classified as a small island developing state in South Asia. The Maldives is an archipelago in the Indian Ocean composed of 1191 islands. The Maldives was governed as an Islamic sultanate under Dutch and then British protection until 1965, when it gained independence. Three years later in 1968, it became a republic. The Maldives remains a member of the Commonwealth. Ibrahim Nasir, a former Prime Minister during the late sultanate period, became President for the first ten years after independence. President Maumoon Abdul Gayoom ruled for 30 years from 1978, elected to six successive terms by single-party referendums. In August 2004, the President and his government pledged to embark upon democratic reforms including a more representative political system and expanded political freedoms. Mohammed Waheed Hassan was sworn in to the President's office on January 7, 2012, when his predecessor, Mohamed Nasheed resigned, following a series of protests led by police.[7] In the presidential election held in November 2013, Abdulla Yameen Abdul Gayoom was elected as the President of the Maldives for the presidential term that began on November 11, 2013.[8]

Nepal had a traditional monarchical autocracy until May 28, 2008, but Nepal was able to maintain its constitutional monarchy. On that date, the Constitution was altered by the Constituent Assembly to make the country a republic. Nepal had maintained its traditional monarchical autocracy until the democratic breakthrough in 1990. Since then Nepal has functioned within a framework of a republic with a multi-party system. The system of government has been parliamentary since the introduction of its 1990 Constitution. After 10 years of Maoist insurgency, Nepal has had two elections for its Constituent Assembly, one in 2008 and the other in 2013. Since the first Constituent Assembly was dissolved in 2012 after failing to deliver a new Constitution, a second election was conducted on November 19, 2013 to obtain a fresh mandate from the people. Yet the recent election has delivered landslide gains to some political parties and produced massive setbacks for others, leading to a dramatic change in national politics. In particular, the Unified Communist Party of Nepal (a Maoist party), which had become the largest party in the first Assembly, suffered a great loss in the recent election. Along with other Madhesi regional parties, it has advocated a transformative agenda for the Nepalese polity and society.

The politics of Sri Lanka reflect the historical and political differences between the two main ethnic groups, the majority Sinhala and the minority Tamils, who are concentrated in the north and east of the island. Neil DeVotta (2002: 84, 96) argues that the "ethnic outbidding" plunged Sri Lanka into a protracted conflict and reduced democracy to a hollow shell and its citizens of all backgrounds have paid a heavy price for their country's misguided ethnic policies.[9] But Sri Lanka has been relatively stable in recent years due to an armistice between the government and the Tamil Tigers. Sri Lanka has a multi-party democracy that enjoys stability given the high levels of political violence, especially that which occurred under the UNP (United National Party) regime of 1977–93. Recent elections in Sri Lanka have seen decreasing election violence between the SLFP (the Sri Lanka Freedom Party) and the UNP, compared to the period 1977–94. Thus elections have been cleaner, without the rampant impersonation and vote-rigging which characterized the 1982 Presidential election.

Since independence, Pakistan and Bangladesh have witnessed several political hiccups, including a number of army coups and major political movements that caused the downfall of political regimes. Pakistan's record with parliamentary democracy has been mixed, Pakistan, after lapses, has returned to this form of government. The Constitution of the Islamic Republic of Pakistan in 1973 provides for a federal parliamentary system with a president as head of state and a popularly elected prime minister as head of government. Bangladesh is a parliamentary representative democratic republic, whereby the Prime Minister of Bangladesh is the head of government, and of a multiparty system. One observer (Kamal 2000) notes that in the past few decades polity in either Bangladesh and Pakistan has given birth to the idea that this society is condemned to oscillate between autocracy and democratic rule.[10] In the present world order, it seems that autocracy and democracy, viewed as permanent possibilities, are in constant mutual tension in politics in some South Asian countries.

With huge populations, most South Asian countries have per capita gross national income (GNI) of US$600. In 2010, 36 percent of the population on average were living in extreme poverty in South Asia, falling under the international 1 dollar-a-day poverty line. A further 47 percent fell under the 2 dollars-a-day poverty line. For example, in Bangladesh total net official development assistance (ODA) to the country in 2010 was US$1.4 billion, though this accounted for just 2.4 percent of GNI.[11] Poverty is still acute and persistent in South Asia in spite of remarkable progress in meeting the targets of various indicators set by MDGs. There is mounting evidence that poverty is associated with poor governance. Yet, the instrumental nature of the governance agenda implies that the main pillars of "good governance" (accountability, transparency and rule of law) are universally applicable, i.e. they can be implemented regardless of the economic orientation, strategic priorities or policy choices of a country's government (World Bank 2000).[12]

Political, institutional and governance-related factors play a central role in explaining growth and developmental outcomes in South Asia. As such, they receive a lot of attention from the various donors who operate in these recipient countries. In the 1980s and the 1990s, an important aspect of a great deal of aid in South Asian countries was the fact that it came with explicit governance conditions. The importance of foreign aid has declined over the years in the Third World; currently foreign assistance accounts for no more than 2 percent of GDP in South Asia.[13]

The recent trend shows that it is the grant part of foreign aid which has declined rapidly. Contemporary data shows that less than 16 percent of the total national budget comes from foreign grants and loans in major South Asian countries. Increasing amounts of foreign aid have come through the NGO sector in recent years. It is the ongoing program assistance of the IMF and the World Bank that has helped maintain the soft loan part of foreign aid in the past 3–4 years.[14] Governments in South Asia will have to realize that many reform programs have already been undertaken in different sectors of the economy on the advice of different donor agencies. Almost half (49 percent) of the Annual Development Plan of Pakistan, Nepal and Bangladesh was largely donor-dependent in the fiscal year 2011–12. Now, the donors may tend to impose fresh conditions on South Asian countries in respect of them receiving aid from their soft loan windows. If that happens, this will be an issue of great concern for the governments in this region. The International Development Association (IDA), established in 1960, complements the World Bank's other lending arm such as the International Bank for Reconstruction and Development (IBRD), which helps develop countries with capital invest-ment. IDA provides credits and grants to the poorest developing countries in South Asia.

Recently the political economy in South Asia has undergone important changes, particularly with the rise of India as an economic powerhouse, on the one hand, and the gradual reduction of South Asia's aid dependence on the other. There is a lot of optimism and skepticism about South Asia's development potential. South Asia is one of the fastest growing regions in the world currently, however, it is a region in which the highest concentration of people are living below the poverty line, and facing human suffering, gender disparities and conflict (Figure 2.1).

Recently the number of people living in extreme poverty[15] has been falling in South Asia since 1990 and accelerated growth in India could lift millions

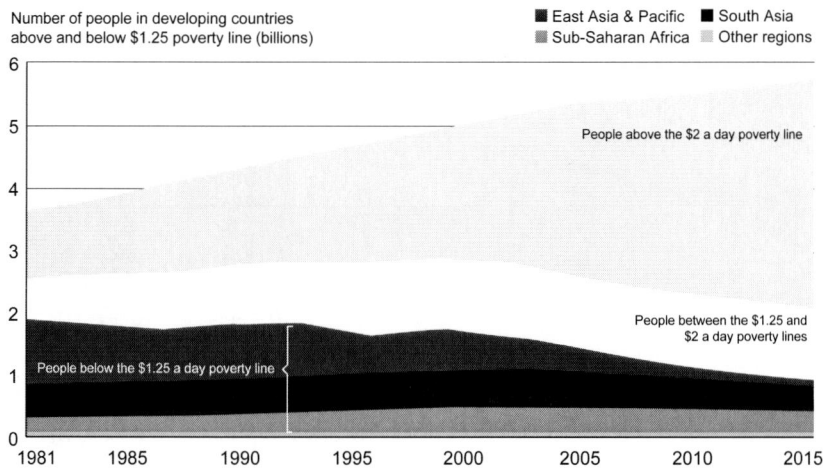

Figure 2.1 Extreme poverty in South Asia

more out of poverty. We know that rising productivity is the key to increasing incomes and reducing poverty. Over the past two decades output per worker has grown faster than estimated in the entire Asian region, including South Asia.[16]

The Food and Agriculture Organization (FAO) of the United Nations estimates that the number of people worldwide who receive less than 2100 calories a day rose from 873 million in 2004–6 to 915 million in 2006–8 and could rise further in the next two yearrs.[17] Even before the recent food crisis, about a quarter of children in Sub-Saharan Africa and two-fifths in South Asia were underweight (see Figure 2.2). Different data analysis in India has raised concern about the lack of convergence between rich and poor regions, richer states have grown faster so that inequality across states is increasing (Ahluwalia 2000; Ejaz 2010; Kochhar *et al.* 2006).[18]

Over the past three decades, the perspectives of the development partners (DPs) have also undergone a significant worldwide metamorphosis with consequences for the countries in the region. Nowadays the range of policies of international donors to the recipients has extended to areas of interest far beyond the policies derived from the Washington Consensus. To donors, the new approach places more and more emphasis on the non-governmental sector, and more particularly, on upholding human rights, democracy and "good governance." The new aid agenda is being incorporated into the design of the Poverty Reduction Strategy Paper (PRSP) so as to help aid recipients to achieve the Millennium Development Goals (MDGs), but unlike in the past, the recipient countries, including those of South Asia, are now expected to assume ownership of new aid priorities (the Paris Declaration of March 2005 gave emphasis to country ownership).

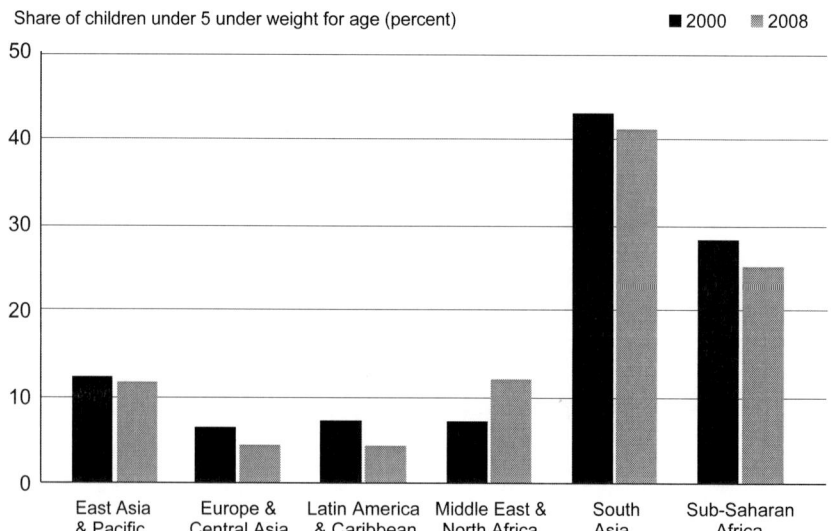

Figure 2.2 Child malnutrition rate in South Asia

The PRSP Forum was organized under the leadership of the governments of the recipients in South Asia to formulate strategies to implement and monitor progress of the PRSP. In the PRSP Implementation Forum (PIFM), 11 key action points were jointly agreed, as the targets to be achieved, by the governments and the DPs. One joint committee and eight subgroups were formed to follow up and to implement these decisions. The joint committee consists of representatives from both governments and DPs and is responsible for monitoring and implementing the progress of the PRS along with donor coordination. The PRS will guide the budget allocation process, particularly for pro-poor allocation programs for the next fiscal year, and will also rationalize annual development plans to match the PRSP.[19]

The administrative apparatus

In a vibrant democracy, the political process is supposed to find answers to governance problems, but this does not always happen in South Asian countries. The political system that is very common in South Asia is that the states are accountable not to the people but to those who are having power: these are often contractors, the mafia, corrupt bureaucrats, and manipulators who have made money through using the political system, and are therefore very interested in the continuation of the patronage-based administration.

The first-past-the-post (FPTP) electoral system in most South Asian countries contributes to creating the enabling environment that issues virtual absolute power to the party which wins the elections and influences the development process. Every time one party wins,they shape a winner-take-all system, where the ruling party gains control over the state institutions, including those allegedly in charge of check and balance roles. Like many other developing countries, and especially those in South Asia (e.g., India, Pakistan), patron–client relationships underlie South Asian politics. The distribution of rents helps to maintain long-standing patron–client relationships. The absence of legal rents in Bangladesh and other South Asian countries implies that rent-seeking goals can only be pursued through the creation of informal rents (Khan 2011). As North *et al.* (2009) highlight, the creation and distribution of rents secure the loyalty of clients to patrons and elites to the system, thereby protecting rents and limiting violence.

By limiting access to valuable resources and activities, as well as contract enforcement, the dominant coalition maintains the balance of power and facilitates cooperation and order. The expectation that violence will threaten to reduce rents decreases the likelihood of trouble. Shocks, such as changes in demography, technology, and the balance of power between the military and political parties, can incite violence and force the renegotiation of the distribution of rents. For our purposes, the concept of political settlements provides a useful framework to understand Bangladesh's industrial policy with respect to the garments sector. Since Bangladesh's independence in 1971, various manifestations of patronage politics have materialized in Bangladesh. Khan (2011) provides a detailed account of Bangladesh's transition from a system of "constrained patrimonialism" (1971–75) to "clientelistic authoritarianism" (1975–90), culminating in "competitive clientelism" (1990–present), in which two dominant political parties and the military are competing for popular support almost exclusively on different concepts of "the nation." In practice, competitive clientelism increasingly breeds weak political governance, yet engenders a surprisingly stable and consistent economic policy environment in Bangladesh that emphasizes privatization and export-led growth.

The state resources in South Asian countries seem to be lucrative to both politicians and their constituencies, which leads to a patron–client relationship between the holders of state power and those seeking favors. Patronage in South Asian countries is largely controlled by individuals, not established institutions bound to follow set procedures. In most cases, power is highly personalized and centralized and the decision-making process is influenced by arbitrary and behind-the-scene transactions. In such an environment, the exercise of power for its clients demands a fudging of the rules, dependence upon corrupt practices and the decay of governance. Eventually all these hurdles leave little chance of equitable development reaching the poor in the region.

The bureaucracy is viewed as disinterested in public welfare and corrupt. Bright men and women join the civil service, but adverse work environments, constant political interference, meaningless transfers, and rampant corruption all contribute to the erosion of their ethics and inspire them sometimes to misuse their authority. It should be noted that honesty, neutrality towards party politics, and efficiency in the civil service have been vaguely defined in South Asia, with less attention paid to public satisfaction.

A high degree of professionalism ought to be the dominant characteristic of a modern bureaucracy, which is largely absent in South Asian countries. The fatal flaw of the bureaucracy has been its low level of professional competence. In the present day administrative climate, there is little incentive for young civil servants to acquire knowledge or improve their skills. An important factor which contributes to the surrender of autonomy of the civil servants to their political masters is the lack of any market value and lack of alternative employment potential. Most civil servants end up being politicized within a few years of joining the service and their skill lies only in manipulation and jockeying for positions within government.

If power is abused, or exercised in weak or improper ways, those with no power, particularly the poor, are most likely to suffer. For instance, teachers need to be present and effective in their jobs, just as doctors and nurses need to provide the care that patients need. But they are often mired in a system where the incentives for effective service delivery are weak, and political patronage is a way of life. Highly trained doctors seldom want to work in remote rural areas. Since those who do work there are rarely monitored, the penalties for not being at work are low. Even when they are present, they treat poor people badly. Administrative and political values have to coincide in the long run to ensure good governance. Authority has been by and large uncoupled from transparency and accountability at most levels, and in respect of most functions. As a result, most state functionaries have realistic and plausible alibis for their non-performance and the harm caused by indecision cannot be attributed to any particular individual or political party. Thus the goal of 'development' does not appear attractive to the rulers, resulting in an unclear and vague road map to the ultimate destination. Many civil servants hold the view that it is the nature of politics which largely determines the nature of the civil service and the ends to which it would be put, and, therefore, civil service reforms cannot succeed in isolation. The politicized administration leaves little choice to the politicians but to resort to populist rhetoric and sectarian strategies. Almost all the organs in South Asian countries have been affected by the malaise of governance.

The vicious circle of distortions in politics leading to bureaucratic apathy (and vice versa), with both resulting in poor governance, can be set right through taking a large number of simultaneous measures. A discussion on political and electoral reforms (restriction on the number of ministers by law is a good beginning), though absolutely vital, is beyond the scope of this work. However, many states in South Asia, especially the poorer ones, have lost the dynamism and capacity to undertake reforms on their own without any external pressure. In India, Pakistan, Bangladesh and Sri Lanka, central governments play the key functions in every sector, sometimes they have been backed by civil society action. However, it seems that the governments do not have the moral authority to promote good governance, as they have done little to take similar steps to reform their own administration, whether it is downsizing or reducing subsidies on fertilizers, food, gas and higher education, or passing a Freedom to Information Act (which is languishing for want of rules!), or reducing the number of centrally sponsored schemes, or providing long tenure to its senior civil servants. The track record of the governments is almost as dismal as that of the many recalcitrant states in South Asia. Therefore, South Asian countries must first of all improve governance through central governments in every respect and then they should go for decentralization to ensure transparency and accountability by accelerating credible interactions with non-state actors such as non-governmental organizations (NGOs) and cicil society organizations (CSOs).

The governance agenda

The notion of "good governance" has served as a general guiding principle for donor agencies in South Asia and elsewhere in recent years: they demand adherence from the governments to proper administrative processes in the handling of development assistance. The main components of the governance agenda in South Asia are as follows:

1   To build the country's capacity for governance and increase ownership of the formulation of the relevant reform programs.

2   To ensure synergies and coherence between the different donor policies and instruments.

3   To reinforce the partnerships for development in order to achieve coordination between the donors' priorities and the partner country's agenda through policy dialogue as well as to benefit from the complementarities among the various donors.

4   To contribute to the protection of human rights and to the spreading of democracy, good governance and the rule of law.

The effect of foreign aid[20] on South Asia is widely debated.[21] The collapse of the Soviet Union in the post-cold war era has enhanced the effectiveness of Western aid conditionality. Strong arguments have been proffered from various quarters that without "good governance" structures, the poor and developing regions, like South Asia, cannot achieve economic growth or reduce poverty. Bad governance is being increasingly viewed as the main cause behind all ills confronting these societies. By linking governance as a conditionality for development aid, the international donor community has given prominence to governance issues. Pushed by powerful international financial institutions, "good governance" has become the cornerstone of development cooperation. The World Bank, in particular, has been a leading proponent of "good governance."[22]

Donors nowadays expect better governance in South Asia, in order to continue or increase aid. This is just another addition to the prevailing notion of aid conditionality. The notion of good governance differs from the generic paradoxes attached to political conditionality. Lack of policy ownership by the recipients sometimes causes "moral hazard" and a crisis of legitimacy.[23] Lack of ownership emerges from the belief of the critics that donors are attempting to buy policy reform, a problem that was identified as long ago as 1987. The critical question attached to this paradox was, if a given set of policies were so beneficial to poor countries in South Asia, why did these policies need to be forcefully pushed?

In the context of development aid, the notion of "moral hazard"[24] refers to the counter productivity of aid conditionality since giving aid money may risk reducing the incentive for the recipient country to carry on with a given set of reforms. We should note that moral hazard is a serious problem in a donor organization like the World Bank. Agents, usually the bureaucracy, generally possess an information advantage over their political masters and principals. The moral hazard problem is further exacerbated by the fact that there are no well-defined or quantifiable objectives against which a staff member's performance can be assessed. As it is difficult to clearly define, observe and evaluate an agent's efforts objectively, it is much easier for an agent to manipulate information to mitigate any potential adverse effects that it may have for him or her.[25]

Several studies conducted both locally and globally have established that reforms led by the World Bank have had some positive effects on reform-exposed countries.[26] South Asia has continued to introduce significant reforms that show, be it sometimes rhetorically, the desired results in the form of much-improved development outcomes with modest gross domestic product (GDP) growth. Even so, this approach has largely widened the gap between rich and poor, and the benefits of such development do not reach those who need them most. The countries keep struggling with high levels of corruption, political instability, natural disasters, and half billion of the poor in South Asia are still living in deprivation.

Notes

1 Easterly, W., "The Effect of IMF and World Bank Programmes on Poverty," Policy Research Working Paper No. 2517 (Washington, DC: The World Bank, 2000).
2 Collier, P., "The Failure of Conditionality," in Gwin, C. and Nelson, J. (eds) *Perspectives on Aid and Development* (Washington, DC: Overseas Development Council, 1997).
3 Collier, P. and Dehn, J., "Aid, Shocks and Growth," Policy Research Working Paper No. 2688 (Washington, DC: The World Bank, 2001).
4 Estimated on the basis of data provided in Haq, M., *Human Development in South Asia 1997* (Karachi: Oxford University Press, 1997).
5 Ministry of Law and Justice, Government of India, *Constitution of India, Updated to 94th Amendment Act*, p. 26. Available at: http://lawmin.nic.in/coi/coiason 29july08.pdf.
6 Ganguly, S., "India's Multiple Revolutions," *Journal of Democracy*, vol. 13, issue 1, (2002), pp. 38–51.
7 Magnier, M., "Maldives President Resigns after Weeks of Protest," *Los Angeles Times*, 7 February 2012.
8 http://zeenews.india.com/news/south-asia/mohammed-nasheed-graciously-accepts-defeat-as-yameen-wins-maldives-run-off_890440.html.
9 DeVotta, N., "Illiberalism and Ethnic Conflict in Sri Lanka," *Journal of Democracy*, vol. 13, issue 1, (2002), pp. 84–98.
10 Kamal, A., "Democracy and Poverty: A missing link?" AAB Paper, May 2000.
11 These are estimated annual compound growth rates for 2007–8 and 2009–10 and are based on the official national income statistics, see the Bangladesh Bureau of Statistics, *Statistical Yearbook of Bangladesh* (Dhaka: Bangladesh Bureau of Statistics, 2011).
12 World Bank, *Taming Leviathan: Reforming governance in Bangladesh* (Dhaka: The World Bank, 2000).
13 Nabi, I. and Devarajan, S., "Economic Growth in South Asia: Promising, un-equalizing, … sustainable?"*Economic and Political Weekly*, vol. XLI, no. 33, (2006), August 19.
14 Ministry of Finance, *Economic Review* (Dhaka: The Government of Bangladesh, 2005).
15 Extreme poverty is defined as average daily consumption of $1.25 or less.
16 See http://data.worldbank.org/news/rgns-on-track-to-meet-poverty-reduction-MDG (accessed June 26, 2012).
17 Ibid.
18 Ahluwalia, M., "Economic Performance of States in the Post Reforms Period," *Economic and Political Weekly*, May, 6, 2000, pp. 1637–48. Chen, S. and Ravallion, M., "The Developing World is Poorer Than We Thought, But No Less Successful in the Fight against Poverty", World Bank Policy Research, Working

Paper No. 4703; 2008; Kochhar, K., Kumar, U., Rajan, R., Subramanian, A., and Tokatlidis, I., "India's Pattern of Development: What happened, what follows," International Monetary Fund,Working Paper No. WP/06/22; 2006; Ghani, E. (ed.) *The Poor Half Billion in South Asia: What is holding back lagging regions?* (Oxford: Oxford University Press, 2010).

19 Ministry of Finance, *Economic Review* (Dhaka: The Government of Bangladesh, 2007).

20 The term "foreign aid" is defined broadly to include all financial or technical transfers (in the form of loans, grants, etc.) from governments, international organizations, multinational financial institutions or private charities in OECD countries, on the one hand, to either government or NGOs in economically less-developed countries (LDCs), on the other.

21 Siddiqui, K., *Towards Good Governance in Bangladesh: Fifty unpleasant essays* (Dhaka: University Press Limited, 1996), pp. 10–20.

22 It is important to stress here that the World Bank is not the only multilateral aid agency promoting "good governance." There are other important multilateral and regional developmental agencies that actively promote governance issues: the IMF, the UNDP, the OECD, the European Bank for Reconstruction and Development (EBRD), etc. For instance, the Asian Development Bank (ADB) was the first regional development bank to adopt an official "governance" policy in 1995. In addition, a host of bilateral donors spend millions of dollars each year to support governance-related programs in several Third World countries, to name but a few: the US Agency for International Development (USAID), the British Department for International Development (DFID), the Swedish International Development Cooperation Agency (SIDA) and the Official Development Assistance (ODA) of Japan. Many of these bilateral donors have also constituted special units to coordinate their governance-related activities. Unfortunately, the governance agenda of the bilateral donors continues to be set by the IFIs.

23 Dijkstra, A.G., "The Effectiveness of Policy Conditionality: Eight country experiences," *Development and Change*, vol. 33, issue 2, (2002), pp. 307–34.

24 Vylder, D.S., "Why Deficits Grow: A critical discussion of the impact of structural adjustment lending of the external account in low income countries," paper presented at conference, Stockholm, 1994; United Nations, *UNDP, Human Development Report* (New York: UN, 2001).

25 Dixit, A., *The Making of Economic Policy: A transaction cost of politics approach* (Cambridge, MA: MIT Press, 1996), pp. 174–92.

26 Ibid.

3 Governance and development in South Asia

Foreign donors and national governments

This chapter discusses the role of the major donors and governments in South Asia with regard to governance and development in the region. The World Bank leads much of the behavior of the donor community and is the most influential source of advice on all growth-related issues for South Asia. As a consequence, the approach, strategies and programs of the major donors (and their different perceptions) have a critical impact on the development effectiveness of aid through governance in South Asia. It is therefore necessary to discuss the basis of their advice and support.

The World Bank relates "good governance" to the countries or societies of South Asia as a whole and looks at the way in which power is exercised in the management of the economic and social resources that help improve development. The United Nations Development Programme's (UNDP) notion of governance includes three separate but interconnected authorities, i.e. political, economic and administrative aspects. Exercise of these authorities should help manage the affairs of South Asia at different levels. ADB's governance approaches include: (1) core governance; (2) sectoral governance; and (3) project governance.

A Joint Country Assistance Strategy has been adopted in recent years and the World Bank, the Asian Development Bank (ADB), the British Department for International Development (DFID), and the Official Development Assistance (ODA) of Japan (these four donors contribute more than 80 percent of total aid) and government officials organize a joint meeting to discuss the joint country assessment strategy for individual countries in South Asia. This coordinated effort defines a common outcome, strategies and an activity plan to avoid overlap in the development process in South Asia. The World Bank desk reviews, which form the basis for the baselines/targets for some of the indicators of development, demonstrate that some progress has been made towards meeting the standards of aid effectiveness set out in the Paris Declaration. However, various significant challenges remain. The main challenges and priorities for the future of South Asia are as follows.

Ownership

Ownership is crucial to achieving development goals and is central to the Paris Declaration. Ownership is defined as a country's ability to exercise effective leadership over its own development policies and strategies. Achieving this is very difficult for South Asia against the backdrop of the domination of the World Bank and other donors vis-à-vis the recipients. Nor, of course, can ownership be measured by a single indicator. It requires a combination of cross-cutting factors that engage both donors and the government. For donors, it rhetorically means supporting countries' leadership and policies, largely visible on paper, but not in practice to some extent. It is meant also to be gearing their overall support to countries' national development strategies, institutions and systems. This is commonly referred to as "alignment." Donors demand alignment when governments set out priorities and operational strategies. This was the main focus of Indicator 1 of the Paris Declaration.

The governments of South Asia identified poverty reduction as the key element in their development strategy in 2000. Although a long-term strategy has not been comprehensively laid out, aspects are included in the Poverty Reduction Strategy Paper (PRSP). Some sector policies (e.g. education) are already in place. The PRSP sets out preliminary development targets linked to the Millennium Development Goals (MDGs), and some even go beyond the MDG targets. The PRSP prioritizes targets through a policy framework, highlighting pro-poor growth, human development and governance. It provides a good basis for furthering a development strategy.

The governments are in the early stages of linking the budget process with national priorities through a Medium-Term Budget Framework developed as part of the PRSP. The framework brings together the recurrent and capital budgets and should increase funding for priority programs. 2006 was the first year of PRSP implementation, and there were signs that revenues and expenditures will be broadly in line with the new budget framework. Most South Asian countries received a C rating in the World Bank's 2005 Comprehensive Development Framework assessment, which provides the baseline for Indicator 1. This puts them within the reach of the 2015 target to achieve a B or an A rating.[1] The governments will need to further refine their long-term vision and medium-term strategies, particularly at the sectoral level, and continue to reform the budget process if this target is to be met.

Alignment

South Asia is at an early stage of alignment between government priorities and systems, on the one hand, and donor policies and procedures, on the other. However, the government is playing an increasingly active role in managing its aid. Moreover, the agreement of undertaking the task of PRSP has facilitated a more government-led dialogue with donors.

Indicator 2a

Indicator 2a provides an indication of the quality of public financial management systems in most South Asian countries. The score is based on the World Bank's Country Policy and Institutional Assessment (CPIA Indicator 13). The World Bank's 2008 Aid Effectiveness Review describes how public financial management (PFM) in South Asia remains weak. However, the individual governments have now prepared a financial management improvement plan that includes all the key elements of effective public financial management. The World Bank judges public financial accountability in South Asia to be at an early stage. The process of bringing audit standards in line with international standards has been launched, and the individual governments are considering a Public Expenditure Framework of Accountability. However, progress to date has been limited. The governments will need to prioritize PFM reforms if South Asian countries are to meet the target of a score of 3.5 on the CPIA Indicator.[2]

Indicator 2b

No score was available for Indicator 2b on the quality of South Asia's procurement systems a few years back. The World Bank's 2008 Aid Effectiveness Review noted that procurement had been a major source of corruption in South Asia. New public procurement regulations were introduced to usher in uniform procurement regulations for all public sector bodies, consistent with international standards. In addition, the governments adopted proper public procurement legislation.

Aligning aid flows to national priorities

PRSP implementation in South Asia purportedly has encouraged donors to align their strategies with national priorities. Comprehensive and transparent reporting on aid, and how it is used, is critical not only to ensure that donors align aid flows with national development priorities but also to achieve accountability for the use of development resources and results. The aim of the indicators is to increase the credibility of the budget as a mechanism for governing actual allocation and utilization of development resources. They are an important criterion for making alignment a reality rather than a loose principle. To this end, the indicators seek to encourage a reasonable degree of congruence between how much aid is reported in the budget and how much aid is actually disbursed.

Coordinating support to strengthen capacity

It is said that the governments are also assuming more and more responsibility for planning, managing and implementing capacity-building projects. For their part, donors have taken steps to coordinate their technical assistance with country programs, including sector-wide approaches (SWAPs) in education and health. However, coordinated technical assistance, including assistance to implement the SWAPs, accounted for only 31 percent of all technical assistance to South Asia in 2005. As part of the follow-up to this survey, the government and donors are working together to define standards and also to coordinate technical assistance. The introduction of a comprehensive capacity development strategy would increase coordination among donors, which in its turn would help South Asian countries reach the target of 50 percent coordinated technical assistance by 2015. Here it should be noted that donors increasingly have preferred SWAPs in recent years. But it is argued that instead of adopting the short-term SWAPs, South Asia could have benefited more from nationwide programs with a longer-term planning horizon.

Avoiding parallel implementation structures

The Paris Declaration instructs donors to avoid, to the maximum extent possible, creating dedicated structures for day-to-day management and the implementation of aid-financed projects and programs. Although many parallel project implementation units (PIUs) are currently in place, few donors make use of them. Steps are nevertheless being taken to reduce the number of PIUs, for example, by consolidating multiple PIUs in the education and health sectors.

Providing more predictable aid

A greater concern is that most aid is not disbursed on a timetable that coincides with the budget cycle. Predictability of aid can be looked at from two different angles. The first angle is that of the donors and the governments' combined ability to disburse aid on schedule. The second angle is that of the donors and the governments' ability to record disbursements that have been comprehensively made by donors for the government sector.

Harmonization

Donors in South Asia have been attempting, some studies claim, to coordinate their activities more effectively, predominantly through pooled funding, shared procedures and SWAPs. This has been facilitated in part by the fact that a number of major donors have delegated significant implementation responsibilities to staff in South Asia. An "Aid Governance" initiative was launched in 2003 to address questions of harmonization. However, the efforts that the donors have made in this regard seem to be very promising.

Using common arrangements and mutual accountability

More than 41 percent of aid to South Asia is channeled via program-based mechanisms, and thus makes use of common procedures. Budget support from the World Bank accounted for 40 percent of this on average, with the remainder disbursed via SWAPs in health and education. Some major donors have also drawn up a joint result matrix to measure progress on their projects and programs. In addition, they can also make an effort to bring the countries closer to the 2015 target, i.e. 66 percent of aid is to be disbursed via program-based approaches. The governments have requested that donor missions should be conducted jointly, in light of concerns about uncoordinated and numerous country missions.[3]

The governments and donors have established task forces to follow up on this. The implementation process should help South Asia meet the target for Indicators by 2015. The Local Consultative Group and the Joint Committee for Monitoring the Implementation Progress of the Poverty Reduction Strategy vis-à-vis Donor Coordination also act as a forum for governments and donors to hold each other to account, though neither of them currently meets the criteria for this indicator on mutual accountability set by the Paris Declaration in 2005. Both donors and governments should create a genuine mechanism for mutual accountability.

The development plan and poverty reduction

The Annual Development Plan (ADP) had been prepared in the light of PRS policies and strategies in South Asian countries to give priority to socio-economic development, employment generation, poverty reduction and human resource development. Projects and programs in different important areas have been undertaken through ADP to implement PRS. Both the Mission Directors of USAID and the World Bank's country directors suggested increasing the utilization of resources and rationalizing ADP with PRSP.[4] The first PRSP was introduced for the period between 2005 and 2008 and the time limit was extended afterwards. It was prepared mainly on the advice of the IMF and the World Bank. But the governments have yet to assess the failures and successes of the first PRSP. For example, in Bangladesh, the PRSP-II, entitled "Moving Ahead: National Strategy for Accelerated Poverty Reduction II (NSAPR)," came into effect in October 2008 and had set ambitious targets of 26.3 percent and 27 percent gross domestic investment out of GDP for the fiscal years 2009–10 and 2010–11.[5] In the case of Nepal, privatization and large cuts in the civil service are strongly endorsed by the PRSP and in the staff review by the international financial institutions (IFIs). These reforms have been on the political agenda in Nepal for several years but have made little real progress.

Since 1992, the World Bank has used the Country Assistance Strategy (CAS) process to set lending levels for countries and to periodically reassess them on a well-reasoned basis. The CAS was followed by the Policy Frame-work Paper (PFP) and finally the Poverty Reduction Strategy Paper (PRSP).[6] By the end of the 1990s, democracy and governance programs had become the major pillars of development aid in South Asia. A new approach to governance aid, however, incorporates the provision of public sector reforms as well. In recent years, support for strengthening governance through the NGOs has gained momentum, relative to other programs. South Asian countries will continue to require substantial external assistance in the decade to come, given the low tax effort and the limited extent to which private sector resources can likely be mobilized for infrastructure, services and other poverty-reducing investments.

The World Bank has forwarded a 70-point agenda to the governments of South Asian countries on financial, social and judiciary issues, i.e. the organization of elections, the control of corruption and the adoption of good governance, all of which are intended for implementation in the fiscal year. The global lender's interests ranged from local government institutions to the planning ministry, from small and medium-sized enterprises to the Election Commission and from banks to the Anti-Corruption Commission. The donor agencies have made it clear that future borrowing from the World Bank and the IMF is dependent on the implementation of the key issues of the 70-point agenda in South Asia.

The global lender wants commitments to eliminate average nominal protection rates, to separate tax policy and planning from tax administration and to combine the two large taxpayer's units (tax and value added tax). A special agenda, dedicated to public finance, suggested a time-bound action plan for the separation of the audit and accounts cadre as well as the extension of the Medium-Term Budgetary Framework to ministries. The public finance agenda was meant to ensure full compliance with international public standard accounting standards; it also aimed to improve public financial management through the enforcement of procurement law and by piloting an e-government procurement system in the planning ministry.[7] We see that the major agenda of the World Bank and the IMF in South Asia is geared towards economic liberalization and privatization of the state-owned enterprises (SOEs), which has been considered by many to be an extension of the Structural Adjustment Program (SAP) conditionality in a new form.

In the past few years, South Asia has witnessed the field-testing of a number of new strategies from structural adjustment to sector-wide approaches and the various Poverty Reduction Strategy Papers (PRSPs). For example, the Government of Nepal published their Tenth Plan and Poverty Reduction Strategy Paper, which provided a comprehensive economic strategy up to 2007 and beyond. Its PRSP contained much that warrants warm endorsement of reforms.

Yet, despite all these efforts to alleviate poverty in the presence of a large number of donors, the South Asian countries have steadily slipped down the Human Development Index (HDI) and have also failed to achieve some of the targets set by the MDGs. Major development actors and national governments should pay more attention in order to learn from the lessons of their organizational past. Notions of partnership and participation are frequently used as tools to implement their development agenda; but they rarely practice it carefully in most of their development programs in South Asia.

Development aid in South Asia

The ideas of what foreign aid means and what it hopes to accomplish have changed over the years. Recently attention has shifted to new areas because of "changing aid faddism," and also in response to genuine concerns regarding aid effectiveness.[8] The empirical findings suggest that the approach either has inherent defects (in many parts of the "Third World" there are doubts about the efficacy of using conditionality to improve policies) or has been implemented in a manner that contributed to its failure to improve governance. Collier and Dehn argue that the instrument of conditionality is largely flawed.[9] In the 1980s, the experience of stabilization and structural adjustment and in 1990s the governance reforms raised concerns about their impacts on the poor, which led to a reassessment of the role of the state.

The new conceptualization of aid has given a "human face" to the market-oriented economic reforms. As a result, a broad consensus has emerged that emphasizes, at least rhetorically, the quality of development assistance rather than purely its quantity. This new concern arose from the donors' belief that much aid in the past has been wasted. It fits in well with the modified version of the so-called Washington Consensus that now incorporates institution-building and good governance as essential ingredients of the reform agenda. A consensus on goals for poverty reduction and social development also emerged in the 1990s in the form of MDGs and the Poverty Reduction Strategic Paper (PRSP).

The flow of foreign aid to South Asia has been affected by this new shift in aid ideas: the World Bank together with the other donors has been imposing "good governance" conditions in every sector while delivering assistance to South Asian countries. The perception of donors is that the weaknesses of the institutions of economic and political governance reduce the country's aid-absorptive capacity and keep economic performance below their full potential. Before we discuss all these points in detail, it is important to first analyze the socio-economic and political scenario of South Asia; this will help us assess whether governance conditionality as prescribed by the donors can bring about genuine good governance in South Asian countries sooner rather than later.

In South Asia, democracy as an institution is relatively new and still fragile. Since achieving independence, India, Pakistan, Bangladesh, and Sri Lanka have witnessed several political hiccups, including a number of army coups and major political or separatist movements, which caused political instability in different periods. One observer (Kamal 2000)[10] notes that in the past few decades South Asian polities have given birth to the idea that these societies are condemned to oscillate between autocracy and democratic rule. With a population of about 1.4 billion, South Asia has a per capita gross national income (GNI) of US$2510 in 2012. Thus, South Asia consists of over one-fifth of the world's population, making it both the most populous and most densely populated geographical region in the world, and yet it is home to half the world's poor. In 2009, 36 percent of the population was living in extreme poverty, falling below the international 1-dollar-a-day poverty line. A further 47 percent fell below the 2-dollars-a-day poverty line.

According to the Global Economic Prospects, in 2012, growth in South Asia slowed to 7.1 percent in 2011 from 8.6 percent in 2010, as the Euro area crisis caused a steep deceleration in exports and a reversal of portfolio inflows. Growth in India and Bangladesh was particularly weak due to monetary policy, stalled reforms, and electricity shortages, which, along with fiscal and inflation concerns, cut into investment activity. But, relatively resilient remittances and good harvests have supported consumption demand in the region. In the case of Sri Lanka, growth further benefitted from reconstruction spending. Key challenges are policy uncertainties, fiscal deficits, entrenched inflation and infrastructure gaps that will continue to weigh negatively on investment activity and are expected to limit South Asian regional growth to a relatively modest 6.4 percent in 2012, 6.5 percent in 2013, and 6.7 percent in 2014.

The World Bank Group is a key development partner in South Asia, with a portfolio of 223 International Development Association (IDA)/International Bank of Reconstruction and Development (IBRD) projects and total commitments of $36 billion as of September 2012. The Bank's strategy for South Asia was updated in March 2012. With a lending program of about $8 billion in the fiscal year 2012, the strategy comprises four pillars: (1) creating more and better jobs by mitigating constraints on growth; (2) building skills and improving health and nutrition outcomes, both closely linked to a focus on women; (3) promoting regional cooperation; and (4) strengthening governance. The Bank's strategy also provides a road map to accelerate growth and foster human development. In the fiscal year 2012 the World Bank approved 54 projects in the region.[11] Total net official development assistance (ODA) to Bangladesh in 2008 was US$1.4 billion, though this accounted for just 2.4 percent of GNI.[12]

Poverty is acute and persistent in South Asia. There is mounting evidence that poverty is associated with poor governance. Yet, the instrumental nature of governance conditionality implies that the main pillars of "good governance" (accountability, transparency and rule of law) are universally applicable, i.e. they can be implemented regardless of the economic orientation, strategic priorities or policy choices of a country's government (World Bank 2000).[13] Political, institutional and governance-related factors play a central role in explaining growth and developmental outcomes. As such, they receive a lot of attention from the various donors who operate in the recipient countries of South Asia. In the 1980s and 1990s, an important aspect of much aid in South Asia was the fact that it came with explicit governance conditions. Thus, the importance of foreign aid has declined over the years in the Third World.[14]

South Asian governments have experienced many reform programs undertaken in different sectors of the economy on the advice of different donor agencies. From now on the donors may tend to impose fresh governance conditions on the governments as a condition for receiving money from them.

If that happens, it will be an issue of great concern for the governments in South Asia as elsewhere.

Resurgent India has received more foreign aid than any other developing nation since the end of World War II, which has been estimated at almost US $100 billion since the beginning of its First Five-Year Plan in 1951. Moreover, it continues to receive more foreign aid in spite of impressive economic growth for almost a decade. At the recent G20 meeting, India asked the World Bank to raise the amount of money India can borrow from the bank for its infra-structure projects.[15]At present, India can borrow up to US$15.5 billion according to the SBL (single borrower limit) in soft loans fixed by the Bank. After the increase of British aid to US$500 million (£300 million) a year, India will still remain the biggest recipient of Japan's ODA in the near future.[16] The BBC have reported how India is using some of the British aid amounting to US$500 million. It said that in 2009 Britain gave almost US$500 million to India in development aid. But India plans to spend more than US$1billion on its space program.

Pakistan receives international aid from several different sources, including countries and the international community. Much of this money goes to the development of stability and civil development within the country. The bulk of foreign aid to Pakistan is from the Coalition Support Fund (CSF) which is reimbursement to Pakistan for expenses already incurred and compensation for facilities made available to the Coalition Forces, such as the Shamsi Airfield and Dalbandin air bases by Pakistan, as well as US$4 billion billed to the CSF for the training and services provided by the American military and its contractors. The amount transferred to the Pakistani Treasury in cash from 2001 to 2011 has been US$8.647 billion. From 2002 to 2010, Pakistan received approximately US$18 billion[17]in military and economic aid from the United States. In February 2010, the US administration requested an addi-tional US$3 billion in aid, for a total of US$20.7 billion.[18] Western officials have claimed nearly 70 percent (roughly US$3.4 billion) of the aid given to the military has been misspent in 2002–2007 and used to cover the civilian deficit. However, the US-Pakistani relationship has been a transactional-based one and US military aid to Pakistan and aid conditions have been shrouded in secrecy for several years until recently.

Between 1972 and 2008, Bangladesh received US$42 billion in foreign aid, of which US$19.3 billion was in the form of grants, and the remaining US $22.7 billion was in concessional loans; the Asian Development Bank (ADB), the World Bank and Japan provided approximately 60 percent.[19] The International Development Association (IDA), established in 1960, com-plements the World Bank's other lending arm such as the International Bank for Reconstruction and Development (IBRD), which helps developing coun-tries with capital investment. IDA provides credits and grants to the poorest developing countries.

Different forums were organized under the leadership of the governments to formulate the implementation process and monitoring of progress of the

PRSP. In the PRSP Implementation Forum (PIFM), different key action points were jointly agreed by governments and DPs to be achieved before the PIFM held in around 2006–2007. One joint committee and eight sub-groups were formed to implement these decisions. The joint committee consists of representatives from both governments and DPs and is responsible for monitoring and implementing progress of the PRS vis-à-vis donor coordination. The PRS will guide the budget allocation process, particularly for pro-poor allocation programs for the next fiscal year, and will also rationalize annual development plans to match PRSP.[20]

Annual Development Plans (ADP) in South Asian countries in recent years have been prepared in the light of PRS policies and strategies to give priority to socio-economic development, employment generation, poverty reduction and human resource development. Projects and programs in different important areas have been undertaken through ADP to implement PRS. Few steps have been taken yet by the Finance Division to assess the utilization performance of the Ministries/Divisions under the Medium-Term Budgetary Framework (MTBF), which is directly involved in poverty reduction and has been given 68 percent of total ADP allocation in recent financial years.

The World Bank's agenda for the financial sector in Bangladesh includes the following demands: bringing the Agrani Bank to the point of sale, revamping the boards of the Agrani, Janata and Sonali Banks, amending guidelines for provident funds and insurance funds to energize Treasury bond market and reforming the insurance law.[21]

Should donors pause to consider whether they need to stop trying out new approaches and instead focus on long-term activities? South Asian countries were the countries to undertake the PRSP process since 2001, though the period varies from country to country. The rushed decision has not helped those who are living in poverty.

The governance–growth nexus

To understand the governance–growth nexus of South Asia, one needs to consider its unique context, i.e. a context in which institutions, historical and cultural settings and its stage of development all play an important part. Most of the international comparisons show very poor perceptions of governance in South Asian countries. Constitutions provide for equality of political citizenship, but fail to deliver on the promise of democracy that most people want. Political parties remain unable to act in a democratic and transparent manner or offer meaningful choices to voters. This has resulted in a low level of trust.[22]

Transparency is the second fundamental aspect of good governance. In relation to South Asia, lack of transparency and the absence of effective monitoring of public spending are major factors contributing to the poor governance. Corruption in South Asia is persistently on the rise. Transparency International ranks Bangladesh, the Maldives, Pakistan and Nepal among the highest on the Corruption Perception Index (CPI) (see Table 3.1).

Table 3.1 Ranking of South Asian countries on the Corruption Perception Index, 2013

Country ranking	Country	Score
36	Bhutan	5.7
87	India	3.3
91	Sri Lanka	3.2
134	Bangladesh	2.4
143	The Maldives	2.3
143	Pakistan	2.3
146	Nepal	2.2

Earlier, India was ranked 84th on the CPI with a score of 3.4 in 2009. But the recent corruption charges in the Commonwealth Games have made it drop down to 87th position. This decline indicates that the country continues to be perceived as more corrupt than in the past. However, India seems more honest in comparison with other countries' ranking in the region. According to Transparency International estimates, corruption cost Pakistan more than Rs.3 trillion from 1999 to 2011—more than a trillion rupees per annum with 15–20 percent annual increase. In 2008, the CPI ranked Sri Lanka at 92nd position out of 180 countries with a score of 3.2.

In 2010, Pakistan's score remained static at 3.2 with a position of 91st and equal in rank to countries such as Bosnia, Guatemala and Zambia. The score remained stagnant due to the absence of independent institutions in the country to address corruption-related issues, even the Bribery Commission is not functional. Bangladesh is the third most corrupt country in the region with a score of only 2.4 out of 10. It keeps on scoring low and is ranked equal to countries such as Nigeria, Togo, Sierra Leone and Zimbabwe. Last but not least, Nepal got the top position with a score of 2.2 in the region. It falls in the group of "highly corrupt" countries with Iran, Yemen, Libya, Cameroon, Haiti, Paraguay and the Ivory Coast sharing the same score. Comparatively, results from 2009 and 2010 indicate a downward movement.

In the governance data set released by the World Bank Institute for 2011, Bangladesh's ranking among 210 countries varied from the bottom seventh to the thirty-second percentile for the six indicators: 6.6 for political stability, 14.9 for regulatory quality, 19.8 for rule of law, 7.9 for control of corruption, 21.1 for government effectiveness and 31.4 for voice and accountability. Bangladesh's position is significantly worse compared to its South Asian neighbors on most indicators. Only in respect of voice and accountability, it is ahead of Nepal and Pakistan. Most of the information from the surveys by the Investment Climate and Doing Business (ICDB) is not encouraging with respect to South Asian countries either.[23] Even more discouraging is the country's poor ranking in the economic competitiveness index prepared by the World Economic Forum.[24]

However, there are some cases of governance in which Global South countries do relatively well. For instance, according to the World Bank's

Doing Business survey of 2011, South Asian countries ranked among the top 50 percent of the countries in terms of the ease of doing business. They actually ranked higher than many developing countries in terms of investor protection.[25] It should also be noted that the corporate tax regimes are relatively liberal in South Asian countries and that profits are fairly high in formal sector enterprises.[26]

In order to assess the state of governance, Dr Mahbub ul Haq of the Development Centre, Islamabad, in 1999 worked out an assessment of governance of 58 countries using the Humane Governance Index (HGI), later published in its annual report. According to the report, South Asia was one of the most poorly governed regions in the world with the lowest HGI values. Out of 58 countries, India was ranked 42, while Pakistan was 52, Sri Lanka was 53 and Bangladesh was 54. In 2002, a pilot testing of 16 countries was conducted under the new governance indicators by the World Governance Assessment (WGA) Project. Only two countries, India and Pakistan, came from South Asia. On a scale of 7 points, India scored 3.27 and Pakistan got only 2.17. There was no sharp difference observed in these two findings; from 1999 and 2002.

Progress remains poor. The recent World Bank Governance Indicators (WGI) are a more refined form of assessment criteria. They measure the governance of any country on the basis of voice and accountability, political stability and absence of violence, government effectiveness, and regulatory quality, rule of law and control of corruption (Table 3.2). WGI analyses voice and accountability by capturing the perception of the extent to which a country's citizens are able to participate in electing governments, as well as enjoying freedom of expression, freedom of association and freedom of the media. Political stability and absence of violence are measured through the perception of the likelihood that the government will be destabilized or overthrown by unconstitutional or violent means.

The third indicator, government effectiveness, analyses through perceptions of the quality of public services, the quality of the civil service, and the degree of its independence from political pressures, the quality of policy formulation and implementation and the credibility of government. Regulatory quality is measured from perceptions of the quality of the government to formulate and implement sound policies and regulations that permit and promote private sector development.

Rule of law in any country is measured by capturing perceptions of the extent to which agents have confidence in and abide by the rules of society, and in particular the quality of contract enforcement, property rights, the police, and the courts, as well as the likelihood of crime and violence. The last indicator, control of corruption, is judged by capturing the perceptions of the extent to which public power is exercised for private gain, including both petty and grand forms of corruption, as well as capture of the state by elites and private interests. In all of the above-mentioned indicators, the South Asian region is lagging behind.

Table 3.2 World Governance Indicators, 2009

Country	Ranking						
	Voice and accountability	Political stability and absence of violence	Government effectiveness	Regulatory quality	Rule of law	Control of corruption	Average
Bangladesh	35.1	7.5	16.7	23.3	27.8	16.7	21.1
Bhutan	29.4	71.2	64.8	13.8	59.4	75.2	52.3
India	60.2	13.2	54.3	44.3	55.7	46.7	45.7
The Maldives	44.1	39.2	42.4	37.1	52.8	29.5	40.8
Nepal	30.8	5.2	18.1	23.8	17.9	25.2	20.1
Pakistan	20.9	0.5	19.0	33.3	19.3	13.3	17.7
Sri Lanka	32.2	11.8	49.0	43.3	53.3	44.8	39.0

Any country's progress in delivering good governance can also be judged by its ability to reduce poverty. Unfortunately, malgovernance in the region has resulted in failure to alleviate poverty, which is widely considered a breeding ground for terrorism and extremism. South Asia's share of global income is only 7 percent while its share of global poverty is about 43 percent and its share of the world population is 22 percent. Per capita income is US$594, which is the lowest in comparison with any other region in the world—even Sub-Saharan Africa has a higher figure than South Asia. The South Asian countries, which have the largest concentration of the poor in the world, have little to no safety net. Figure 3.1 shows the increase in both rural and urban poverty between 1993 and 2011.

The human development balance sheet for the South Asian region, from 1993 to 2004, shows that South Asia's share of the world population remains the same, 22 percent, as it was in 1993–95, but its share of the world's absolute poor has increased from 40 percent in 1993–95 to 47 percent in the year 2004. In education, South Asia has shown a little progress, however; the literacy rate has increased from 47 percent to 58 percent. However, the pace is slower compared to other developing countries including Sub-Saharan Africa. Currently, 212 million people are without access to safe water and the number of people without access to basic sanitation has even increased from 830 million to 897 million. And though the percentage of malnourished children has declined to 46 percent from 52 percent, South Asia still has the highest proportion of malnourished children in the world. Maternal mortality ratio rose to 510 per 100,000 in 2004 from 430 per 100,000 in 1993–94.

South Asian countries have tried to develop their private sectors by using various donor-prescribed policy reforms aimed at maintaining macroeconomic stability, i.e. keeping fiscal deficits low so as not to crowd out bank lending to the private sector, providing access to imported inputs through import liberalization, increasing competition by reducing entry barriers and improving the central bank's oversight functions in respect of commercial banking. The successive democratically elected governments have, since 1991, been able to make relatively good public expenditure choices. The disaster management capacity of the government has also improved significantly over the years. The state has created space for, and established partnerships with, NGOs and the private sector to

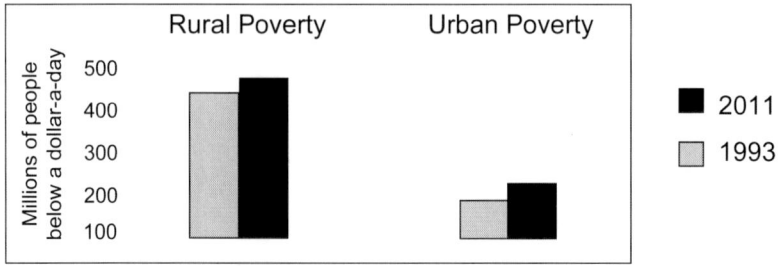

Figure 3.1 Numbers of the poor that rose in South Asia from 1993 to 2011

help deliver social services. And there has also been a certain degree of continuity in policy in spite of changes in the government. After all, it is the fact that most of these recent development goals are set by the donor agencies rather than by the governments. Tangible improvement in governance system is still far off. Leaders in South Asian countries have brought about cosmetic changes through lip service to satisfy their donors and to secure the further inflow of aid money.

Notes

1 The World Bank, *World Bank's 2006 Aid Effectiveness Review* (Dhaka: The World Bank, 2006).
2 External Relations Division, *Report of the External Relations Division (ERD) of Bangladesh* (Dhaka: Government of Bangladesh, 2010).
3 World Bank Section, *Report of the Economic Relations Division* (Dhaka: Government of Bangladesh, 2008).
4 External Relations Division, *Report of the Poverty Reduction Strategy Section* (Dhaka: Government of Bangladesh, 2010).
5 Available at: bangladesheconomy.wordpress.com (accessed October, 24 2008).
6 Shahiduzzaman, K., "PRSP-II: Is Bumpy Ride Ahead?" *The Financial Express*, August 28, 2008.
7 "World Bank Sets Agenda for Government," *The New Age*, July 21, 2007, Dhaka.
8 Easterly, W., "The Effect of IMF and World Bank Programmes on Poverty," Policy Research Working Paper, No. 2517 (Washington, DC: The World Bank, 2000).
9 Collier, P. and Dehn, J., "Aid, Shocks and Growth," Policy Research Working Paper, No. 2688 (Washington, DC: The World Bank, 2001).
10 Kamal, A., "Democracy and Poverty: A missing link?,"AAB Paper, May 2000.
11 Available at: worldbank.org/en/news/2012/09/25/south-Asia-Regional-Brief.
12 These are estimated annual compound growth rates for 2006–7 and 2008–9 and are based on the official national income statistics. See Bangladesh Bureau of Statistics (2008).
13 World Bank, *Taming Leviathan: Reforming governance in Bangladesh* (Dhaka: The World Bank, 2000).
14 *The Daily Star*, June 1, 2010, Dhaka.
15 *The Times of India*, March 20, 2010.
16 Available at: www.defence.pk/forums/world-affairs/51219-massive-foreign-aid-india-continues.html#ixzz2EeySYXoh.
17 Available at: www.thenews.com.pk/daily_detail.asp?id=226110.
18 "Pakistan got $18bn aid from US since 2001," *The Times of India*, February 23, 2010.
19 Bangladesh Bureau of Statistics, *Statistical Pocket Yearbook of* Bangladesh (2008), *Foreign Aid Indicators* (Dhaka: Government of Bangladesh, 2008).
20 Ministry of Finance, *Economic Review*, April (Dhaka: Government of Bangladesh, 2007).
21 "World Bank Sets Agenda for Government," *The New Age*, July 21, 2007, Dhaka.
22 www.idea.int/asia_ pacific/sod_south_asia.cfm.
23 World Bank, *Main Report*, Vol. II (Washington, DC: World Bank, 2011), Chapter 7.
24 Bangladesh ranks 98th out of 102 countries in business competitiveness, according to the World Economic Forum's Global Competitiveness Index, Report of the World Bank, 2011. Available at: www3.weforum.org.
25 In terms of investor protection index, Bangladesh scores 6.7 compared to the OECD average of 6.0 and the South Asian average of 5.0.
26 The World Bank's Doing Business report does not take account of business profitability.

4 The poverty reduction and governance paradox

Introduction

In recent years, it has been argued that poverty should be independently targeted because of the fact that economic growth does not necessarily result in the reduction of poverty. The main thrust of donor policy and aid flows should therefore be to support so-called Poverty Reduction Strategies (PRS). The intellectual basis for this approach has been provided by "trickle-down" theories. Although the debate on these issues is still continuing, the World Bank has decided that the primary focus of aid programs[1] should now be poverty reduction and all low-income countries, including Bangladesh, should adopt this approach and prepare a Poverty Reduction Strategy Paper (PRSP), the centerpiece of dialogue between donors and recipients.[2]

Problems with orthodox structural adjustment loans in South Asia and elsewhere have led the development community to accept that poverty reduction efforts should address poverty in all its dimensions, not only lack of income, but also the lack of health and education and poor people's lack of control over their lives. Therefore, recent approaches to development have included an increased focus on "good governance" to deliver public services to vulnerable groups properly and to more quickly disclose information that poor people can use. The World Bank's Poverty Reduction Strategy makes governance the core, embracing the two pillars of governmental strategies: (1) improving the investment climate; and (2) empowering the poor while addressing the core governance issues common to these two pillars.

Pillar 1 of the World Bank Poverty Reduction Strategy under the Country Assistance Strategy (CAS) seeks to improve South Asia's investment climate; the World Bank group will build on the country's strengths by continuing to help maintain macroeconomic stability and accelerate its progress towards an open and market-based economy. Pillar 2 is about empowering the poor; the World Bank group will attempt to build on South Asia's impressive social gains by helping the governments meet the Millennium Development Goals (MDGs) relating to human development while also enhancing the quality and efficiency of service provision to the poor through sector governance, accountability and enhancing voice and participation as well as local governance. [3] Progress under the two pillars is believed to depend on successful reforms of the core governance reforms under the framework of PRSP.[4] All these governance issues have been given emphasis in the PRSP so as to formulate a more effective strategy of growth and poverty reduction.

The new development strategies have aimed to develop a key focus on the quality of growth.[5] Most of the development literature and donors' PRS emphasize the key role of market-oriented macroeconomic policies, a favorable instrumental environment, good economic and political governance, and private investments in achieving high growth.[6] Poverty reduction strategies should also include an individual country's social, political and cultural conditions to improve the governance system to trigger high economic growth.

Historically, the economy of South Asia was subordinated to the guidelines and targets laid down in the Policy Framework Paper (PFP) prepared by the IMF and the World Bank in the 1980s. Since 1992, World Bank has used the CAS process to set lending levels for a country and periodically reassesses them on a well-reasoned basis. The CAS was first followed by the PFP and then by the PRSP.

The governments of South Asia have undertaken the task of preparing the PRSP in order to have access to soft loans from the World Bank and the IMF. Since the late 1990s, recent foreign aid money has been emphasizing country 'ownership' and putting the recipients in the driver's seat in designing and managing development aid and strategies resulting in a worldwide process of PRSP. However, the policy agenda of the PRSP has to a great extent been pre-empted by the medium-term policy framework that is supported by the World Bank and the IMF.[7] The PRSP was developed following the 'advice' of the World Bank and the IMF in tandem and was prepared by Bangladeshi bureaucrats. It is said that PRSPs do not always reflect the will of the people and strategic papers sometimes ignore their choices. However, this PRSP is the main guide that will be used to decide how the money will be allocated. There is deep concern regarding the positions of governments and donors on the export of natural resources, the lease of the seaports and the critical effects of privatization. People sometimes resist the kind of development agenda that the governments and donors commit to in connection with aid utilization.

The PRSP process started in South Asia in 1999 and this is the generic name for a policy product marketed by the twin powers (the World Bank and the IMF) as the latest reform package. Claims of national ownership and alignment with national plans were further confounded by the involvement of the staff of both the World Bank and the IMF at various stages in the PRSP preparation. They provided "policy advice" not only on fiscal management, but also on structural, institutional and sectoral reforms, budgetary targets and expenditure priorities; in addition, the staff were also invited to carry out joint staff assessments (JSAs) to ensure that the final product could be presented to their Boards for approval. Staff were instructed to consider whether the document provided a "credible framework within which the Bank and Fund are prepared to design their programs of concessional assistance."[8]

The PRSP is prepared by local consultants. Nevertheless, if we consider the text of the document and people's experience, we realize that there are certain mechanisms that can unlock its potential, but it is said to be far from ensuring genuine country ownership at this stage. The donors largely formulate the essence of the strategy and they monitor its implementation.[9] Moreover, the policy matrixes of the PRSP are similar to those of the policies written in the Country Assistance Strategies prepared by the World Bank itself. It is also said that the PRSP and related documents such as those pertaining to Poverty Reduction Support Credit (PRSC) take primacy over a country's own national medium-term plans. There was concern whether a participatory approach and the openness as stated in the text of PRSP could be truly ensured in the PRSP, i.e. that they would also extend to implementation. The question was also raised whether the governments in South Asia truly were committed to a transparent and accountable process of monitoring.[10] PRSP processes have been narrow to some extent in both their substance and participation. Participation has by and large been limited to inviting prominent and well-resourced NGOs to state their views on pre-planned documents. The PRSP is viewed by many as the sugar coating for the reform process which can potentially face the same fate as the earlier generation of reforms due to some persistent problems.[11] Country ownership can be enhanced only by the fact that the governments should be given more autonomy to manage the PRSP process as a whole, depending on their own proposals based on local needs and demands.

The role of donors and poverty reduction

Ideas about the nature of foreign aid have changed over the years. Recently, the focus of aid has started to revolve around aid effectiveness and the quality of development assistance rather than quantity; after all, a lot of aid was believed to be wasted by the recipient countries.[12] Poverty is a broad issue that includes income levels, food security, quality of life, asset bases, human resource capacities, gender inequality, vulnerability and coping. All these aspects correspond to the various MDGs.[13] South Asian countries have taken huge strides towards achieving the MDGs by having poverty in check before 2015. Competent governance can be the key to poverty reduction. The phrase "good governance" has been used as rhetoric, but also here actions speak louder than words: only through competent governance can an equal distribution of public goods be ensured by reducing poverty.

The negative impact of the Structural Adjustment Policy in the 1980s raised concerns about the possible marginalization of the poor and led to a reassessment of the role of the state in more market-oriented economic reforms. In the 1990s, a broad consensus was reached on realizing poverty alleviation and social development in the form of the Millennium Development Goals.[14] In the Paris Declaration of March 2005, a growing number of national and multilateral agencies emphasized notions such as "ownership, harmonization, alignment, results and mutual accountability" and made the following pledges: (1) to align aid efforts according to country-owned PRSPs; (2) to link the aid partner country's PRSP implementation and to refrain from aid conditions that are not consistent with PRSP; and (3) to have mutual accountability between donors and the partner country.[15]

In its World Development Report called *Agriculture for Development*, the World Bank admitted that the process of trade liberalization that it prescribed in the 1990s had in fact resulted in skyrocketing food prices that afflicted the rural population of South Asia (World Bank 2012). This report, released by the World Bank on 19 October 2007, also said that the trend of reducing farm size in agricultural economies like countries in South Asia constituted another major cause of rural poverty, adding that such a reality could well generate further social tensions, leading to civil conflict.[16]

The report also claims that the liberal trade policy which was imposed had generated massive imports of rice by hundreds of small traders during the floods in different parts in South Asia and that it helped the governments stabilize prices without building up any large stock. Trade liberalization that raises food prices hurts net buyers, i.e. the largest group of the rural poor in India, Pakistan, Nepal and Bangladesh, while it benefits net sellers.

The recent priority of donors under the Washington Consensus incorporates institution-building and good governance as essential aspects of reform and Poverty Reduction Strategy plans.[17] The development community is taking an increasingly intrusive approach in the recipient countries through these new approaches to aid. Donors are convinced that the institutional weaknesses of economic and political governance have seriously reduced South Asia's aid-absorptive capacity and utilization.

The IMF and the World Bank have adopted the Poverty Reduction Strategy approach in delivering assistance to developing countries. In order to be eligible for concessional loans issued by the World Bank or the IMF, the PRS process involves the preparation of a Poverty Reduction Strategic Paper (PRSP).[18] For example, the preparation of PRSP was undertaken in Bangladesh after a new government came to power through democratic elections in October 2001. An Interim PRSP (I-PRSP) entitled "A National Strategy for Economic Growth, Poverty Reduction and Social Development" was finalized in March 2002[19] and a draft of the complete PRSP was produced in December 2004. The final version of the PRSP, under the title "Unlocking the Potential: National Strategy for Accelerated Poverty Reduction" came out in October 2005 (Government of Bangladesh 2005). The governments in South Asia applied for IMF program lending under the so-called Poverty Reduction and Growth Facility (PRGF) and the World Bank's Development Support Credit (DSC) under the PRSP umbrella; both these credit programs were negotiated under a medium-term policy framework involving disbursements of funds in a series of installments.[20] A joint assessment by the World Bank and the IMF approved the PRSP. All the other development partners that work in Bangladesh (several UN agencies, the Asian Development Bank and the bilateral donors) have accepted the need to align their aid operations with the PRS approach so as to pursue their own agency-specific goals more effectively. Some critics say that though consultations were held prior to the preparation of PRSP-II, the suggestions made and opinions voiced by some stakeholders were not incorporated into the document because of the government's tendency to uncritically swallow the lender's recipe.[21]

In South Asia, the World Bank's strategy has strongly focused on "good governance," which has been aligned with the PRSP in the national development plan of individual countries. PRSP has increasingly become the centerpiece for support from other international aid agencies. However, due to the gloomy picture required by the PRSPs to reduce poverty drastically in South Asia, most of the countries have gone back to their original five-year plan, putting aside PRSPs. Sweeping policy changes have occurred in the World Bank's Country Assistance Strategy since the mid-1990s, the ADB's Country Strategies and Program from 2006 and the United Nations Development Assistance Frameworks from 2006, the latter being the joint document of the individual governments in South Asia and the UN agencies on the ground and other bilateral donors.[22] To improve aid effectiveness, the donors nowadays prioritize country ownership of pro-poor development strategies and better alignment or harmonization of donor policies to reduce the transaction costs of delivering aid.[23]

Weaknesses of the PRS

The policy shift of donors to poverty reduction in recent years has given rise to "aid populism." Investments in key areas such as infrastructure, energy and technology development were under-funded as the emphasis was on directly targeted poverty interventions. This kind of policy shift is explicit in the World Bank's global aid portfolio and visible in its policy towards South Asia. However, this was compensated for to some extent by two other big donors like the ADB and Japan, which continued to remain engaged in the above sectors. All the donors in South Asia have taken official initiatives to align their aid operations with the PRSP and have been referred to in their country assistance strategies. As a step towards donor coordination and harmonization, the World Bank prepared its CAS jointly with ADB, DFID and Japan. The four development partners are called "the Gang of Four" as together they currently provide 80 percent of all development assistance in South Asia.

The PRSP covers a much wider range of strategies and policies than the CAS does, and the period is also slightly different sometimes. For example, the PRSP's medium-term policy agenda was for the three-year period of FY 2005–FY 2007, while the 'outcome/milestones' of the CAS referred to the four-year period of FY 2005–FY 2009. Although the alignment between the joint CAS and the PRSP appears promising, most of the strategic goals of PRSP are broad enough for a range of policy items to fit in. It is not very clear whether the policy agenda in the CAS is guided by that of the PRSP in every matter or not.[24] There are some minor but significant differences between the PRSP policy agenda and the CAS milestones in some key governance issues. For instance, both incorporate enactment of the law regarding the right to information, but the PRSP puts it only under future priorities. Regarding the improvement of government procurement procedures, both include similar actions including the introduction of e-procurement; however, the CAS agenda goes one step further to include compliance with procurement regulations to be monitored "through independent annual procurement review" and through civil society surveillance.[25]

Although the PRSP puts forward many policies, particularly to improve the quality of governance in the countries of South Asia, it sometimes prescribes what the government should do rather than telling them what the government actually proposes to do. The PRSP consists of many policy matrices covering macroeconomic management, sectoral policies and many cross-cutting development themes, such as governance, food security and women's rights. Under different strategic goals, each of the policy matrices shows the PRSP policy agenda along with future priorities. Of these policy matrices; governance is set as a crucial issue for poverty reduction and growth. Some specific actions are suggested to improve governance and stimulate investment such as optimizing the public procurement process through online tendering.[26] This was also done through separation of the judiciary and executive branches of government and also through the reduction of the role of the Members of Parliament in local development strategies. Implementation of different programs solely by different local government bodies may be politically difficult in South Asia, considering the critical nature of national politics in the individual countries.

The PRSP has focused on the reiteration of qualitative assertions to improve governance and to make the anti-corruption institutions more effective by strengthening watchdog bodies, using fiscal resources, enhancing reforms for revenue mobilization, minimizing the losses of State-Owned Enterprises (SOEs), etc. These are some major policies stipulated in PRSP. In addition, sector-wide approaches (SWAPs) will be used to reform the state-owned banks through management contracts, to rationalize power tariffs, to modernize the central bank, and to implement much of the policy agenda for health, population and education programs, etc. This policy agenda has been agreed under the ongoing World Bank–IMF fund program lending, in spite of many inherent problems and deficiencies.

The perceptions of weak governance and fiduciary and other risks have discouraged donors in South Asia from operating through the available country systems, leading to the creation of parallel implementation structures and excessive fragmentation of donor activities. Adopting a multi-donor program-based approach or SWAP does not always create the desired outcomes, as can be seen in the SWAPs in the health sector. For example, the Health and Population Sector Programme (HPSP) was the first SWAP in Bangladesh, a multi-year program (1998–2003) led by the World Bank, designed as a blueprint for the program action of the 1994 International Conference on Population and Development (ICPD). It aimed at integrating family planning and reproductive health and promoting rural healthcare by setting up an extensive network of community-driven rural health centers across the country, by acquiring agricultural lands. The program looked perfect on paper but did not work properly in practice. It lacked local ownership and was clearly over-designed in terms of resource needs and institutional arrangements, because the plan was made to restructure the entire health administration and mobilize community participation. It did not work properly because the plans were too ambitious.[27]

Thousands of newly established health centers remained unused and empty in many countries in South Asia. Moreover, the family planning service was withdrawn and both the administrative restructuring and community partici-pation proved unworkable.[28] A SWAP for the health sector, called HNPSP (N is added for nutrition), had been launched in Bangladesh to cover the period from 2005–10.[29] It lacked effective local ownership though there was more local participation in its project design. A number of project support units had been set up as a provision of the project, which would be tantamount to running a parallel administration along with the government system. The notion of centralized bulk procurement through international bidding was found to be time-consuming, and burdensome for small local purchases.

Sometimes, donors complain about the difficulty of finding enough capable or trustworthy officials within the government agencies in South Asia to set up a project or program with local ownership. The lack of trust leads to a tendency for donors to try to micromanage the aid-financed projects and to arrange too many project appraisal and performance review missions. Through all these activities the donors try to exert pressure on the governments to implement development projects in the proper way.

The Paris Declaration stipulates that "donors draw aid conditions, whenever possible, from the partner's national development strategy" and that "other conditions would be included only when a sound justification exists" to act otherwise. When a lack of local knowledge is combined with universalistic preferences and assumptions, this may lead to a project design that either potentially can create problems or can be counterproductive sometimes.[30]

Although an internationally accepted idea of best practice in this respect shifted back and forth, another "inclusion" of the public expenditure support facilities (PESF-II) is to target school children from poor and vulnerable groups; the exact mechanism for achieving these objectives is left up to the expatriate consultants to find out (one condition of the project is to appoint such expatriate consultants). Thus, governments and donors sometimes offer what they want to provide, not what the poor can use. The projects designed by the governments and the donors usually have the characteristics of a top-down approach that is inadequately informed by knowledge of what works and what does not; they tend to apply global templates in designing projects without adequate feedback on local cultural traditions or institutional charac-teristics. As a result, poverty reduction strategies and governance reforms largely fail to work properly in South Asia. Moreover, vast amounts of aid money are being wasted, putting the interests of the elites first while at the same time allowing poverty conditions in South Asia to become critical, as marked by the sharp inequality between the rich and the poor and widening the gap between them.

MDGs and poverty reduction

The Millennium Development Goals (MDGs) are developmental targets that were globally adopted in September 2000. There are eight international development goals:

- eradicate extreme poverty and hunger (MDG1);
- achieve universal primary education (MDG2);
- promote gender equality and empower women (MDG3);
- reduce child mortality (MDG4);
- improve maternal health (MDG5);
- combat HIV/AIDS, malaria, and other diseases (MDG6);
- ensure environmental sustainability (MDG7);
- and develop a global partnership for development (MDG8).

Initially MDGs were embraced by 189 countries, including those in South Asia, by signing the Millennium Declaration – a resolution adopted by the UN General Assembly in order to improve development and reduce poverty (McArthur and Sachs 2003).

MDGs are a historical initiative taken by the UN to commit to halving poverty across the globe by 2015 (Vandemoortele 2004). The term 'poverty' is used in the same context as it is defined by the UN statement signed by the heads of all UN agencies in July 1998. The UN had defined poverty as "fundamentally, poverty is a denial of choices and opportunities, a violation of human dignity. It means lack of basic capacity to participate effectively in society." Therefore, poverty can be defined as having few or lack of opportunities. Moreover, the same poverty measurement indicators were adopted in South Asian countries, allowing the MDG Country Reports 2005, 2007 and 2010 to identify poverty levels in the country concerned. On the other hand, the term 'development' is used inter changeably to mean advancement or progress in MDGs. Thomas (2000) characterized development as "a vision or measure of progressive change," while Gore relates it to "performance assessment." In this chapter, MDGs which are policy-related, indicator-led and have medium-term horizons will be considered development indicators. Thus, a positive indicator in MDGs will be considered a progressive development which reduces poverty in the Maldives.

The PRSP and poverty reduction strategies of the donors were aligned with the MDGs in South Asia. It should be noted that MDGs are sometimes claimed to be ambitious; in many respects the MDGs and good governance are the products of the triumph of capitalism in the post-cold war era.[31] The political framework to achieve the MDGs was provided by the new global deal between the Global North and the Global South in 2002 in Monterrey, Mexico. World leaders endorsed a relatively ambitious agenda at the United Nations Millennium Summit, held there in September 2000. The United Nations Development Programme (UNDP) links and coordinates global and national attempts to achieve the Millennium Goals.[32] The UNDP, in collaboration with the Government of Bangladesh, is coordinating and reporting on progress towards the UN Millennium Development Goals, which includes eight goals set out in the UN Millennium Declaration, and presents specific timetables for reducing extreme poverty and chronic hunger. The MDGs have specific timeframes which run until the targets are met by 2015. There are ongoing efforts in South Asia to achieve the MDGs by 2015, but progress on this front has been slow and uneven.[33]

A report by the ADB on the MDGs, published in February 2012, has stated that the South Asian nations are making the least progress in the Asia-Pacific region in meeting the MDGs they had pledged to achieve by 2015. These goals include reducing child and maternal mortality, halving poverty and hunger, providing universal primary education, gender equality, and halting the spread of HIV/AIDS. The report also added that all South Asian countries, with the exception of Sri Lanka, have fallen behind in achieving MDGs on poverty reduction, eliminating hunger, completion of basic education, gender parity and provision of tertiary education.[34] The 2010 Millennium Development Goals report painted a dark picture for South Asia, including India.[35] The report was alarming, predicting the inability of these countries to meet the MDGs of halving poverty and extreme hunger by 2015 and to eliminate gender disparity up to secondary education by 2015 (India has already missed that target). The situation is equally grim when it comes to child mortality and maternal mortality rates in India.

The number of people in extreme poverty in India is likely to drop by 188 million by 2015, according to the report that warns South Asia of the danger of missing the MDGs. UNICEF India representative Karen Hulshof agreed with the warning, saying 70 million Indians still lived below the poverty line. On most other MDGs, South Asia is closer to Sub-Saharan Africa than to the advancing East or South-East Asia. The 2008 financial meltdown has worsened the situation here, with India adding to its numbers of hungry poor. In South Asia, the percentage of the population suffering from hunger rose between 2002 and 2007 from 20 to 21 percent. India and Pakistan together account for the bulk of under-nutrition in South Asia, having witnessed an 80 percent rise in food prices post-2008. Data analysis shows that South Asia has the highest child malnutrition rates globally, with 46 percent of children below 5 there being underweight. This marks a poor 5 percent decline from 1990 when the rate was 51 percent.

In South Asia, only 9 percent of women are managers and just 20 percent are employed outside agriculture. Reductions in infant mortality rates (IMR) and maternal mortality rates (MMR) are also far from successful. "The annual rate of reduction of IMR and MMR is well short of 5.5% which was needed to meet these MDGs." Over 99 percent of women who die globally in childbirth are in South Asia, with just one in four rural women getting any antenatal care. Pakistan has made a little progress in reducing maternal mortality and providing universal access to reproductive health as required by MDG 5, by attaining an average annual reduction in maternal mortality of 3 percent between 1990 and 2010. However, this is still 2.5 percent less than the 5.5 percent target to be met by 2015.

The Maldives is a small South Asian nation with a population about 350,000 people, dispersed across 196 islands spread over 300 miles; it is one of the most dispersed countries in the world. The developmental policies of the country are outlined in a framework called the National Development Agenda, which is drawn up with the help of subordinate ministries. The Department of National Planning, the former Ministry of Planning and National Development (MPND) plays a vital role in the framing process. The National Development Agenda aims to reduce poverty and achieve development. To do so, top priority is given to the MDGs (discussed later). Adequate policies are included in all the development agendas in the Maldives to achieve MDGs.[36]

The 6NDP and 7NDP in Maldives, adopted between 2000 and 2008, followed a path of progressive development by achieving three MDGs. These achievements were realized following adequate importance given to MDGs in the NDP. The 6NDP, as the first truly participatory consultative development agenda, paved the way to include policies to attain MDGs. "Government officials, and the private sector, as well as local administrators and Chiefs in the atolls were actively involved in the preparation process for the 6th NDP."[37] Apart from this, a fairly high priority was given to the MDGs in the 7NDP. One reason could be that the MDG Country Report 2005 was published when the Maldives government was framing the 7NDP.

Gender inequalities persist in education too. India, despite small gains, missed the 2005 deadline of achieving gender parity up to secondary level, and it may not meet the 2015 target of equality across all education levels.[38] Nepal, Bangladesh and Sri Lanka have done better. The South Asian nations need to accelerate the pace of poverty reduction from 1.5 percent per year observed in the 1990s to 3.3 percent for the period 2000–15. Calculations show that if the past trends of income inequality persist into the next decade, the nations will have to sustain a GDP growth rate of about 7 percent per year over the next 15 years to be able to reach the income-poverty reduction target.

The priority of MDGs is identifiable, as the key principles in the 7NDP are the focus of some MDGs. These include "promote gender equality" and "ensure environmental sustainability," which accords with MDG1 and MDG7. In addition, five of the 12 targeted goals in the 7NDP are directly associated with MDGs. These five goals are: Goal 4: Create a sustainable built environment that ensures preservation; Goal 5: Protect the natural environment; Goal 6: Invest in people through providing equal opportunity for education; Goal 7: Improve access to housing and health care; and Goal 8: Empower women.

Achieving these goals would make a positive impact on MDG2, MDG3, MDG6 and MDG7. Therefore, it is clear that these strategies are embedded in national development planning to prioritize MDGs and attain progress.

Good governance is imperative to achieving MDGs as set by the UNDP and the World Bank. Governance issues are described in the PRSP but various reforms that have been undertaken in this regard have proved less effective to ensure transparency, accountability and rule of law in a proper way. There is a risk of having good intentions derailed under the pressure to make large and quick increases in expenditure to meet the timetable to achieve the MDGs.

The World Bank has come to see the relationship between state entities and economic markets as lying at the core of a "governance" agenda, and therefore, as a means of advancing towards the materialization of the MDGs.[39] Having said that, the governance agenda remains more market-centric than state-centric. As one study concludes, "The World Bank's faith in market mechanisms underestimates the significant challenges posed by institution-building and the need to protect the vulnerable."[40] The governments in South Asia can easily get involved in corruption by giving emphasis to deregulation and partnerships with the private sector and NGOs, because of the lack of credible interactions between them.

MDGs and good governance (as interpreted by the international financial institutions) both set out with the assumption that rapid economic growth will effectively address their respective aspirations. However, different studies have pointed to the limitations of the "growth response," indicating that the emphasis on quick growth has come at the expense of equity and equality. The actual outcome may not be satisfactory from a social standpoint if one applies narrow managerial and numerical criteria to determine what poverty is or what kind of appropriate governance it entails. Simultaneously, governance reforms sometimes discourage direct intervention by governments to regulate, mitigate or prevent negative social impacts. There is also a critical contradiction seen largely between poverty eradication, on the one hand, and the narrow application of good governance as a development strategy, on the other. Those contradictions must be acknowledged and unpacked in order to enable a genuine discussion about possible alternatives.[41]

Incompetent high-level political leadership is one of the major factors which prevent most South Asian nations from meeting the targets of the MDGs. Three important targets on poverty, slums and water have been positive in most of the South Asian nations. However, meeting the remaining targets, while challenging, is possible, but only if governments do not waiver in their commitments made over a decade ago. Much depends on the attainment of MDG8 calling for the global partnership for development. The current financial crisis besetting much of the developed world should not be allowed to decelerate or reverse the progress that has been made so far. South Asian nations should build on the successes they have achieved so far, and should not give up until all the MDGs have been attained.

Policy reforms

South Asia managed to implement broad-based structural-adjustment type reforms in the early 1990s, but has since failed to pursue more politically challenging second-generation market reforms. This raises important questions about what political, economic and social forces drive or block policy change in the region, and how these have changed over time. Not surprisingly perhaps, the current policy paralysis appears to be the outcome of incentives created by strengthened client–patron relationships permeating the policy-making process across the region. Institutions, historical and cultural settings, and the stage of development matter for an understanding of the political economy of policy-making. Across South Asia, there are differences in the way institutions and governance structures have developed. India and Sri Lanka have relatively mature and established democratic institutions and systems. Bangladesh and Pakistan, on the other hand, have been subject to frequent authoritarian military rule. Yet the commonalities across the region are far greater, emanating from a shared colonial history that saw each country inheriting very similar political and administrative structures.[42]

A need to repudiate links with the past saw South Asian governments strive for national self-sufficiency by enthusiastically adopting inward-looking economic policies. Despite rising evidence that such policies were failing to deliver the desired development goals, the democratic forms of government practiced in the region were slow to react, owing largely to the need to build consensus. A hesitant reform process that began in the late 1970s and progressed through the 1980s only became a more comprehensive effort in the early 1990s when India began a major reform initiative.

Many of the key elements that drive reform in developing countries, such as the presence of domestic economic difficulties, pressure from international financial institutions, a break from groups with vested interests and strong political leadership, were present in each of the major reform episodes. Notwithstanding the presence of international financial institutions, national policy-makers played a leading role, as evident from the sequencing, pacing and design of the reforms. Bangladesh tackled its agricultural inputs market first, before moving on to more contentious import tariff reforms. Where difficult reforms were implemented, such as the withdrawal of food subsidies, compensatory policies such as public works programs were built in, even when they had an obvious fiscal cost. Yet despite the inroads made, South Asia's reform efforts have attracted considerable criticism for their narrowness of scope.[43]

Nonetheless, no reversal of reforms occurred. More importantly, since the mid-1990s, there has been a convergence on economic policy across mainstream political parties in the region. It is thus even more paradoxical that South Asia has been gripped by policy paralysis over the last decade. The failure to strengthen institutions and governance structures lies at the heart of this paralysis. Indeed, the region's record in most global governance indicators is very poor, with India doing marginally better than its neighbors. The typical rent-seeking activities under a license regime have been replaced by stronger patron–client relationships between politicians and other key actors in the policy-making process. The concentration of state power has intensified, with political parties dominated by a handful of families, stifling democratic practice within parties, and centralizing decision-making.

Most South Asian countries implemented extensive reforms during the early 1990s to facilitate their integration into the global economy. The impact of these reforms on trade and economic growth has so far been weak. The significant initial effect of globalization on trade has not been robust. Further-more, the favorable initial effect of globalization on economic growth has not been sustained and the inequality in the distribution of income has continued to rise. More inequality and slow growth have contributed to the increase in the incidence of rural poverty. Since 1990, all the countries in the South Asian region have been following the path of economic reform. However, despite this, there has not been any significant improvement in the levels of poverty, unemployment, demographic features, health and distribution of incomes and opportunities. Most South Asian nations are not able to maintain coherence between their economic and social set-ups during the period of economic reforms. The main beneficiaries of their new growth process are the elite classes of society, i.e. the white-collared workers, the skilled workers in the information/ communication technology sectors. South Asia's growth (5.8 percent) during 1980–89 fell to 5.4 percent during 1990–98 and has been on average 6 percent in recent years.

The liberalization and the globalization of markets have compelled domestic industries to face a highly competitive world. In South Asia, the numbers of people living below the poverty line have increased despite the 6.5 percent growth rate of the largest country, India. Inter- and intra-regional inequalities have increased, leading to a highly skewed income distribution pattern in favor of high income groups during this period. Under-development in South Asian countries involves three major features: (1) the low level of living; (2) the low self-esteem of the people; and (3) limited freedom of choice. These three forces act and react upon each other as cause and effect. Along with these, international forces in the form of international transfer of values (communication, fashion, technology) and cultural vulnerability again strengthen the vicious circle.[44] Although there has been a continuous heated debate over the basis of ascertaining the percentage of people living below the poverty line and there have been significant differences between the data provided by the Planning Commission, the National Sample Survey (NSS) in India, Pakistan, Nepal, Bangladesh, and Sri Lanka, this shows that there are two groups of intellectuals who are debating the poverty line phenomenon.

The first group, called the pro-liberalization lobby, claims that the pace of financial growth led by the economic reforms of the post-1990 Indian govern-ments has brought a significant decrease in the numbers of the poor and therefore, the percentage of people living below the poverty line has gone down. On the other hand, the opposers of liberalization claim the economic growth is 'so-called' and find that the fruits of liberalization have essentially been grabbed by an inflated middle class and the plight of the poor has remained the same. Even when India has reached self-sufficiency in food grain production and the Union government is often faced with the problem of plenty and the increasing demands of a hike in prices, with the proper storage facilities, and fuller use of the food grain, the other part of the story remains shabby and shameful with the account of starvation deaths in Orissa and Bihar and suicides of hundreds of farmers in different provinces, along with the disturbing statistics on malnutrition.

This problem has to be seen not only in economic terms but also in terms of political decision-making because there are much larger problems in the field of public distribution system (PDS). The extent of corruption and mismanagement in the PDS requires serious attention by researchers as well as policy-makers in order to reach a proper understanding of the problem of public distribution. It is clear that the way out of the vicious circles of cause-and-effect relationship is to raise the standard of living of people in the developing nations for this purpose, and economic reforms can play an important role in this.

Organizational development (OD) was used as a tool for the achievement of the reform and development goals in Bhutan. An important part of this reform agenda has been the retooling and refocusing of the civil service. A series of reforms were enacted and these are linked to the internationally popular goal of instituting good governance to reduce poverty. In the Bhutanese case, this has been tied to four important pillars: transparency, accountability, efficiency, and professionalism.[45] There is considerable potential to use OD in the pursuit of the multi-level goals and, in fact, there is a high level of fit between the principles and values of OD and the stated reform agenda in Bhutan. However, it is argued that the implementation of this approach is problematic and several tensions are emerging. These tensions have the potential to undermine both the OD approach itself, and the ability of Bhutan to use OD to achieve a complex set of organizational and social goals. Given the unique development approach of Bhutan, this represent a lost opportunity to use OD to achieve significant social outcomes.

OD in Bhutan pursues multi-level goals and it has been connected to other government policies and is viewed in the Bhutanese approach as a tool to enact the organizational change accompanying the major reform agenda. For example, in the Position Classification System, OD is seen as a tool for monitoring and evaluation which could "help to assess the overall health of the Civil Service" (RGoB 2007, p. 64). OD is also included in the Bhutan Civil Service Rules and Regulations of 2006 where it is mandated that every "Agency … undertake OD exercises regularly to enhance both organisation and individual performance" (ibid., p. 2). In the *Good Governance Plus* report, OD was specifically linked to the right-sizing agenda and it was stated that the outcomes of the OD exercises were expected to form the basis for all decisions that would relate to restructuring, staffing and capacity building.

As part of the Bhutanese OD policy, every government agency is required to undertake OD exercises every three to five years and it is expected that this will include an assessment of achievements, formulation of vision, the mission, values and strategies and revisions to structure and staffing.

The use of OD to try and achieve multi-level, complex economic or social goals is something that has been alluded to in the OD performance but the way in which it is playing out in Bhutan is unprecedented. There appears to be a high level of fit between the unique reform approach adopted by Bhutan and the values and principles of OD. Philosophically, it appears that the Bhutanese have attempted to balance the tensions between human and institutional development using OD, the ultimate challenge as set out by Friedlander and Brown (1974).[46] In practice, however, it appears that OD is being used to undertake audit processes, indicating that it is institutional reform and development which have taken precedence over human development. In the context of its unique development philosophy and the rhetorical claims at least to focus on linking individual and national development, this approach is problematic. And while there is still considerable research to be done on this experiment, it is believed that the early stages of implementation suggest a lost opportunity in using OD to achieve multi-level development goals and better balance institutional and human development needs.

The Maldives is coming to terms with a reformed tax system, following the introduction of a General Goods and Services Tax in 2011. The Finance Minister said that the new system, which had raised the eyebrows of businesses, consumers and politicians alike, was a natural consequence of recent political changes and required everyone's support to function well. After the 2005 democratic reform, costs increased. These costs had to be met by additional revenue. The Maldives had a state deficit of Rfl.3 billion (US$85 million) in 2011–12. Since democratization, the Maldivian government has surpassed other national governments' employment rates by employing 10 percent of the national workforce. One-third of government spending goes to state employees, and nearly half of the 2011 budget was spent on salaries and allowances.[47]

The Goods and Services Tax (GST), which became operative in October 2011, has raised a 3.5 percent tax on certain items. Contrary to an earlier tax which was paid for at the point of import and effectively invisible to the customer, the GST requires most businesses to charge an additional 3.5 percent directly to the customer at point of sale. Certain items are tax-exempt in the Maldives, a detail which has allegedly made it difficult to implement in stores selling a variety of products. The government is optimistic that the new tax reform system will cut costs and improve business operations. Many businesses are compliant with the new measures. Business owners will have to crunch the numbers, and that will show them more about what is happening in their businesses. They will be able to better see how things operate in the near future.

The GST is part of a larger tax reform system described in "a package of policy reforms that will help stabilise and strengthen the Maldives' economy" agreed to by the Maldives and the IMF in May 2011. The policy reforms included raising the Tourism Goods and Services Tax (TGST) from 3.5 percent to 6 percent from January 2012, and to 10 percent in January 2013. Tourism is one of the Maldives' leading economic contributors. Policy-makers stressed that the tax was a step towards self-sufficiency for the Maldives. The international community will not give Maldives the money required to balance the deficit, therefore, the people of the Maldives are the ones who have to raise that money and it is everyone's responsibility to make sure that they can stand on their own feet.

Meanwhile, the opposition party (DRP) in the Maldives has expressed concern over the tax, after supporting its initial pass through parliament. They claimed that businesses were not sufficiently prepared for the transition, and requested a six-month delay. Noting "administrative confusion" and the country's heavy reliance on imports, the DRP also suggested levying a customs duty at the entry point to the country as a more effective means of raising revenue. The opposition party believed that the GST is a regressive expense. The government does not have the infrastructure to support it, and implementation of the GST will require the hiring of a lot of people. The government claimed that the tax system had not been implemented prematurely; rather it would only benefit large businesses while harming smaller ones.

The opposition party has claimed that the government is doing the opposite of what it preaches. The main problem with the bill is that the government has decreased the tax burden on the very rich, especially in the tourism sector. The current tax system should be overhauled and replaced with a modern one along with progressive taxes. The DRP was in favor of the recently announced plan to decrease import duties starting in January 2012. A policy to reduce import duties would bring prices down starting the next year. Waiving certain import duties would be significant and once the new tax system is fully operational, all will fall into place. The only issue was that many businesses had a shortage of coins. Maldivians have a habit of rounding up amounts to avoid coin transfers, but in a successful economy coins are important. The Maldives Inland Revenue Authority (MIRA) has been doing a commendable job in distributing coins, and the Maldives Monetary Authority (MMA) foresaw the issue and has a distribution system in place.

It was alleged that the party's motives were political but the president was advised by his advisors and economic experts that a taxation system needed to be implemented. It is argued that the very rich have not been taxed appropriately as per their earnings. Once the tax system is fully in place, things should stabilize. Tax reforms were seen as an economic and social issue, concerning the distribution of wealth. Even with the new taxes, the Maldives still has the most generous tax system in South Asia, even compared with other island nations, and its neighboring countries such as India and Sri Lanka.

The mammoth numbers of the population of India cause alarm. South Asia's share of the world's population is massive and the population policies of the country have failed miserably, thus causing a serious impediment to development efforts. The National Population Policy 2000 in India aimed at providing and ensuring education for all up to the age of 14 years, reducing infant mortality and maternal mortality, providing universal immunization, delaying marriages, increasing institutional and supervised deliveries,providing 100 percent registration of births, deaths, marriages and pregnancy, tackling communicable diseases, promoting the small family norms, and linking family planning to other social sector programs. In the demographic arena, the population explosion has been a huge challenge for India. India's population is likely to exceed even China's by 2020. All its development gains will be lost if India fails to control the size of its huge population. Due to the high population growth rate, about one-third of the population in India is unproductive, In other words, a major proportion of development expenditure in the form of healthcare, childcare, and primary education is spent on current and not on capital heads. This is a matter of serious concern for a developing nation like India. One of the important development indicators is the percentage of the urban population. In India, excessive rural to urban migration has resulted in a 28 percent urban population. But rapid urban migration without adequate civic amenities in the cities has ultimately led to the massive growth of slums or *jhuggis*, again escalating the urban misery and calamity in the form of pollution, lack of sanitation, mismanaged administration, poor law and order, widening urban disparities, the excessive pressure of the workforce on the highly capital-intensive and low employment flexible manufacturing and service sectors, and ultimately resulting in excessive urban unemployment. Widening economic disparities with the high growth rate of the economy show the worsening distribution framework of the economy. In a welfare state, distribution is just as important as growth and development.

But the most disturbing aspect of India's development pattern is the social sector. Capital is a necessary but not a sufficient condition of development. It means that the human resources are equally important in the development of an economy. Too much emphasis upon absolute high growth rates in terms of income, in the industrial, agricultural and external sectors, along with the poor growth of the social sector (health, education and the environment) will fail to sustain the high levels of development in the long term. It is essential for the government of a welfare state to give enough attention to this sector, especially in the era of economic reforms, i.e. liberalization, privatization and globalization.

The paradox of reforms

Governments in South Asia are gradually withdrawing from public sector expenditure and the biggest victims of this disinvestment privatization process are the health and education sectors. This process must be stopped. A developing welfare state with a high poverty rate cannot afford to leave this sector to the mercy of market forces (privatization), otherwise it will lead to further marginalization of the middle- and low-income groups of society as well as agricultural laborers and casual workers. Such a highly skewed development pattern is undesirable in South Asian conditions.

South Asia's bureaucracy is more politicized and powerful, performing both administrative and political functions, as politicians rely on a few hand-picked technocrats to formulate and implement policy. The dual role and discretionary powers these people enjoy mean a greater blurring of transparency and accountability in policy decisions, and a distancing of policy-makers and elected politicians from their constituencies. While democracy has spread in South Asia, political party rivalry and confrontational politics are more pronounced, particularly in countries such as Bangladesh and Pakistan. The growth of small parties representing narrow interests is giving rise to minority coalition governments in India and Sri Lanka. They not only hamper reform efforts, but strengthen patron–client relationships. Coalition arrangements require that posts and privileges are dispensed freely, and polarization in party politics encourages the practice of competitive populism to the detriment of sound policy-making.

In the absence of credible channels through which the public or interest groups can influence policy-making, the region is increasingly seeing judicial intervention being sought as a compensatory mechanism. In Sri Lanka and Pakistan, interest groups have successfully petitioned the Supreme Court to halt or reverse privatization deals. India has witnessed judicial intervention in corruption scams, as well as petitioners seeking court intervention in pushing forward civil service reforms. But judicial intervention is not an appropriate compensatory channel to fix the weaknesses in institutionalizing a reform process. More often than not, governments view judicial intervention as an over-reaching of court powers whereby any ensuing tussle runs the risk of compromising judicial independence. Instead of seeking judicial intervention, South Asia should focus on reinvigorating its politico-institutional structures to institute norms and rules that will restrain the drift towards arbitrary action and corruption.

This dynamics reveals how reforms operate within the context of a particular administration system, particularly in administrative systems that exhibit the traits of hybrid systems, and shows the importance of matching the values of the reforms to the values of the administrative systems. These discussions conform to studies which show that successful reforms are culturally sensitive, and that there should be a match between rules, identities and situations. The disparities are more pronounced when considering the application of NPM-type (a platform for inclusive finance) reforms from the developed countries to the developing countries or from Western Anglo-Saxon countries to the Asian countries. In such circumstances, inherent differences in culture and values require the recipient countries to either accept or adapt the new culture and values embedded within the reforms, or acknowledge the differences and change the reforms to suit the local context. This emphasizes the need for Asian management researchers to use indigenous knowledge to contribute to reforms with a global relevance.[48]

Governance and human development

It is clear that a high literacy rate in a nation will lead to better participation of the people in democracy and power sharing, a scientific temper and attitude among people, higher levels of labor productivity and above all the progressive and enthusiastic attitude of people towards development. Indicators such as life expectancy at birth (in years), and female and male life expectancy show that the Indian government still has a lot to do to improve the quality of its manpower, which will ultimately lead to higher levels of productivity and income levels.

Gender inequality and bias show a poor attitude towards females. Such miserable conditions of half of the productive manpower of India indicate the underutilization and ill planning of human resources. Health, education, social security, participation in decision-making processes and economic freedom are some of the issues which need to be properly and urgently tackled to utilize this resource in an optimum manner. Similarly, the high infant mortality rate (IMR) and the high maternal mortality rate (MMR) in India demand serious attention. A high IMR essentially leads to high population growth rate, which is unthinkable at this juncture of development. Inadequate primary health facilities, especially in rural and backward regions, insufficient immunization measures, malnutrition, unhygienic housing conditions and larger family sizes lead to such high IMRs. The high MMR is also the consequence of high fertility and high IMR. In other words, all these variables act as cause and effects. Such causation relationships must be tackled intelligently.[49]

Public administration is unlikely to function efficiently when the rule of law is in question, when there is public disorder, or when there is little consensus on fundamental issues. Acute conditions of class, tribal,or religious conflict within a society will usually be reflected in the management and operation of government departments and public agencies. The size of the vote in politics is also an important cause of high fertility, and the high population growth rate in certain sections of society. "More and more the number, more and more the participation in power" is the slogan of certain political parties and groups of Indian society and this has led to the Indian demographic profile in favor of certain religion groups in certain states, thus distorting the development process and th social pattern of these states (e.g. Uttar Pradesh Bihar), as is clear from the 2001 census. Highly populous countries like India will lead to higher environmental degradation. The model of development accepted by the policy planners has landed India in an ecological crisis, resulting in loss of forests, poisoning of air and water, erosion of land and rendering millions homeless. The causes of environmental degradation have been classified as the use of inappropriate technologies and gross mismanagement of the resources.

Even the liberalization process has intensified the environmental and social crisis. The Government of India has been trying to eliminate poverty since achieving independence. A series of Five-Year Plans, numerous schemes for poverty eradication and various populist slogans and movements have endeavored to alleviate poverty but the success rate of all of them has been insignificant. The NDA government had announced a time-bound poverty eradication program with an eye on: GDP growth rate of at least 6 percent per annum over the next ten years, provision of universal access to safe drinking water, 100 percent coverage of primary healthcare centers, universalization of primary education, extension of midday meal scheme throughout all primary schools, public housing assurance to homeless, road connectivity to all villages and the streamlining of the public distribution system; giving priority to the poor and the socially disadvantaged groups.

The present-day development discourse is largely based on the phenomenon of governance. Public sector management, transparency, the legal framework, accountability and information have been listed as the main elements of governance. The crisis of governance in India is most important, bearing in mind the proportion of the poor people in the population and India's high rank among the most corrupt countries. Good governance in India essentially involves fighting corruption, improving bureaucratic and political accountability and promoting people's participation and public–private partnership.

In conclusion, it may be said that poverty and economic disparity are two such issues, which require proper and adequate attention in a highly populated nation like India, which has started moving down the path of economic reforms. The problem of development planning is one of assuring that there be sufficient productive investment, and then of directing the productive investment into such channels as will provide for the most rapid growth of the production power of national economy. Any comprehensive development planning must make use of all the resources which the country has: there should be no ideological blocks to the employment of both, as much state activity and as much private activity can be possibly executed. The political economy of the Indian state clearly suggests a strict supervisory and regulatory role on the part of government.

Governance for development should really aim at all-round development of the country using every available agency. To bring about better development results both public and private sectors have to play their appropriate roles. Numerous associations of the civil society such as NGOs, trade unions, commercial and industrial bodies, labor unions, welfare associations of residents, associations of women and housewives, professional bodies of doctors, engineers, teachers, students and intellectuals, etc. have all to contribute their respective shares to healthy growth and development. It is ultimately the government and not the market forces, which should decide the priorities and pattern of the development process even in the era of economic reforms. Despite repeated insistence on disinvestments of public sector enterprises and off-quoted benefits of the withdrawal of the government from the service sector, the superiority of the market over state sovereignty must be an area for concern. Social and political changes must precede economic reforms, otherwise the policy implementation will be severely hampered.

There are no easy options, and there does not appear to be any clear-cut solution to the various Third World situations. Social movements for an autonomous, equitable and culturally satisfying development are necessary, even to provide the conditions for the regulation of the MNCs. In the changed scenario of the twenty-first century, governments of the developing nations need to be the watchdogs of their nations, otherwise the superpowers of market rule (privatization, liberalization and globalization) will distort their judicious distributional pattern in favor of a few elite classes. The Indian state is said to be highly interventionist.[50] It controls a major proportion of India's resources and potential initiatives. In these circumstances, the state's growing ineffectiveness is a matter of considerable concern. India's problems are likely to grow, but the state's capacity to deal with them may not. This could be a long-term recipe for accumulating crises of governability. There is urgent requirement for administrative and bureaucratic reforms along with economic reforms.

Elimination of corruption from public offices and government departments must be the topmost priority of the decision-makers. There are various sources that contribute to an increase in corruption. The quality of life, human values, moral values, discipline, integrity and honesty, etc. are the factors that determine the commitment to the nation, the people and services. The increasing number of scams and highly publicized corporate scandals are examples of poor governance in India. The strengthening of public audit, accountability, better functioning of local self-government institutions, publishing the citizens charters, the spread of e-governance initiatives, greater public–private partnership through NGOs are the approved ways of good governance and civil society. Therefore, it can be safely suggested that the path of development in India may be approached only through proper legislative acumen, perfect implementation efforts, an equitable judicious system, perpetuation of the national interest by political actors, the continuous cooperative attitude towards industry, faith in social responsibilities of the administration, eradication of corruption from public offices, and a wholesome reform process at different levels of governance. This may not only lead to overall development of the state but will also pave the way to good governance, which has become essential in the present-day political world. Our policy planners will have to strive their best in these directions and the road of success is not far away. The ancient texts pray for the socio-economic development of all the sections of the society and happiness, health, wealth and prosperity of everyone in the society is the aim. This must be the guideline of our socio-economic and political ruling elite.

The poverty-reduction potential of more significant urban growth was also offset by the rapid rise in urban inequality. India, Pakistan, Bangladesh, Sri Lanka, Nepal, Bhutan and the Maldives should find a way of translating their integration with the global economy into higher growth and sustainable development by carrying out complementary policies to enhance supply elasticities and offset some of the adverse outcomes by taking action through cooperation among South Asian countries. However, these should be supplemented by offsetting policies to promote greater equity and poverty reduction.

Initiatives and responses

While South Asian nations have struggled with poor governance and perceptions of high corruption, significant reforms have been undertaken to reduce the opportunities for corruption. South Asian nations have enacted, for example, world-class procurement law, established the Anti-Corruption Commission and overhauled financial management. The countries have also agreed to sign the UN Convention on Anti-Corruption and are addressing the fiscal losses of state-owned enterprises, i.e. organizations that are often associated with mismanagement and poor governance arrangements.

The governments want to set up elaborate institutional frameworks to monitor PRS. The existing National Steering Committees have been established to watch over the PRSP preparation and to review the progress of its subsequent implementation. Moreover, National Poverty Focal Points have been created to keep charge of the necessary documentation relating to PRS implementation. Technical committees, made up of the top officials from the Planning Commissions and other related ministries, have been set up, in which technical experts will monitor the consistency of projects and programs with the stated PRS goals.[51] Different working groups composed of government officials, donors, experts and practitioners have been formed around the ministries similar to the PRSP thematic groups. Recently, the governments have also established high-profile independent advisory committees in which experts, researchers and civil society leaders will meet to provide guidance and advice and to commission studies for an annual assessment of the progress being made towards PRS implementation and the attainment of the MDGs.

If the present trend of corruption and administrative inefficiency persists in the South Asian nations, there is little hope of any success in the implementation of PRSP-II. Unless the present administrative machinery in the individual countries is totally revamped and relieved of political and partisan pressure, corruption cannot be controlled to a reasonable extent in South Asia. Only when corruption has been defeated, can a viable and long-term reform agenda be developed through political will and commitment. Otherwise, the goals of PRSP or the target of MDGs will not be attained unless the countries are able to escape from the vicious circle of poverty and the low-income trap.

The main concern of the governments is, however, the capacity and manpower in different ministries. Current staff performance and organizations have to be enhanced by involving outside experts and researchers to do the additional work of monitoring and evaluation. The success of this arrangement will surely depend on the political will of the governments and their ownership of the whole PRS process.

While strongly linked to western countries, which represent the greatest source of foreign direct investment (FDI) and the most important markets for its exports, South Asian countries are also looking for enhanced partnership and cooperation with their Asian neighbors. South Asia's history and geopolitical position give India a disproportional role in the foreign affairs of other South Asian countries. India's influence in other South Asian countries' international agenda and internal politics is strong. Notwithstanding the power imbalance, other countries have some negotiation entry points with India due to their proximity to South-East Asia and the East Asian countries and their locations in the South–South-East Asia corridor. India holds a strong position as other countries like Bhutan, Nepal need to go through its territory in order to transit goods. Bilateral relations for India with other countries in South Asia are complicated by a series of long-standing issues such as illegal migration, drug trafficking, smuggling and allegations of sheltering "terrorists" and insurgents, the Tipaimukh Dam and Tista Agreement, and the management and sharing of water and rivers.

The India–Pakistan conflict paralyses what should be the most important regional cooperation organization for other countries in the region, the South Asian Association for Regional Cooperation (SAARC), and it undermines the smooth implementation of the South Asian Free Trade Area (SAFTA), and the South Asian Preferential Trade Agreement (SAPTA). Enhanced and effective regional cooperation in South Asia would not only have positive impacts in terms of trade, circulation of people, political dialogue and resolving conflicts, but it could also unlock the immense hydropower potential that characterizes the region as a whole. Regional cooperation in the sustainable energy sector would represent important progress for South Asian countries, considering the energy deficit, which affects both economic growth and people's quality of life in South Asia.[52]

South Asian countries are trying to strengthen their relations with their South-East Asian neighbors through the Bay of Bengal Initiative for Multi-Sectoral Technical and Economic Cooperation (BIMST-EC)[53] and the Asia Cooperation Dialogue (ACD),[54] of which Bangladesh was a founding member. The most interesting regional initiative is, however, the Bangladesh, China, India, Myanmar Forum (BCIM), promoting a regional platform for a new regional cooperation setting. China plans to use the Bangladesh–Myanmar corridor to foster the creation of the "Chindia"—China+India—which many economists and think-tanks see as the world's strongest future economic bloc.

Relations with bordering Myanmar are mild and focus mainly on the influx of the Rohingya refugees and their status on the Myanmar–Bangladesh border. China has flourished rapidly, and China has surpassed India as the favored trade partner of some South Asian countries. China has gained naval access to Chittagong port and is cooperating on the Bangladesh–Myanmar–China road project to link Kunming with Chittagong. Pakistan and Bangladesh were the second biggest Chinese arms importer globally, amounting to over $350m.[55] At the same time, Chinese and South Korean investments in the private industrial sector have been growing steadily in South Asian countries. In addition, South Korea and China are increasing development assistance, mostly in infrastructure,and China is interested in investing in the building of deep-water ports in South Asia.

The balance in South Asia's international relations is gradually changing with a shift from dependency on Western countries' FDI and markets towards more integration with Asian countries. Moreover, considering the weak regional cooperation mechanisms existing today in South Asia; and notwithstanding India's privileged position with regard to other small countries in South Asia, that shift implies an increasingly strong presence of South Korea and China in South Asian countries. Beyond the positive economic implications of enhanced cooperation with Asian big players, there may be consequences for the "classic" donors' leverage capacity with regards to democratic governance and human rights. While, on the one hand, China's growing interests in the country will certainly contribute to economic growth and poverty reduction, on the other, increased Chinese influence may weaken other international partners' capacities to advocate for economic development accompanied by enhanced human development.

South Asian countries are passing through a transformation process, which will imply deep changes in many socio-economic areas in the near future. Private sector-led economic development, urbanization, modernization and a generational change, are the main features of this process, which, however, involves many other trends and actors, and requires a multidimensional interpretation. All trends and stakeholders are linked to each other, and change within a certain area affects another, and so on. While the evidence of a deep process of change is clearly visible, what is less clear is where this change will lead. The near future will witness a struggle between the traditional power-holders and the new players. However, it is difficult to predict whether this struggle will end in the assimilation of the newcomers within the old power structure, or whether it will lead to more profound socio-political changes, beyond economic development.

Notes

1 Cash, K. and Sanchez, D., *Reducing Poverty or Repeating Mistakes? A Civil Society Critique of Poverty Reduction Strategy Papers* (Stockholm: Church of Sweden Aid, Save the Children, Sweden, and the Swedish Jubilee Network, Sweden, 2003).
2 Matin, I. and Hulme, D., "Programmes for the Poorest: Learning from the IGVGD program in Bangladesh," *World Development*, vol. 31, issue 3 (2003), pp. 647–65.
3 World Bank, *Country Assistance Strategy for Bangladesh, Nepal, Pakistan, Nepal 2006–9* (Dhaka: The World Bank, 2006), pp. 29–41.
4 Ibid., pp. 28–9.
5 Cohen, D., Jacquet, P. and Reisen, H., "*Beyond Grants vs. Loans": How to use ODA and debt for development*, December (Paris: Paris Press, 2005); and Caliari, A., "The Debt-Trade Connection in Debt Management Initiatives: Need for a change in paradigm," paper prepared for the UNCTAD Expert Meeting Debt Sustainability and Development Strategies, October, Geneva, 2005.
6 Rehman, S., *Challenging the Injustice of Poverty: Agendas for inclusive development in South Asia* (London: SAGE, 2010).

7 Eastwood, R. and Lipton, M., "Pro-Poor Growth and Poverty Reduction," paper presented at "Asia and Pacific Forum on Poverty: Reforming policies and institutions for poverty reduction", Manila, Asian Development Bank, 2001.

8 Guidelines for Joint Staff Assessment of Poverty Reduction Strategy Paper, IMF and World Bank, April 18, 2001 and Poverty Reduction Strategy Paper-Operational Issues, IMF and World Bank, December 10, 1999. An Independent Guide to PRSP, EURODAD, 2000.

9 Jenina, C.M. and Shalmali, G., *Structural Adjustment in the Name of the Poor: The PRSP experience in the Lao PDR, Cambodia and Vietnam* (Hanoi: Government of Viet Nam, 2002).

10 Abugre, C., "Still Sapping the Poor: A critique of IMF poverty reduction strategies," ISODEC, June 2000.

11 See Centre for Policy Dialogue, "Poverty Reduction Strategy for Bangladesh: Views of Civil Society," Dhaka, Bangladesh, available at: www.cpd-bangladesh. org/work/irbd_docs/INT02–04.doc.

12 Rodrik, D.B. (2005), "If Rich Countries Really Cared About Development", available at: www.ictsd.org/dlogue/2005–7-01/Docs/RODRIK-BRIDSALL_SUB RAMANIAN_what-rich-can-do_April2005.pdf.

13 Vandemoortele, J., "Are the MDGs Feasible?" *Development Policy Journal*, vol. 3, issue 1, (2003), pp. 1–22.

14 Sachs, J.D., *Investing in Development: A practical plan to achieve the millennium development goals* (London: Earthscan, 2005).

15 Available at: www.aidharmonization.org/secondary-pages/Paris2005.

16 Khawaza, M.U., "Trade Liberalization Induces Food Price Hike," *The New Age*, 22 October 2007.

17 Structural Adjustment Participatory Review International Network, *Structural Adjustment: The SAPRIN Report: The policy roots of economic crisis, poverty, and inequality* (London: Zed Books, 2004).

18 For a comprehensive critique of the PRSP and PRGF, see the World Bank website: www.worldbank.org/poverty/strategies/overview.htm and the IMF website: www. imf.org/external/np/prsp/prsp.asp.

19 The draft I-PRSP was posted on the government's website in April 2002.

20 For a comprehensive critique of the PRSP and PRGF, see Agubre, op. cit.

21 Shahiduzzaman, K., "PRSP-II: Is bumpy ride ahead?" *The Financial Express*, 28 August 2008.

22 International Monetary Fund, "Aligning the Poverty Reduction and Growth Facility (PRGF) and the Poverty Reduction Strategy Paper (PRSP) Approach: Issues and operations," SM/03/94, and Corr.1 (2003).

23 The new aid consensus was embodied in the Paris Declaration of March 2005, which was a follow-up to the Rome Declaration of 2003.

24 The common policy agenda includes such actions as establishing a private seaport, introducing e-governance for procurement and rationalizing agricultural subsidy.

25 World Bank, *Country Assistance Strategy for Bangladesh, Nepal, Pakistan, Nepal 2006–9* (Dhaka: The World Bank, 2006), p. 107.

26 This item is also mentioned in the policy agenda for Roads and Highways.

27 Some donors, however, saw this as a merit of the project.

28 World Bank Section, External Relations Division (ERD) Sher-e-Bangla Nagar, (Dhaka, Bangladesh, 2006).

29 Ibid.

30 Under same-school enrollment, children with disability are found to drop out frequently because of teasing and bullying. Interviews with children under the same-school enrollment scheme and with ministry officials were held in August 2006, Dhaka and Gazipur, Bangladesh.

31 Vandemoortele J., "Are the MDGs Feasible?", in Black, R. and White, H. (eds) *Targeting Development: Critical perspectives on the millennium development goals* (London: Routledge, 2004), pp. 124–44.
32 United Nations, *UNDP, Human Development Report* (New York: UN, 2009).
33 Ministry of Finance, *Economic Review* (Dhaka: The Government of Bangladesh, 2006).
34 Available at: www.mdgasiapacific.org/.
35 Available at: http://southasia.oneworld.net/news/indias-mdg-status-critical.
36 Government of Maldives, "Aneh Dhivehirajje: The strategic action plan national framework for development 2009–2013," 11 November 2009. Available at: http://planning.gov.mv/en/images/stories/publications/strategic_action_plan/SAP-EN.pdf (accessed 17 May 2014).
37 Ibid.
38 Available at: www.undp.org/.../mdg/the-millennium-development-goals-report-20. See European Commission (2003) "Country Strategic Paper Maldives 2003–2006," (10 October 2003) http://eeas.europa.eu/maldives/csp/03_06.pdf (accessed 15 May 2014).
39 World Bank, *Costing the 7th Millennium Development Goal: Ensure environmental sustainability* (Washington, DC: The World Bank, 2002).
40 Collingwood, V. (2000) "Good Governance and the World Bank." Available at: www.brettonwoodsproject.org (accessed 20 April 2011).
41 Sharma, K.S., "Development Crisis and Governance in South Asia: Some Issues and Suggestions: A case of India," *Samaj Vigyan Shodh Patrika*, vol. v, no. 1, April–September 2007, pp. 19–29.
42 Weerakoon, D., "An Uncertain Future for Policy Reforms in South Asia," *East Asia Forum*, 20 October 2011, ANU: Canberra.
43 Ibid.
44 Sharma (2007), op. cit.
45 Royal Government of Bhutan, *Organisational Development (OD): Toward excellence in the civil service* (Bhutan: Royal Civil Service Commission, 2007).
46 Friedlander, F. and Brown, L.D., "Organization Development," *Annual Review of Psychology*, vol. 25 (1974), pp. 313–41.
47 http://minivannews.com/politics/democratisation-has-its-costs-maldives-comes-to-terms-with-tax-reform-26478.
48 Ugyel, L. (2013) "Dynamics of Public Sector Reforms in Bhutan: Interaction of values within a hybrid administration," Crawford School Working Paper, No. 13–01, 2 January, Australian National University, Canberra.
49 Sharma (2007), op. cit.
50 Gedam, R., *Economic Crisis and Political Disaster* (New Delhi: Heritage Publishers, 1993), p. 1.
51 This committee will have representatives from the Implementation, Monitoring and Evaluation Division (IMED) of the Planning Ministry.
52 Available at: www.powerdivision.gov.bd/user/brec1/30/1.
53 Available at: http://news.outlookindia.com/item.aspx?632563.
54 Available at: www.acddialogue.com.
55 Available at: www.dhakatribune.com/safety/2013/nov/12/bangladesh-comes-second-chinese-arm s-purchase-last-year.

5 Poverty dynamics and empirical evidence

Introduction

Post-cold war geopolitics has made possible a more direct targeting of aid in order to reduce poverty worldwide. Over the last two decades, however, recipient countries underutilized aid money to promote growth and economic reforms for a sustainable development. This inability has compelled international donors, such as the World Bank, to set certain preconditions of good governance in exchange for loans. There has been increasing recognition of the need to make aid more effective through governance conditionality; this approach is believed to help reduce poverty while promoting economic growth.

The World Bank was the first major donor agency to adopt the concept of "good governance" in the 1990s as a condition for lending to the developing countries.[1] Bangladesh, in line with other recipients, has been receiving foreign assistance under this new system and thus, it is hoped that the "good governance" conditionality prescribed by the donors will reduce poverty and stimulate development. The World Bank claims that in a country with poor economic and social policies and no political movement to change those policies around, aid cannot promote structural reform nor help along development to fight poverty.[2] One of the targets of the Millennium Development Goals is "good governance."[3] This is an agenda for improving living standards through poverty reduction; it was adopted by world leaders at the Millennium Summit in September 2000.[4]

Poverty alleviation

The idea of poverty alleviation originated in the disillusionment with the "trickle-down" theories in the 1960s.[5] These contended that development at the national level would automatically improve the well-being of all sectors of the population. However, in reality, it was soon understood that by and large it did not benefit the poor even in those cases in the Third World where growth did occur. In Sub-Saharan Africa, South Asia and Latin America, the situation significantly worsened and the numbers of people who lived in absolute poverty even rose.

This led to the recognition of "poverty alleviation" as a development objective in itself in the late 1970s. The structural adjustment policies in the 1980s[6] reversed the previous philosophical trend towards equity and solicitude for the poor by putting at the center of its programs not people but neo-liberal market forces.[7] By betting on the economically strong and by arguing against "affirmative action," the World Bank and the IMF forsook in fact the small producers and the poor and reverted to the old orthodoxy of trickle-down theories and the reliance upon macroeconomic indices to measure development.[8] All these have proved to be extremely controversial, however. And their impact has been disastrous, especially in the case of the Structural Adjustment Policies, which only produced negative outcomes.

The Bretton Woods Institutions themselves had recognized the failure of their policies by the end of the 1980s. In 1989, the IMF, in its publication *World Economic Outlook*,[9] introduced the concept of "high quality growth:" the emphasis was not just on economic growth but on "equitable growth," taking into account the plight of the poor and vulnerable groups. To this end, the IMF took the initiative to open a dialogue with the UN agencies, which were becoming increasingly critical of the development policies of the World Bank and the IMF. The new policy ideas of the IMF and the World Bank were welcomed by the UN agencies, as is clearly shown by the UNDP *Human Development Reports*[10] for the years 1990 and 1991.[11] Regardless of the policies embraced by the Bretton Woods agencies, their empirical agenda has remained more or less same over the years.

Deacon (1997)[12] has identified the trend of this growing influence as the beginning of a "globalization of social policy and a socialization of global politics." Alleviating poverty might be on the global political agenda, but this is a time when it is generally accepted that the "golden age" of welfare state protectionism is past[13] and prescriptions for welfare reform are informed by a perceived need to limit public spending and sustain labor market flexibility. The new paradigm promulgated by the International Fund for Agricultural Development (IFAD), and cited by Mafeje (2001),[14] conceptualizes poverty alleviation as a mobilization or integration of the poor in the cause of economic growth. This view is similar to what the World Bank is prescribing to alleviate poverty in the developing world. It seems that the poor will be helped to accept responsibility for their own destiny, but in the context of a world order that depends on their own destiny.

We can say that the discourses of the major development agencies, particularly the Bretton Woods institutions, reveal the inevitable presence of Northern Hemisphere orthodoxies. Mafeje (ibid.)[15] has argued clearly how in the 1980s elements of the Thatcher–Reagan orthodoxy came to represent a significant element in the policy prescriptions that were made for developing countries by the IMF and the World Bank (see also Deaton 1997).[16] In the 1990s and in the twenty-first century the Blair–Clinton and the Bush–Blair–Obama orthodoxies respectively grew in dominance and in their hegemonic influence around the globe. Here we see the acceptance of the economic liberal agenda and socially conservative communitarianism that are the hallmark of economic orthodoxy. The new paradigm is said to be not so new in reality; rather, it is defined by many a recombination of old and new paradigms.

Capital markets in South Asia

South Asia was the second fastest-growing region in the world in the aftermath of the global crisis in 2008. However, its recent performance has been less stellar, and it has been sustained by potentially volatile portfolio inflows. More stable foreign direct investment (FDI) in the region is low, half that of other regions relative to GDP; inflation is twice that of other regions and fiscal deficits and debt-to-GDP ratios are high. South Asia has been struggling to return to the growth rates achieved before the global financial crisis of at least 8 percent a year so that it can significantly reduce poverty. South Asia is critical to the World Bank Group's goals of ending extreme poverty and boosting shared prosperity by 2030 and they are working with governments in the region to overcome barriers to growth and provide greater opportunities for all.

Recent global capital rebalancing, driven by fears of the unwinding of easy monetary policy in the US, has highlighted structural weakness and vulnerability in South Asia. This is a wake-up call for policy-makers not to lose focus on tackling key economic and investment constraints. Regional GDP has grown by 4.4 percent in the 2013 calendar year, 5.7 percent in 2014, and potentially 6.2 percent in 2015, driven by an improvement in export demand, measures to speed up the implementation of large infrastructure projects in India, stronger private investment activity, and a good monsoon. India, the region's main economy, with around 80 percent of South Asian GDP, was projected to grow by 4.7 percent at factor cost in the fiscal year (FY) 2014–15, a slight decline from an estimated 5 percent real GDP growth in FY 2012–13. Although partly reversed, India's rupee depreciation of around 20 percent between May and August 2013 reflected changing market sentiment toward the region and the increasing vulnerability to external shocks.

Other countries across South Asia are either growing slowly or slowing down. Overall, South Asia's regional growth was moderate in 2013 compared to prior projections. Regional growth had deteriorated in the second and third quarters of 2013, mainly due to supply-side constraints and weak domestic demand. Bangladesh's projected growth for 2015–16 at 6 percent notes a 0.2 percentage point decrease vis-à-vis 2012, reflecting political uncertainties, supply-side constraints and lower investment. Bhutan's real GDP growth fell to 6.9 percent in 2012–13, down from 8.1 percent. Nepal's real GDP growth fell to 3.6 percent in 2013 from 4.9 percent in 2012. In Pakistan, a marginal 0.1 percentage point decrease to 3.5 percent for 2013 was estimated. The Maldives and Sri Lanka, on the other hand, saw a slight increase in their growth rates. The Maldives' real GDP growth increased from 3.4 percent in 2012 to an estimated 4.3 percent in 2013 and Sri Lanka's increased from 6.4 percent in 2012 to 6.8 percent in 2014–15.

Despite recent volatility in international capital flows, fundamentals determining long-run growth and stability in South Asia have not changed significantly over the last 12 months. Like other developing regions, South Asia is facing greater turbulence as markets reassess sources of global growth and risks. The World Bank report stated that exuberance had given way to deep pessimism, particularly in the case of India, while the underlying potential remains somewhere in-between. However, short-term capital market turbulence is manageable and the return to sustainable growth in the developed world is a positive development for South Asia.[17]

India's slowdown had significant spillover effects on the rest of South Asia, even more so after the financial crisis. Overall, while South Asian countries vary in terms of political, economic and financing challenges, accelerating the long-term reform momentum remains the best policy for coping with turbulent global capital flows, not dramatic shifts in short-term fiscal or monetary policy. Two highly complementary policy areas are central building blocks of much needed higher and sustainable growth.

Continuing with a gradual tightening of fiscal and monetary policy, macroeconomic stability and higher tax revenue will create fiscal space and reduce volatility. In this context, letting exchange rates adjust will allow depreciation to enhance the region's competitiveness and stimulate exports. Removing supply side constraints, both regulatory and physical, will pave the way for increasing investment and growth. Both regulatory efforts to ease doing business in the region and attract investment, and providing the necessary infrastructure to avoid structural bottlenecks remain at the center of any policy strategy aimed at bringing South Asia back to its potential and previous performance.

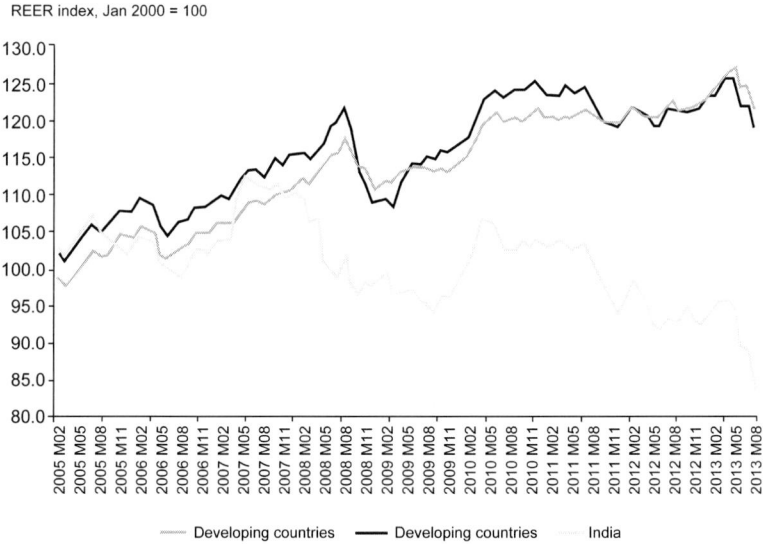

Figure 5.1 India's real exchange rate has been depreciating for several years

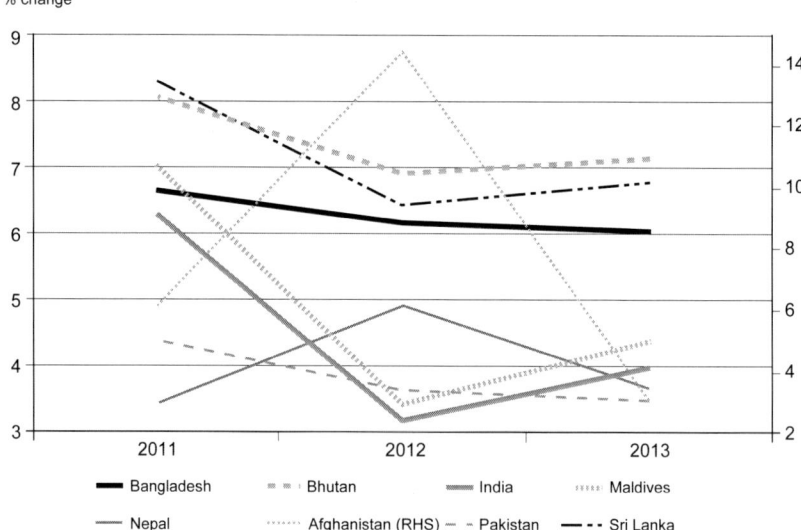

Figure 5.2 Real GDP growth remains respectable, but it is on a declining path

Poverty trends

In South Asia are living there the highest numbers of poor people, estimated at 135–190 million people. The vicious circle of poverty in the region is most pronounced in areas that have significant minority populations,[18] that are economically stagnant, where agrarian class structures and gender relations are exploitative, and where governance is weak. Some 44 percent of the population of India live below the international 1-dollar-a-day poverty line.[19] The respective figures are also relatively high at 38 percent, 31 percent and 29 percent in Nepal, Pakistan and Bangladesh. Although accurate data are unavailable in Bhutan and Afghanistan, the proportion of people living on US$1 a day is much higher. Furthermore, South Asia has the worst indicators of female illiteracy and very poor rates of child mortality. It is noteworthy that the headcount ratio for the chronically poor has been declining in many parts of the region, particularly in southern and western India, and in Bangladesh, and most human development indicators also have improved over the past two decades.

The Indian National Sample Survey in 2012 reported that the number of poor people increased by 13 million between 1987–88 and 1993–94, while data from 1999–2000 show a very large reduction in the second half of the decade. This finding is intensely disputed, however, due to changes in the way the national figures have been calculated, and as such it remains difficult to estimate the absolute numbers of chronically poor people today. Due to the very nature of chronic poverty, however, it is unlikely that the proportion of people in chronic poverty has declined at anything like the rates of poverty in general. For instance, village-level research in Rajasthan, where headcount poverty has unambiguously declined, suggested that about 18 percent of the total population was poor, both 25 years ago and in 2011. This figure ranged from 8 percent to 31 percent across districts, and was highest among scheduled tribes, more than two-thirds of whom had remained in poverty over the past 25 years. The poverty ratio in India fell steeply to 21.9 percent in 2012 from 37 percent in 2004 and the unemployment rate has been steadily declining in recent years.[20]

The pace of poverty reduction in India has been faster over the years. Between 2005 and 2012, India lifted 137 million people out of poverty and reduced the poverty rate to 22 percent. India has also improved its performance on shared prosperity, with the consumption growth of the bottom 40 percent accelerating significantly since 2005. At the same time, however, more than half of India's population remains vulnerable—living between one and two poverty lines—and growth in the bottom 40 percent continues to lag slightly behind average growth.

India has become the fourth largest economy in the world due to strong economic growth but still has a low per capita income, the Economic Survey revealed:

> India has emerged as the fourth largest economy globally with a high growth rate and has improved its global ranking in terms of per capita income. Yet, the fact remains that its per capita income continues to be quite low.

The survey added that: "India has moved up the ranks, but is still the poorest among the G-20, but the per capita income of India stood at $1,527 in 2011,"[21] which is claimed to be the most visible challenge. Nevertheless, India has a diverse set of factors, domestic as well as external, which could drive growth well into the future. The survey also stated that between 1980 and 2010, India achieved a growth rate of 6.2 percent, while the world as a whole registered a growth rate of 3.3 percent. As a result, India's share in global GDP more than doubled from 2.5 percent in 1980 to 5.5 percent in 2011. Thus, India's rank in per capita GDP showed an improvement from 117 in 1990 to 101 in 2000 and further to 94 in 2009.

For Pakistan, different approaches to defining chronic poverty and the poverty line have led to a wide range of estimates of chronic poverty. In Pakistan, estimates of rural chronic poverty, based on mean income over five years, are at 26 percent, which represents about 50 percent of households classified as poor in the first year of the survey, and about 6 percent of households classified as non-poor in the first year. In Sri Lanka. it is clear that though per capita GDP passed the US$800 hurdle in 2009, poverty is still a persistent problem. The proportion of the population living on less than US$1 a day, and the nutritionally "ultra poor," both seem stable at just above 5 percent of the population. The extent to which the 40 percent of

Sri Lankans who survive on between US$1 and US$2 a day are likely to be chronically poor is an empirical question.

Bangladesh has been witnessing a modest poverty reduction rate of around one percentage point a year since the early 1990s. Reports by the Bangladesh Bureau of Statistics and the World Bank show a decline in poverty from 58.8 percent in 2000 to 49.8 percent in 2008.[22] However, the proportion of the poorest people (defined through a lower poverty line) remains extremely high at around 20 percent of the population in 2000.[23] In Bangladesh, 6.7 percent GDP growth rate (during fiscal year 2006) was associated with rising inequality, which tended to offset part of the gains from economic growth that flowed to the poor. Overall, the Gini index of inequality increased from 0.259 to 0.306 over the 1990s.[24] The per capita income at the end of the fiscal year 2008–9 stood at US$611, according to a review of the Bangladesh economy circulated in July 2009, by the Ministry of Finance.[25]

The national savings GDP ratio was also the highest ever at 29.15 percent in 2006–10 and led to higher investment and a wider spread of its multiplier and accelerator effect in the economy.[26] The Economic Review, as part of more comprehensive budget documents, usually is circulated at the time of presenting the budget to parliament. The economic progress was seen in the national economy during fiscal year 2012–13. It has been calculated that in that fiscal period, per head GDP increased to US$482 while per head national income reached US$611. Both figures were US$447 and US$476 respectively in the fiscal year 2005–6. GDP growth in recent years is around 6 percent on average.[27] The growth registered by Bangladesh demonstrates the supreme resilience of its economy.[28]

The largest group of extreme poor people in rural India are casual agricultural laborers; cultivators are the second largest group. Most of the chronically poor are either landless or near-landless, and highly dependent on wages. Agricultural wages have been rising slowly in much of the sub-continent, and this is probably the best single explanation for the slow but steady reduction in the depth of consumption poverty. However, getting work does not always translate into exiting poverty. In agrarian economies with large casual labor markets, the number of days of work obtained in a given period, is almost as important as the wage level. Migration is often part of a broader set of livelihood strategies employed by poor wage laborers. Chasing scarce, short-term, insecure, and low-paid wage labor from area to area, migrant laborers often find themselves in a constant battle to repay debt and maintain household consumption levels.

Hunger and ill-health are both contributors to and results of chronic poverty. Malnutrition is not specially associated with poverty, but it may be with chronic poverty. Those below the poverty line tend to spend a large proportion of their earnings on food, often without meeting minimum energy and nutrient requirements. Families facing chronic food insecurity are caught in a hunger trap. The inadequacy and uncertainty of their food supply make it difficult for them to take advantage of any development opportunities that might emerge. Despite India's position as a net food exporter, 268 million people are still considered to be living in food insecurity in India. Almost half the women aged between 15 and 49, and three-quarters of children, are anemic. Of the 204 million people that are currently undernourished in India, there is a significant subset of those who are unable to access two meals a day throughout the whole year.

In the Maldives, economic growth has brought significant social progress by reducing poverty, particularly in the area of education. Since 2002, the Maldives's primary and lower secondary school enrollment rate has neared 100 percent. Literacy rates are among the highest in the region, with 94 percent of its population aged 15 years and older being able to read and write. In 2009, gross domestic product (GDP) was estimated at US$1.4 billion, or about US$4600 per capita. Nevertheless, 16 percent of the total population live below the poverty line. The Maldives is a service-based economy, with services contributing 77 percent of GDP, of which 27 percent comes from tourism and tourism-related activities. Fishing, a traditional economic activity of the country, contributes 7 percent of GDP. The scarcity of arable land and water shortages mean that agriculture contributes just 2 percent of GDP. Most food staples have to be imported. An ambitious tourism expansion plan has fueled construction, and contributed to the deployment of the telecommunication and transport infrastructure. For further poverty reduction there is clearly a need for economic diversification. Diversifying the economy beyond tourism and fishing, reforming public finance and increasing employment opportunities remain major economic challenges for the government.

The Bhutanese economy continues to grow strongly by reducing poverty, albeit from a small base. Bhutan has a history of fiscal prudence and good governance, very little debt, and is assisted by the nominal anchor provided by the currency peg to the Indian rupee. Bhutanese products enjoy free access to the large Indian market and India is Bhutan's main trade, investment and development assistance partner. Agriculture and forestry dominate Bhutan's domestic economy, while hydropower and tourism are major export earners. Steep mountains and swift-flowing rivers make hydropower production a natural fit in Bhutan. It is estimated the country has a total potential hydropower generation capacity of 30,000 megawatts. Bhutan is likely to see significant increases in export and tax revenues as new hydropower projects become operational. Bhutan's Tenth Five-Year Plan (2008–13), launched in February 2008, has a central focus of poverty reduction and is underpinned by Bhutan's transition to democracy and the Millennium Development Goals (MDGs). The United Nations Development Programme (UNDP) *Human Development Report* (2013) ranks Bhutan 140 out of 185 countries in terms of the human development index (HDI), which measures countries' relative standing in terms of life expectancy, educational attainment and adjusted real income. Bhutan faces the challenge of matching gains from strong economic growth (6–8 percent per annum since the mid-1980s) with rising expectations of employment opportunities and welfare improvements, while preserving its environment and culture.[29]

In 2000, the United Nations announced a series of eight Millennium Development Goals to reduce poverty, improve health,etc. The impact of such initiatives in South Asia has been marginal at best. The economic slowdown due to the global recession can be seen in the context of South Asia. Slowdown also was attributed to a slight setback in some crop subsectors and livestock production in recent years. However, this slowdown was more than compensated for by the manufacturing sector in South Asia. The growth is based on this sector, and particularly in the heavy manufacturing industries.[30] The pick-up in inflation could become entrenched, however, in the absence of corrective policies. The rise in inflation to over 7 percent reflected increases in both food and non-food prices. Gross domestic product (GDP) growth stayed around 6 percent in the fiscal year 2009, despite the global economic recession and supply-related disruptions, with lower agricultural growth offset by strong manufacturing and service activities.[31]

Economic growth in South Asia has been modest in recent years. Keeping at such a pace, however, the goal of ending extreme poverty by 2030 will not be attained. Governments must work harder on reforms to raise growth in a region where most of the world's poor live. Weak revenue collection, poor infrastructure, low skill levels, and corruption are likely to hamper sustained growth and undermine further poverty reduction in South Asia.

Research findings

Although the first post-transition governments in South Asia had high levels of support, this support began to weaken as the extent of economic recession became palpable. One of the main issues generating anxiety among citizens has been the growth in the scale of poverty. Estimating poverty levels is difficult, and the scale of poverty can vary, depending on how poverty is defined and measured in the country concerned. Nonetheless, it is clear that though poverty rates have been improving and fluctuating since the beginning phases of the economic restructuring program, extreme poverty has not been addressed as succesfully as expected.

When they embarked on their simultaneous political and economic transitions, according to the Statistical Office of different South Asian countries, it is estimated that about 40 percent of the population on average were living in poverty. During the first few years of reform, as a consequence of rising unemployment, a fall in real wages in many sectors, and the decrease in the value of savings, the number of people affected by poverty in some areas grew. Particularly harmful were the lifting of price controls, inflation, the imposition of fiscal discipline, and the cutting of huge subsidies on the price of basic commodities.[32]

As important as the actual poverty levels are the public perceptions of poverty in South Asia. Public assessments of the growth prospects of the economy as a whole and people's own personal chances for improvement in material conditions have become increasingly pessimistic. However, while the actual poverty levels have fluctuated, the public perceptions of poverty have remained remarkably stable. Not only do people tend to overestimate the percentage of the population that can be classified as poor, but expectations that poverty will remain in the future have tended to dominate. Thus, the respondents estimated that 40 percent of the population was poor, and that estimate changed only slightly in recent years. In fact, on the eve of the accession, 46 percent of respondents expected that the levels of poverty would most likely decrease in the near future, with only 16 percent anticipating that corruption, lack of good governance, inflation and commodity price hikes in South Asia would put many people into poverty trap (Table 5.1).[33]

Poverty was seen primarily as the consequence of unemployment and hunger as well as the difficulty of finding new work in South Asian countries, with a substantial majority of people believing that finding employment with smart salary is very hard. Simultaneously, at the beginning of the transition, most people felt that if they were unemployed, they could count on the state to ensure the necessary support or could turn to the state in their times of need. At the same time, the number of people reporting that they had savings put away for unexpected expenses due to price inflation in South Asian countries fell. Adding to the people's concerns has been the fact that the rate of unemployment and extreme poverty has remained stubbornly high in most South Asian countries even during periods of high economic growth. These high unemployment rates, in turn, have translated into widespread anxiety about the possibility of losing one's job.

Various data have confirmed that unemployment and hunger in South Asia have been one of the primary causes of long-term poverty. This study has found that repeated poverty seems to be closely associated with long-term unemployment both at the aggregate and at the regional level. However, poverty does not affect all socio-demographic groups to the same extent in South Asian countries. Rural households were much more likely to suffer from long-term poverty than urban households. Along with place of residence, the most important factor affecting the probability of a household slipping into poverty was education. The higher the education level attained by the head of the household, the smaller the probability that the household would experience poverty. The research finding shows that people with an academic education

Table 5.1 Do you think that in the coming years the numbers of poor people will be declining? (%)

Indicator	%
Substantially greater	24
Somewhat greater	16
The same	40
Somewhat less	9
Substantially less	2
Hard to say	9

are almost never reduced to the subsistence level (0.4 percent) whereas in families where the head of the family has only lower educational qualifications, 10.3 percent of people live below this minimum and 63.2 percent below the social minimum. The research findings of this study confirm these propositions concerning the incidence of poverty and inequality in South Asian countries.

The data analysis shows that the transition from the planned to the market economy has witnessed increasing inequality in South Asia. Increased inequality is thus accompanied by the hollowing out of the middle class. The rise in inequality, moreover, has proven to be a vital phenomenon. It has resulted in long-term poverty, leading to what one respondent called, "A real risk of an entrenched poor and underclass emerging." Furthermore, because internal migration from rural areas to urban areas has increased dramatically since the 1990s, there are substantial regional differences in the level of poverty and unemployment rates.[34] In many urban areas, unemployment has over the years been much lower than the national average in South Asia. In the large cities like New Delhi, Mumbai, Islamabad, Dhaka, Kathmundu, Male, Colombo, Thimphu, etc. the national unemployment rate has fluctuated between 6.2 and 8.6 percent in recent years.[35] Outside of these urban centers, unemployment has always been higher, in some areas reaching 35 percent.[36] In fact, what has become increasingly apparent in South Asian countries as the reforms progressed is that there is an increasing disparity both between social classes as well as between various regions of the countries.

The prosperous and well-educated urban population appears to be growing and the increasingly impoverished people of small towns and rural areas are largely lagging behind in South Asia. These differences, moreover, rather than decreasing with the progress in reforms, have been growing as a result of the uneven distribution of new investments. Not only are employment possibilities dramatically different between urban centers and the small towns and rural areas, but they are also substantially influenced by educational attainment in South Asian countries. Thus, though the transition to a market economy that most of the South Asian countries undertook in 1990s affected all social strata, it affected them in very different ways. Despite regional variations, on the whole, the urban and better-educated segments of the population have been better able to adjust to the new economic realities, while the residents of small towns and rural areas as well as those with less education have fared much worse. These divergent experiences of the socio-economic strata are reflected in the very different ways these groups perceive and assess the changes that have taken place.

The different perceptions of the national economy's health as well as personal chances of success reflected the actual experiences of respondents from different social strata. While the pace at which the economy grew since the initiation of reforms has fluctuated, nonetheless the restructuring measures have tried to curb the inflation rate as well as to ensure the rise of per capita income. However, these undeniable successes mask the uneven distribution of benefits and costs of reforms across different socio-economic groups. While some groups, and in particular the well-educated urban dwellers have benefited from the reform measures, the same cannot be said of the residents of small towns and rural areas as well as those with less education. These differences in costs and benefits of reform are reflected in the divergent perceptions of the restructuring effort among different social strata.[37]

Public perception and data analysis

How do the differing experiences with economic reform affect people's perceptions of the political changes? Most respondents have not been satisfied with the actual functioning of democratic transitions in South Asian countries. For example, in a September 2013 survey, only 1 percent of respondents believed that the political systems is good and does not require any changes, 30 percent thought it was basically good but required small changes, 44 percent believed it was not very good and required many changes, particularly the patronage politics, while 17 percent thought it was bad and necessitated fundamental changes. This dissatisfaction with the actual functioning of democracy is not unique to South Asians but is in fact quite common in other transitional societies as well as in many established democracies. On the other hand, the majority of South Asians declare that democracy is the best possible political system. In other words, the public appears to clearly distinguish between the democratic principles and the way they have actually experienced democracy since the transitions in their respective countries in South Asia.[38] Although they may be dissatisfied with how democracy has functioned, they nonetheless appear committed to the democratic ideal. Field surveys, however, indicate a more complex reality. In the first place, depending on how the question is posed, the commitment to democratic principles appears less unequivocal. Second, the support for democratic principles and the perceptions of how democracy is actually experienced are not distributed evenly across socio-demographic groups

Most respondents thus seemed to agree that democracy was preferable to other political systems. However, when the question was posed differently, this commitment to democracy seemed to be more equivocal. This time, respondents were asked to agree with one of three statements: (1) "Democracy is better than all other forms of rule." (2) "In some instances nondemocratic forms of rule may be preferable to democratic rule." and (3) "For people like me, it doesn't really matter whether a government is democratic or not." Given this wider choice, only 34 percent of respondents agreed with the first statement that democracy is better than all other forms of rule. Twenty percent chose the second and 35 percent chose the third statement, while 11 percent of respondents were uncertain which statement they agreed with. As before, the survey revealed profound differences in how various socio-economic groups viewed democracy and governance, with well-educated, well-off urban dwellers having a much more favorable view of democracy than the poorer, less-educated residents of small towns and rural areas.

These views, despite periodic fluctuations, have proven to be remarkably stable. Although the belief that democracy is the best political system increased somewhat at a point, it could decline again to its previous levels. When the same question was posed in the field survey, the results were almost the same. Thirty-one percent of respondents said that "Democracy is better than all other forms of rule," 19 percent said that "In some instances nondemocratic forms of rule may be preferable to democratic rule," and 40 percent believed that "For people like me, it doesn't really matter whether a government is democratic or not." More important, despite these slight periodic fluctuations, the differences between socio-demographic groups' assessment of democracy as an ideal political system remained equally pronounced. Similar differences emerge among socio-demographic groups when the meaning of democracy is probed further. In a survey conducted in August 2001, respondents were asked to choose between two answers concerning their associations with democracy: "democracy means, above all else, human freedom," or "democracy is, above all else, mess and chaos." In other words, this survey asked for responses that more clearly related to the way South Asians actually experienced democracy rather than probing their attitudes toward democratic principles.

In addition, the profession of the respondent had a significant influence on whether democracy was understood primarily as meaning human freedom or chaos. Among managers and the intelligentsia, 91 percent of respondents associated democracy with human freedom, and among the self-employed, 86 percent. On the other hand, among the unemployed, only 55 percent of respondents associated democracy with human freedom, while 30 percent associated it with chaos. In other words, regardless of how the questions probing the meaning of democracy were phrased, deep differences among South Asians of different socio-economic strata were evident.

Many South Asians and in particular those who live outside the large urban centers and those who are less educated and poor, remain quite ambivalent about democracy more than a decade following the political transition and are highly dissatisfied with how democracy has evolved in South Asia, characterized by patronage politics, clientelism, family dynasty, corruption and governance deficit following the democratic transition in the respective countries. Do this ambivalence and dissatisfaction have any influence on how people behave in the new political context? Does it affect political participation? Does it affect how people perceive their ability to have a voice within the democratic system? While supporting democratic principles, most South Asians are dissatisfied with how democracy has functioned since the transition. Furthermore, this dissatisfaction is hovering between 50 and 60 percent of respondents. It is still too early to tell whether this 10 percent jump is the beginning of a new trend or a temporary fluctuation. However, this growth in dissatisfaction with how democracy is functioning in South Asian countries was accompanied by a 10 percent decline in support for democracy as the best possible political system from 70 percent in 2008 in to 60 percent in 2013.

The picture that emerges from our field survey indicates that the dissatisfaction with the quality of South Asian democracy and governance affects how citizens of South Asian countries view the various public institutions and how they perceive their ability to have a meaningful voice within the new political system. There is widespread disrespect and distrust of political parties, organizations, and politicians as well as the media. The majority of respondents feel that rather than being representatives of the interests of their constituencies or of the national interest as a whole, most politicians are active in public life to promote their own interests and advance their own careers. This discrepancy between the interests of society as a whole and the interests which dominate the agenda of government is disturbing to many citizens and it is the main reason for the growing public alienation since the articulation of interests has no transmission into government policy. In survey after survey, most people express dissatisfaction and distrust of the main institutions of the new democratic order, while placing most trust in the army, the police, and religion. Although dissatisfaction with public institutions is hardly unique to South Asians or other transitional countries, nonetheless it is significantly higher than in established democracies.

Furthermore, rather than believing that, thanks to the emergence of a pluralistic political system, they have the ability to change things, there is widespread perception of powerlessness. When asked in field survey whether a person like you has influence over the affairs of the country, 87 percent of respondents said no, with only 10 percent believing they did. This, moreover, reflected a growing feeling of powerlessness among citizens; 19 percent thought that they did have the ability to influence the course of public affairs. Furthermore, 61 percent expressed the opinion that the government is not concerned about them, does not address their needs, and does nothing for them; and 92 percent said that elected leaders are only interested in promoting their own careers rather than representing the views of the electorate. Not only do they feel neglected by the government, but many feel that the government does not respect them. The feeling of abandonment was quite pervasive, as was the belief that a person has no influence on what is going on in the country. These feelings of neglect are further exacerbated by the perception that despite the official rhetoric of the equality of citizens, equality remains an elusive ideal. Most people believe that decent living standards are not guaranteed by the government, something that most citizens feel is one of the main duties of the state in a democracy, and that an individual's chances in life are determined by material conditions. Even more troubling, most respondents think that even the elementary and widely accepted principle of the equality of all citizens before the law does not exist.

However, while most citizens feel abandoned by their representatives and unable to have a meaningful voice in shaping political decisions or the course of public policy, once again, there are significant differences in these perceptions among different socio-demographic groups. As in the case of support for democracy as the best form of rule and support for economic reforms, those living in large urban areas, the better educated, and the materially better off have more faith in the efficacy of their actions. Feelings of alienation have been reflected in the consistently low voter turnouts in general elections.

The alienation of the public is also manifested in the almost complete lack of involvement in political parties and civic activities or associations. While there are many organizations and associations in existence in South Asian countries, relatively few South Asians are actually active in them. The configuration of civil society has been swift in recent years. In the few years following the fall of state socialism, robust and assertive civil societies have emerged. In making their argument, they point to some very impressive statistics that show the swift proliferation of a variety of nongovernmental organizations and movements in South Asia. However, according to Freedom House, most of these organizations are rarely working for the extreme poor at the grassroots levels. Even more important, most poor citizens do not participate in many of these organizations. In the field survey, respondents were asked whether they were active in any of about 30 organizations. Although respondents participated in a wide variety of associations, in none of them were more than 5.5 percent of respondents involved. Similarly, there has been only marginal participation in political parties and other political organizations and almost no participation in the activities of local self-government despite the adoption of the decentralization reform that shifted more responsibilities to the local level. This lack of involvement is perhaps not at all that surprising, given that there is also widespread perception that involvement in civic activities is futile, with 52 percent believing that civic associations have no influence on what is going on in the country. Although there is widespread dissatisfaction with the functioning of democracy and governance, government's perceived lack of concern with the welfare of citizens and only marginal involvement of the public in political and civic activities, there are substantial differences in both perceptions and activities depending on the social position of the respondents.

Certain groups are much more active in civic and political organizations. Those who are active tend to be the same groups that had more faith in the efficacy of their actions, in other words, people with higher education and, in particular, representatives of the managerial class and the intelligentsia, those who reside in large cities, and those who perceive their material situation to be good. Those who feel that they have lost as a consequence of the transition to a market economy, and in particular those who are unemployed, as well as housewives, remain disengaged. One would imagine those people would be precisely those who would organize since they are in a difficult situation and one would expect this to prompt them to seek involvement in groups that seek to help those in the bad situation. But clearly this is not happening. The reason for this is the lack of belief that you can change your situation. In fact, there is a very strong relationship between a difficult material situation and lack of activism and involvement.

In other words, there is an increasingly clear division within society. The majority of citizens devote all their attention and energy to ensuring that their social position, standard of living, and social security do not deteriorate further. The minority, on the other hand, concentrate on seeking social advancement and material success. It is this minority that is also the social group most actively involved in political life. The field surveys confirmed that this pattern of participation in associational life had stabilized at these low levels. About three-quarters of respondents declared that they did not participate in any organizations. Furthermore, the participation rates of different socio-demographic groups remained stable as well. The only change the respondents indicated was a growing activism among self-employed respondents. What clearly emerges from the field surveys is that the worse a person's material situation is and the less that person's educational attainment, the less likely that person is to become engaged in associational life. This dependence of participation on an individual's resources is hardly surprising.

Many studies of democracy in Western countries have noted this correlation between educational and material endowments and a person's propensity for civic and political engagement. In Western democracies, the expansion of the middle class ensured that ever-larger segments of the populations acquired the necessary resources to become engaged in civic and political life. In South Asia, however, the growth of the middle class has been anemic. Rather, the society has been increasingly bifurcated into the well-educated and employed urban minority and the poorly educated, underemployed and unemployed majority that resides in small towns and the rural areas. In spite of the fact that the South Asian economy has been expanding at an impressive rate of about 6 percent annually in recent years, the unemployment levels persist and the levels of poverty have remained high; some estimates place a third of the population below the poverty line. There is little to indicate that these patterns of social stratification are going to change in the near future.

The underlying promise of neoliberal market reforms and public sector reforms was that the temporary hardships of transition would generate not only growth but, in the words of the IMF official, high quality growth, by which he meant not just "growth for the privileged few, leaving the poor with nothing but empty promises." However, it is becoming increasingly clear that these promises have yet to materialize.

Mounting evidence suggests that far from ensuring equitable growth, the structural adjustment programmes have contributed to the widening gap between the rich and the poor in the reforming countries in South Asia. Many studies suggest that the region's societies have had to contend with some of the most rapid increases in class inequalities ever recorded. This research explored how the social changes brought on by the implementation of market reforms have affected the process of democratic governance and political participation in South Asian countries. Some rather troubling questions arise from this analysis. Contrary to initial expectations, the deepening of market reforms has not resulted in a rapid expansion of the middle class. Rather, what has been emerging in South Asia is the increasing bifurcation of society into a small, well-educated, urban sector and the poor,the residents of small towns and rural areas, who are lacking marketable skills.

The differences in the political and civic activism of various social groups are not surprising. As modernization theorists noted some time ago and later studies confirmed, urbanization, educational attainment, and higher incomes tend to go hand in hand with involvement in public life. In other words, as people move up into the middle class, they tend to become more politically active. In South Asia, however, the middle class remains under-developed, as ever larger segments of the population become impoverished. Thus, though most South Asian countries have retained their status in most accounts as a success story of the Third Wave of democracy, establishing a truly participatory political system remains very much a work in progress. Although this work has focused on the experience of South Asian countries as most of them seek to deepen democracy while simultaneously constructing a market economy, many of the patterns of socio-economic and political change are not unique to this case. Other developing countries have struggled with similar challenges. In particular, the new patterns of social stratification and class divisions have been evident in most of the region's countries. How the public in the countries in South Asia perceive these changes, how they assess them and judge them, and how they respond to them are likely to have a profound influence on the processes of democratic promotion and good governance.

Analysis of the survey

As mentioned earlier, a field survey was conducted on both the central and local governments in the major cities and towns of South Asia. At the central level our interviewees were government officials, donor agency officials, academics, journalists and civil society activists. At the local level, we went into rural towns and villages to interview the beneficiaries of aid. This survey was conducted in New Delhi, Islamabad, Kathmundu, Dhaka and Colombo.

Analysis of our respondents' viewpoints, as expressed in the questionnaires and interviews, reveals several critical points. The existing poverty reduction strategies, including PRSP and current governance reforms, drew support from only few respondents. Twenty percent of the total respondents approved the present policy while the rest of the people did not find the present poverty reduction strategies and governance reforms to have much significance. In what follows, we will summarize our respondents' criticism of the donor-driven agenda as well as their governments' lack of political will and other significant issues collected during the field survey.

Policy gaps or deficiencies

1   The policy gaps and lack of viable cooperation among different stakeholders were identified by 80 percent of the total respondents.

2 The bargaining power of the government vis-à-vis donors was identified as weak by the respondents. Aid policies have been pursued persistently and deliberately to serve national interests.

Recommended measures

Some 75 percent of the total respondents recommended the following measures to be taken in order to improve the governance system for poverty reduction and economic growth: In the light of the national interest requirements, more intensified interactions, equal bargaining and proper negotiation between the governments of South Asia and donors should be ensured by identifying the resources needed in the individual country:

1 Mobilization of the various communities co-existing in South Asian countries to undertake comprehensive and in-depth studies on the root-causes of administrative inefficiency and governance problems.
2 Self-reliance, active neutrality of civil society and the establishment of a sustained internal mechanism to prevent corruption and poverty.
3 Intensified diplomacy in order to secure economic, cultural and educational facilities.
4 Common plans of action among the government, donors and civil society for poverty reduction and governance reforms in accordance with local needs highlighting local ownership.
5 Greater affirmative action on the part of governments to have the best possible "good governance" system for economic growth and poverty reduction.

Considering local needs and political culture, political alignments and national philosophies are crucial while implementing different development projects under the programs of development and governance reforms. Lack of in-depth studies and workable commitment of the governments to proper implementation of pro-poor programs is another obstacle to the implementation of the development programs and the governance reforms in the countries of South Asia. Criticism of the governance reforms as well as the government's lack of participatory practice is summed up well by some respondents. They also said that most programs against poverty have less success because of pre-conceived ideas of the dominant actors about what the poor need and what the poor are forced to adopt.[39]

Notes

1 World Bank, *Governance Matters VI: Governance indicators for 1996–2006* (Washington, DC: The World Bank, 2007). Available at: http://info.worldbank.org/governance/wgi2007/.
2 World Bank, *Report on Aid and Reform in Africa* (Washington, DC: The World Bank, 2001).

3 UNGA (United Nations General Assembly), *Millennium Declaration*, A/RES/55/2, 18 September (New York: United Nations, 2000).
4 Alarcon, D., "The MDGs in National Policy Frameworks," *Development Policy Journal*, vol. 3, issue 1, (2003), pp. 37–46.
5 Herfkens, E., "Donors and Recipients," *Development Policy Journal*, vol. 3(April), (2003), pp. 101–6.
6 SAPRIN (Structural Adjustment Participatory Review International Network) (2002), "The Policy Roots of Economic Crisis, Poverty, and Inequality." Available at: www.saprin.org.
7 Deaton, A., "Measuring Poverty," Princeton Research Program in Development Studies, Working Paper No. 230 (Princeton, NJ: Princeton University, 2004).
8 McKinley, T., *Macroeconomic Policy, Growth and Poverty Reduction* (Basingstoke: Palgrave Macmillan, 2001).
9 IMF, *World Economic Outlook* (Washington, DC: International Monetary Fund, 1989).
10 UNDP, *Human Development Report* (Oxford: Oxford University Press, 1990–2005).
11 Gore, C., "The International Poverty Trap," *Development Policy Journal*, vol. 3, April (2003), pp. 107–26.
12 Deaton, A., *The Analysis of Household Surveys* (Washington, DC: The World Bank, 1997) and Deaton, "Measuring Poverty," op. cit.
13 Gosta, E.A., *Welfare States in Transition: National adaptation in global economies* (London: Sage, 1996), pp. 15–29; and Gosta, E.A., "Welfare States in Transition," *Journal of Socioeconomics*, vol. 28, issue 5, (1996), pp. 647–9.
14 Mafeje, A., "Anthropology in Post-Independence Africa: End of an Era and the Problem of Self-Redefinition," in Mafeje, A. (ed.) *African Social Scientists Reflection*, Part 1 (Nairobi: Heinrich Böll Foundation, 2001), pp. 28–74.
15 Ibid., p. 73.
16 Deacon, B., *Global Social Policy: International organizations and the future of welfare* (London: Sage, 1997), pp. 31–45.
17 World Bank, *World Development Report 2012: Agriculture for development* (Washington, DC: The World Bank, 2012).
18 The term minority is used to distinguish groups that experience discrimination and particular forms of exclusion and not only those which constitute a small proportion of national population. In India, for example, this broadly refers to scheduled caste and scheduled tribe populations.
19 See www.commodityonline.com/news/india-gdp-growth-likely-to-be-47-in-2013–14-speed-up-reforms-world-bank-56745-3–56746.html, Oct. 2013.
20 See http://zeenews.india.com/business/news/economy/poverty-recorded-steepest-fall-in-upa-regime-since-2014-govt_91858.html.
21 See http://indiatoday.intoday.in/story/economic-survey-2012-13-india-growth-poverty/1/177886.html.
22 Bangladesh Bureau of Statistics, *Preliminary Report of Household Income and Expenditure Survey 2008* (Dhaka: Bangladesh Bureau of Statistics, 2008) and World Bank, *Poverty in Bangladesh, Building on Progress Report* (Washington, DC: The World Bank, June 2008).
23 World Bank (2012); 33 percent by World Bank poverty line estimate.
24 IMF and World Bank, *Poverty Reduction Strategy Paper* (Washington, DC: The World Bank, 2001), pp. 13–15.
25 Ministry of Finance, *Review of Bangladesh Economy*, June (Dhaka: Government of Bangladesh, 2012).
26 "Per Capita Income is Now $611," *News Today*, June 30, 2012.
27 *News Today*, June 2010.
28 "Macroeconomic Stability, Poverty Reduction Key Goals, National Budget 2011–12," *The Financial Express*, June 12, 2012.

29 See www.dfat.gov.au/geo/bhutan/bhutan_country_brief.html.
30 Asian Development Bank, *Economic Review of South Asia*, June (Manila: ADB, 2012).
31 *News of South Asia*, July 10, 2012.
32 This dissatisfaction with reforms does not always translate into outright opposition to the Reform program. As a recent collection of case studies suggests, often the public is willing to back a government that is implementing painful structural adjustment policies. See Stokes, S. (ed.) *Public Support for Market Reforms in New Democracies* (New York: Cambridge University Press, 2001).
33 Data from April 2013.
34 Erzo, F. and Luttmer, P., "Measuring Poverty Dynamics and Inequality in Transitional Economies: Disentangling real events from noisy data," Policy Research Working Paper No. WPS 2457 (Washington, DC: The World Bank, 28 February 2001).
35 World Bank, *Annual Report on South Asia* (Washington, DC: The World Bank, 2013).
36 Data from employment bureaus collected from different countries by the author in 2013 and also data from the different Statistical Offices in South Asia.
37 Data obtained by the author from the field survey in May 2013. Although this study does not examine the influence of gender on political participation, it is important to note that gender plays a very significant role in affecting political participation.
38 In recent years, for example, satisfaction with the functioning of democracy has plummeted in much of the Global South.
39 Comment by one respondent who does not want to provide his name and designation, but to remain anonymous.

6 Endogenous governance and democracy in South Asia

Governance and democracy

In recent years, much of the analysis of the new agenda of "good governance" has been set within the broader understanding of the previous activities of the state and the neo-liberal critique of it. It is also located in the current effort to rearrange the division of the public–private domain by rolling back the state and expanding the autonomy of the market. "Civil society" is seen as filling the gap left by the withdrawal of the state, in promoting the market as well as democracy. Once democratization became a priority, donors needed a strategy. They turned to theories of how their own democracies had developed, particularly to the work by Alexis de Tocqueville. Western aid donors have professed agreement with the Tocquevillean theory[1] that societal associations contribute to a vibrant "civil society" through their ability to aggregate public opinion, articulate it to the relevant state officials, offer policy alternatives and train the next generation of social and political leaders. They have also agreed that the development of a pluralistic "civil society" is an essential component of democratic consolidation. While civil society is a much-debated term, as discussed in earlier chapters, those who cite its positive characteristics often mention diverse social interactions—from soccer clubs to choirs to neighborhood associations.[2]

The World Bank's construction of good governance starts from the rejection of the past development models. "The post-independence development efforts failed," the World Bank says, "because the strategy was misconceived."[3] According to the World Bank, there is now "a growing consensus" that these strategies "pinned too much hope on rapid state-led industrialization." State failures compounded development failures; private sector and individual initiatives were stifled and institutions were set up that did not reflect a society's characteristics and culture. The "good governance" agenda then underlines the curbing of the role of the state and expanding the space for market forces and competition to play their role.

It furthermore puts emphasis on civil society institutions to strengthen democracy and in constructing an informal sector that can harness people's entrepreneurship through community institutions and inter-personal relationships. In the "good governance" discourse, democracy emerges as the necessary political framework for successful economic development, and in this discourse, democracy and economic liberalism are conceptually linked: bad governance equals state intervention; good governance equals democracy and economic liberalism.[4] "Civil society" is seen as a source of vitality for both the spread of democratic values and economic growth. Its institutions are a countervailing force that curbs authoritarian practices and corruption. They also can create or strengthen associational organizations that provide such goods and services more efficiently than the state.

The space left by a retreating state is said to be filled by such private initiatives; a proliferation of associations that manage local resources or deliver basic services will in turn support the trend towards greater participation and democracy. This belief is nurtured by the contention that social organizations succeed because there is collaborative action based on trust, norms and networks. These relationships are popularized as social capital that builds capacity for participation and self-government. The argument is that associations help generate social capital which, in its turn, strengthens democracy and improves the efficiency of the markets.

In this agenda of good governance, the conceptualization of "civil society" assumes that power and exploitation are associated with the state, while freedom and liberty come under the realm of "civil society." This leads to a kind of romantic view of civil society where the existence of institutions outside the state becomes a sufficient basis to assume that state power is curbed and greater democratization is taking place. Such a perception does not take into account the characteristics of a society where there are associations, those of class or of a religion, that exist primarily to curb the human rights of individuals. There are also many associations that do not have any self-conscious political intentions and do not seek to limit the reach of the state or influence its policies. Other associations, in turn, may espouse authoritarian ideologies and pursue undemocratic strategies and goals. Civil society cannot be seen as inherently democratic or undemocratic. Its character will differ across societies and associations.

The heterogeneous and segmented nature of Bangladeshi civil society cautions against definitions that treat it as inherently democratic. There are diverse traditional, ethnic, class, regional and national interests. Such differences increase the likelihood that some of the associations or voluntary groups formed on these bases may pursue parochial interests. While the state withdraws and allows voluntary associations to step in, intensification of particularism and parochialism may also take place. Rudolph argues that associations are of various kinds and one needs to specify what types of associations are likely to generate democracy.[5] The same study also points out that associations may nurture, as Tocqueville said, "the inner moral life of those who participate, enhancing their sympathies for their fellow human beings," without, however, "nurturing their engagement with wider community."[6]

Associational life, in other words, can make members appreciate each other even while making them self-regarding and parochial. It can generate a form of group selfishness that results in conflicts. In most South Asian countries, the task of ensuring inter-group and intra-group loyalty still remains unfulfilled; this requires support by the state as well as sufficient pressure from society. Universal laws are necessary, and this requires the strengthening of the state rather than abandoning it. Further, within the economic sphere, parallel markets have developed to avoid high taxes, enabling people to buy goods and services at low prices. These and similar activities have weakened the state but failed to ensure a sense of nationhood. The informal sector has not always promoted the market either.

Within this discourse of "civil society," considerable emphasis is being laid on local community institutions. It is this emphasis that is a departure from the past. Of course, from the very beginning of the planning process, local participatory institutions like the Union Council, the village assembly and the cooperatives were perceived as important agencies mobilizing people's support for planning and development. Community action organized to assert the rights of the people living on the margin attracts hostility from the government acting in league with the vested interests. Thus, an associational activity is considered harmless so long as the scope of action is limited and narrow. As soon as it expands into a broader field, it may begin to threaten the established power relationships in society. For instance, to protest the exploitation by the Rural Electrification Board (REB) in Bangladesh and its customers in Kansat, Chapainawabgonj formed the Palli Bidyut Sangram Committee (PBSC), who have been struggling since its inception for an uninterrupted power supply and reduced meter charges by the Rural Electrification Board. On January 4, 2006, following the extreme power shortage, the PBSC members laid siege to the Kansat Palli Bidyut Samity (an REB suboffice) demanding a regular power supply for irrigation and the withdrawal of the minimum usage charge. The demanding voices were getting stronger but REB was quite reluctant to show any interest in its customers' complaints, which made the mob angry, agitated and violent.[7]

Democracy and development

Despite the differences in emphasis on the relationships among governance, democracy and development, a common underlying shape of the agenda of "good governance" becomes clear. Three main levels are thought of as the main components of governance, ranging from the most to the least inclusive: systemic, political and administrative. From a systemic point of view, the concept of governance is obviously wider than that of government, which refers to a looser and wider distribution of both internal and external political and economic power, to a system of political and socio-economic relations or, more loosely, a regime.[8] Currently "good governance" also means a democratic capitalist regime, presided over by a minimal state, which is also a part of the wider governance of the New World Order. Second, in a limited but political sense, good governance implies a state enjoying both legitimacy and authority, derived from a democratic mandate and built on the traditional liberal notion of a clear separation of legislative, executive and political powers.

From a narrow administrative point of view, the "good governance" agenda rhetorically means an efficient, open, accountable and audited public service, which has the bureaucratic competence to help design and implement policies, and manage whatever public sector there is. Good governance is seen not simply as the new technical answer to the difficult problems of development or poverty reduction, though some of its proponents sometimes like to present it in that light. The World Bank's conception of the "good governance" agenda re-identifies precisely the principles of administration, which, by the way, are Weberian in spirit,[9] and that have long been argued as being of benefit to developing countries. The World Bank's notion is naïve, though Weber was not, because it entirely ignores that good governance is not simply available on order, but under country-specific conditions.[10] Political culture, the power structure, the nature of politics and the political parties should be taken into consideration both to institute and sustain good governance. The question is whether such universal notion of a "good governance" agenda, regardless of country-specific conditions and local political culture, can promote real democratic changes and accelerate development in Bangladesh and elsewhere in the Third World. This study contends that the pressure that the World Bank–IMF duo and some Western countries exert on the developing countries to adopt market, "civil society" and governance reforms as preconditions for financial aid has negative effects on the aid-receiving countries. There are also conflicting views about the precedence of democracy or development.

This section explores the effects of externally driven economic development through external governance reforms in most South Asian countries, as prescribed by the World Bank and other Western development partners (DPs), such as raising the performance level of the public sector, increasing public education and setting realistic expectations. Subsequently, the demand for more personal, social and political freedoms will grow and leaders will want to discuss the lack of sustainability in such systems. In the 1960s, democracy was believed to be an outcome of socio-economic development, not a condition of it,[11] which required a high level of literacy, communication and education, an established middle class, a vibrant "civil society" and relatively limited forms of material and social inequality[12] and a secular public policy. The foundations of most modern advanced industrial economies were laid down under non-democratic or highly limited democratic conditions as in Britain (1750–1850) and much of Western Europe.[13] This supports the view that democracy is a consequence of development and hence sustains the earlier arguments in modernization theory. A more prominent argument is that the premature democracy may falter in its early stages when there is "a cruel choice between rapid self-sustained expansion and democratic processes"[14] and when there is a need for effective state action.[15] This is due to the fact that the early stages of development require capital accumulation for infrastructure and investment before an advanced welfare system or high wages can be afforded. These propositions have not gone unchallenged and have stimulated debates that have been reviewed.[16] But, in practice, no examples of sustained growth in the developing world have occurred under conditions of uncompromising economic liberalism, whether democratic or not. From Costa Rica to China and from Botswana to Thailand, the state has played an active role in influencing economic behavior and has often had a significant material stake in the economy itself. So, the important factor in this book is the kind and character of a competent state and its associated political and economic conditions that are crucial in influencing developmental performance. The focus has been on the primacy of political culture, not simply on the donor-driven "good governance" agenda, as the central determinant of development. We can hardly ever say that the combination of democratic politics and economic liberalism has been associated with a critical breakthrough from agrarianism, now or in the past.[17] Of course, this does not deny the fact that democracy is required in South Asian countries, but it should be based on an indigenous process. Actually, evidence from Bangladesh suggests that the "good governance" agenda is flawed in many respects and it has been far from clear that economic liberalization through governance reforms prescribed by the development agencies will generate real democratic practices, or achieve development goals by tackling rising inflation in order to raise welfare across the country. To understand this dilemma, we need to look at the political culture and indigenous governance processes of South Asian countries as these have so far been neglected by the donors' "good governance" agenda.

Political culture

The problem of an externally imposed governance system in the Third World and the donor-driven "good governance" agenda is that they ignore local political culture and a country's specific conditions. The political culture approach, which came to prominence in the late 1950s and early 1960s, attempted to address the problem of overgeneralization. Despite a number of weaknesses, Almond and Verba (1963),[18] in their path-breaking study of five industrialized nations, attempted to set up a classificatory scheme, whereby political culture could be classified, providing the basis on which the political culture approach developed. Under severe criticism for its lack of methodological sophistication, the cultural approach faded in the early 1970s and 1980s, but it was revived in the latter half of the 1980s. The "political culture" concept assumes that particular political institutions of governance arise out of the norms, beliefs, attitudes and values that people hold, and that these institutions will in turn affect beliefs, attitudes and values.

There is now tacit agreement among those adopting the political culture approach of the existence of close interactions between cultural and institutional forces, which makes them difficult to disentangle in practice (Elkins and Simeon, 1979, p. 142).[19] Although the impact of culture on politics is obviously multifarious, it is hard to envisage any element of politics being "culture-free." This is because of the fact that politics has to do with social relations, with ways and means of achieving power to influence decisions concerning societal matters. Lucian W. Pye has described how political power is extraordinarily sensitive to cultural nuances. Therefore, cultural variations are decisive in determining the course of political development.[20] Samuel Huntington goes even further in describing cultural differences as possible or even probable sources of fundamental conflicts.[21]

So we see that it has long been accepted that political culture and cultural orientations play a significant role in the political and economic behavior of individuals and nations. The cultural determinist point of view of politics rests upon what Emmerson calls "ultra-Orientalism,"[22] which assumes the existence of a single set of values upheld by all people in Asia, spreading across dozens of countries, speaking mutually unintelligible languages and believing in different religions. This is then contrasted to a single but different set of values supposedly held by an equally diverse population in the West. Cultural plurality and diversity are reduced to no more than two polar extremes: the East as the East and the West as the West. This culturalist approach has been contested all along by self-declared Western Universalists who see value as rather irrelevant to the economic and political process.

The basic point of departure in the political culture approach to politics is that every political system is a unique socially constructed creation within the confines of a cultural context, which to a greater or lesser degree shapes the pattern of human interaction in the system. Culture here is defined as the values held and the norms followed by a distinct group of people and described as "the software of mind,"[23] the unstated assumptions that characterize that group of people and their standard operating procedures.[24] In the political culture approach, where "attitudes, beliefs and rules that guide a political system"[25] make up the main sphere of interest, an *a priori* definition of democracy is irrelevant. Internalization of values and norms in the various agencies of socialization such as the family, education and news media, on the other hand, become highly relevant. On the basis of these perspectives, it is not difficult to find some of the key East–West differences regarding issues such as democracy and human rights. The most important differences relate to areas like: stability vs. rapid change, order vs. authority; traditional vs. modernization. Differences in these areas indicate East–West gaps between political cultures in their conceptualizations of the human being, society, change, development and values.

Traditionally and historically, the political culture of Bangladesh, as a former part of the Indian subcontinent and East Pakistan, should be understood in the context of South Asian political culture. South Asian political tradition should be identified in the light of the shift of dynasties, of dominating philosophies and religious creeds, colonization and other direct foreign influences.

The architecture of local governance

Unfortunately, with a disregard for South Asian indigenous political culture, the contemporary governance system and the political institutions in Bangladesh were set up according to foreign or Western blueprints. The political and administrative systems that were established during 200 years of British rule on the South Asian subcontinent were a basic inheritance that characterized the newly independent states of the Indian subcontinent.[26] The decision to introduce even a limited version of democracy into the Indian subcontinent, while welcomed by the English-educated moderate intellectuals, was criticized by radical nationalists who, under influence of the revivalist movement, demanded observance of the indigenous traditions of political conduct in India and, thus amendments of British democracy.[27] One of them was Sri Aurobindo Ghos, one of the leading figures of the radical wing of the Indian National Congress.[28] He formulated a critique of European democracy in 1903, explaining the major difference between Asian and European models of democracy and pointed to the weaknessess of European democracy in Asian society by saying that European democracy takes into account the rights of men and not the *dharma* (laws of society) of humanity.[29]

Individual man with his rights and aspirations stands at the center of the European concept of democracy, while the community and *dharma*—the duty to serve the community—is the basis of society.[30] In his critique of democracy, Aurobindo did not reject it, but insisted on amending the European version according to the Asian context.[31] The structure of the contemporary South Asian states and their rhetorical democracy are mainly an inheritance of the colonial past. Elements of parliamentary democracy prevailing in most South Asian countries, introduced into British India under the predominance of a highly centralized bureaucratic state, came to form a special type of colonial democracy, which influenced the South Asian democratic system a lot.[32]

However, the Western ideals of democracy have been considered absolute, i.e. there is only one democratic process, and it has ignored the informal grassroots democracy that existed for several decades in the postcolonial states in South Asia[33] The dynamics, ongoing, and diverse public opinion, which had once the potential to shape South Asian politics through grassroots democracy, has been effectively undermined by a Western necessity to bureaucratize democracy.[34] First of all, the traditional village assembly or *Panchayat* system, as an informal grassroots democracy, that calls for unity in thought and action is an understandably scary proposition to the West, particularly the British colonial power in South Asia, which colonized and exploited this region for centuries.[35]

The history of the village-level *Panchayat* institutions on the Indian subcontinent goes back hundreds of years. In the post-independence period, the *Panchayat* systems were largely neglected. India has now realized that these *Panchayat* institutions at the village level need to be vibrant and responsive to the needs of the people to bring about lasting progress in the villages to benefit people of all classes. This will lead to the empowerment of the poor and weaker sections of society. The new theme of 'Democratizing *Panchayats*' has been taken up on a pilot basis in India with the following aims: (1) promoting and strengthening village-level institutions as functional groups in the *Panchayat* to ensure people's participation; (2) sustaining the *Panchayat* institutions to access resources and reduce their dependence on the state; and (3) integrating the existing traditional systems with the *Panchayat* to enhance the participation of the people and achieve synergy. This kind of village *Panchayat* or village assembly is still ignored in South Asia. For example, the existing tier of local government in Bangladesh, the Union Council, has the potential to learn lessons from the Indian *Panchayat Raj* system, which has already been institutionalized.

Therefore, it is in the interests of Western powers to ridicule and belittle indigenous informal grassroots democracy as an informal mode of social relations lacking the sophistication of bureaucratized democracy. By inheriting the Western democratic system in South Asian countries, the governments try to de-legitimize the pre-existing, home-grown democratic spirit of the South Asian countries. This has caused weak governance and fragile democracy to this very day.

The history of democracy—in theory and practice—is a Western experience created out of specific needs and aims of shifting relevance over a long period of time and in a specific part of the world, namely, the one commonly labeled the West. It can be argued that liberal democracy, in its fully-fledged form, is primarily a characteristic of the economically advanced Western societies and is more a product of social-economic development than its cause.[36] The struggle and compromise among different interest groups in a political system, which are controlled by checks and balances, based on a negative perception of power and on the mutual distrust called "realism," are thought to provide the best possible political system. The universal and general approach of Western political culture, which focuses on individual freedom and rights and also protects individuals from coercion by the state, is too simple and too narrow.[37]

The concept of liberal politics only relates to state institutions, whereas economic and cultural factors are regarded as separate and sometimes irrelevant. This liberal model considers individual freedom to be more important than equality, i.e. material scarcity is not seen as an obstacle stopping individuals enjoying freedom. The flaw is that liberal democracy ignores the fact that in order to feel free, individuals must enjoy a certain degree of political and economic equality.[38] This is not compatible with the local culture and the traditions of the South Asian countries, where poverty is rampant. That is why this kind of narrow concept of liberal democracy has become distorted in South Asian countries where democracy has been characterized by huge corruption, the authoritarian nature of the democratic regime, clientilist politics, weak governance, etc.[39] Politics in the West may currently be said to have lost some of the cultural touch.

The colonial version of democracy in South Asia is intertwined with the imposition of the current form of good governance. The governance agenda prescribed by the donor agencies has led to the formation of a premature and weak democracy characterized by confrontational politics and politics of violence, a situation exacerbated by the lack of intra-party democracy, excessive state patronage and family dynastic politics.

The crisis of governance

South Asia is an interesting case, which represents the contemporary post-modern condition where nothing is clear-cut. Despite moderate economic growth, most South Asian countries are still economically backward and politically not very successful. Democratic transitions have largely produced fragile democracy in most of these countries in recent years. The donor agencies have equated "good governance" with democracy, and development and the capitalist market economy with political freedom. However, this notion fades away when we look at South Asia, a region in which the indigenous process of governance has been ignored. The countries are still at the crossroads in their march towards democratic order. Though most of the countries started their political journey with a democratic system, it failed to sustain a viable mechanism; slowly but steadily the parliamentary government has degenerated into an authoritarian system.[40] Although there was a restoration of democracy in 1991, a genuine form of democracy is yet to take shape while dealing with a fragile scenario and frequent disruptions.

Since gaining independence most South Asian countries have been driven by internal power struggles and economic chaos, while attempting to develop a democratic society. For example, Bangladesh's representative government is battling poverty, official corruption, organized crime and Islamic militancy. Bangladesh has enjoyed more than four decades of independence and it has also witnessed 13 years of military rule or governments dominated by the military. The institutional framework for parliamentary democracy was restored in Bangladesh in 1991. The *Jatiya Sangsad* (Parliament), comprising directly elected representatives of the people, has been the centerpiece of national politics, but democracy in Bangladesh has so far gone hand in hand with corruption, human rights violations and criminalization threatening the state's economy and survival.[41] Professor Ataur Rahman, a noted political analyst of Bangladesh, was among those critical of the two female leaders and their governance by patronage. The only visible outcome for the Bangladeshi people was rising corruption coupled with violence and fear. Bangladesh needs a changed and renegotiated democracy in a good new framework.[42]

We cannot deny the fact that the dominant political party leaders have led South Asians for years against autocracy, and have fought extremely hard to establish democracy. Under their leadership, in the past few years, the economy in South Asia has blossomed with a growth rate of around 5 percent. A strong private sector has developed, and has established itself as the driver of economic development. Various development indicators have shown significant improvement. However, per capita income remains very poor. The political leaders have also failed to protect all the institutions from corruption and rent-seeking. The political parties have become hostage to black money and muscle power. Authoritarian behavior and the activities of the political parties in power sometimes destroy democracy within their parties as well as in the country. Corruption and nepotism are thus bred in society. The personal animosity and rivalry of the two major parties have caused a deep rift in the country, and the interest of the country has always been sacrificed for narrow partisanship. People in South Asian countries nowadays demand that all these misdeeds have to be properly investigated.

Endogenous democracy

Grassroots democracy usually follows the tendency towards designing political processes where as much decision-making authority as practical is shifted to the organization's lowest geographic level of organization. To cite a specific hypothetical example, a national grassroots organization, such as an NGO, would place as much decision-making power as possible in the hands of a local chapter instead of the head office. The principle is that for democratic power to be best exercised, it must be vested in a local community instead of isolated, atomized individuals.[43] As such, grassroots organizations exist in contrast to participatory systems, which tend to allow individuals equal access to decision-making, irrespective of their standing in a local community, or in which particular community they reside. Informal grassroots systems also differ from representative or formal democratic systems that allow local communities or national memberships to elect representatives who then go on to make decisions.

At the policy prescription level, the development discourses have pushed civil society, namely NGOs, up on the agenda in South Asian countries in the hope of promoting democracy and "good governance." "Grassroots democratization" has become the language by which donors and international NGOs alike emphasize the importance of "downward accountability" through so-called "civil society" institutions and especially the NGOs—a focal point for discussions on good governance in the late 1990s.[44] In reality, these are all nothing but the rhetoric of the donor agencies. The donor-driven neo-liberal type of grassroots democracy through so-called "civil society" equated with NGOs has failed to capture the notion of endogenous democracy in South Asia as traditionally practiced in the form of the village assembly called the village *Panchayat* in India, which is of South Asian origin. Direct democracy through the village *Sabha* or meeting has been ignored so far in many parts of South Asia. There is an informal endogenous democracy on the traditional Indian subcontinent, to which South Asian countries belonged, in the form of the village *Panchayat* (Assembly), i.e. village consensus through village meeting, a notable feature of South Asian political culture. At the base is the *gram sabha* (village meeting)—the entire body of citizens in a village participate. This general local body has specific responsibilities. The 'Bengal model'[45] of rural local self-government (*Panchayat*) is considered to be responsible for better governance, and political participation, decreasing the level of political violence, and ensuring some level of popular identification that can be an example of indigenous democracy in South Asia. Against the backdrop of social capital theory, which privileges so-called civil society as a precondition for the success of democracy, this kind of informal democracy is regarded as the case for 'direct democracy without associations' in South Asian countries.

Without denying the importance of associationalism in making democracy work sometimes, the South Asian type of local body shows that the act of associationalism may be performed by agencies and not typically civil societies. There is thus a positive lesson to be learned from India. The political parties and their mass associations can be at work in making local democracy work through a village assembly in a favorable political and institutional context. The irony is that the current participatory programs of the NGOs are based on the associational approach driven by the World Bank and other DPs. These are neither accountable to the government nor to the people that they serve. Nor can the NGOs mobilize people against the backdrop of corruption and rent-seeking to hold the government accountable to citizens. That is why the spirit of arriving at consensus by the common people in both urban and rural areas, the basic spirit of having social space, is not given emphasis, or rather it is missing altogether. Moreover, the most vital element of the grassroots democracy-participation is missing as the donor-supported NGOs rarely care for the indigenous political culture and endogenous democracy of South Asia; rather they serve the interests of the donors.

The traditional governance process

The donors' focus is mainly on one type of organization, the NGOs, and they come under the rubric of organizations of community power and grassroots democracy. By challenging this neo-liberal notion of the donor agencies, specifically of the World Bank, this study places emphasis on that kind of indigenous process and claims that it is the most suitable process for promoting grassroots democracy in the context of Bangladesh. Such grassroots democracy would flourish in a social space provided by a competent state, not through the donor-driven "civil society." There is already an indigenous mechanism in South Asia, the village assembly or *Panchayat* in rural areas, those that are focused on both particular matters and those with wider responsibility for community affairs. Traditional village leaders, *matbar* (leader), still play an important role in settling small-scale village disputes through the village *salish* (meeting), but complicated issues are dealt with by the *Upazila*/Union *Parishad* (council) members and political leaders. This kind of village assembly is a loosely structured, leaderless, largely spontaneous effort, but has been ignored so far, though it is able to solve local problems and disputes successfully in many respects. These assemblies are based at the community level.

In India and Nepal, the *Panchayat* has been institutionalized, but in Bangladesh it has lost its spirit. Instead of reinstating the *Panchayat* in Bangladesh, it has been proposed to create a four-tier local government system. However, only the Union Council is in operation in Bangladesh. This Union Council has the potential to take the place of the *Panchayat* by allowing the necessary social space for the entire community. This Union Council can also learn lessons from the *Panchayat* in India. By community, we mean a geographic community, which, in the case of Bangladesh, would be a village, an urban neighborhood or a rural town. These were also based on common interests because they are places where people live and, in some cases, where people work as well. The village assemblies were not based on political affiliation—though partisan politics might play a role in their operation in some cases—nor exclusively based in the workplace, nor relating exclusively to a particular subgroup within the community, such as women, youth and workers, or an ethnic, religious or color grouping. Taken together, they were potentially unitary bodies able to express and articulate the felt needs of people in relation to everything from the provision of housing, food, water and roads, to the distribution of land, the creation of meaningful employment, matters of security, and particular problems experienced by women. They were, in fact, informal mass bodies open to anyone in a given community.

It is clear that strengthening local governance requires strong political will. The clarity of mind and the iron-clad commitment of the political leaders of West Bengal towards endogenous democracy and their initiatives to this effect make the *Panchayat* system a reality based on indigenous processes. They have a clear vision for the *Panchayati Raj* and they are relentless in making that vision come true. Another aspect of the *Panchayati Raj* that attracted attention is its ability to strengthen grassroots leadership, especially of the women and the marginalized. The *Panchayat* system appears to provide a systematic training ground for the people who will take top leadership positions in the country in the future. Almost all the work that is performed by the NGOs in Bangladesh is the responsibility of the *Panchayati Raj* institutions in India.[46] NGOs appear to work as contractors for the *Panchayats*. Bangladesh should follow this lesson from India to promote endogenous democracy through local and indigenous agencies like the existing Union Council under the guidance of a competent state, as NGOs are increasingly coming under scrutiny and criticism, due the lack of their accountability and legitimacy.

Traditionally popular *Sabhas* and *Samitis*, the latter being the assembly of the whole people and the former a smaller body, settled different kinds of disputes on the basis of consensus in the villages of South Asian countries. These two bodies act as legislative and deliberative bodies, and our claim is that they should be made functional in South Asia. The local government, i.e. the existing Union Council, should be both responsible and responsive to the village *Sabhas* and *Samitis*. But, for that purpose, it is imperative that an institute to train villagers in the task of socio-economic development in its various dimensions should be set up to cater to the needs of a cluster of villages. In this way, the system of planning from above can be assisted or replaced by one from below. Contrary to scholarly misconceptions about local democracy in South Asia, this kind of local and direct democracy, in rural towns and villages, is based on the same principle of modernity as democracy at national and state levels, and it is there that its developmental and progressive potentialities lie.

The other feature is that the traditional village assembly or village mass bodies represented an attempt—explicitly or implicitly, consciously or unconsciously—to capture more power for the population at the grassroots level. Some were quite advanced and self-conscious in this orientation. This is a good example of ensuring accountability from below. Neither NGOs nor groups of bureau-cratized "community development" schemes were involved in this indigenous process, hardly anyone had a chance to abuse power. Thus, we need to look at the indigenous experience, and not at donor-driven Western models of social change through "civil society," to understand the precursors of "good governance." Of course this book is not positing yet another new dogma, that is, that the village assembly is the only locus of change. Rather, the experience of Bangladesh suggests that the village assembly is one of several critical loci of social spaces and change. This kind of social space should be the normative core and the heart of any conception of democracy from below in South Asia. A sustainable civil space provided by a competent state must ultimately depend on the spontaneous mobilization of citizens to demand transparency and accountability from the governments of South Asia and even to seek more effective elections and representation in parliament. Donors can do little to create such civic mobilizations or indeed to promote the accumulation of social capital as it remains an inherently indigenous process.

Patronage politics and governance

It is often argued that there has been a weak governance system in South Asia because of the patronage web, characterized by nascent politics and an ill developed political party system.[47] The "good governance" agenda of donors has failed to address the problems of local politics by perpetuating the status quo, which also contributes to shaping the country's governance system, economic progress and development. Thus, we need to look at the local politics of South Asian countries. A political party, as defined by the country's Election Code, is an organized group of persons pursuing the same ideology, political ideas or platform of government.

The subject of local politics needs to be discussed in light of the approach of political parties and party systems towards political development and democratic consolidation. First, in the new typology of political parties drawn up by Richard Gunther and Larry Diamond, there are two types of elite-based party: the traditional local notable party and the clientelistic party.[48] Under this typology, the political parties in South Asia would be classified as clientelistic parties, i.e. instruments of an oligarchic elite for the predation of the state and its resources through various means—the use of traditional patron–client ties, non-personalistic forms of patronage, rent-seeking, outright corruption, fraud, coercion and violence. Second, the institutionalization of political parties and party systems is often regarded as being very important or even crucial for a country's political modernization and democratic consolidation.

Scholars like Samuel Huntington have developed criteria to rank parties and party systems from weak to strong, from un-institutionalized to institutionalized.[49] Under the traditional characterization of political parties and party systems, the main parties in South Asian countries and their overall party system would be regarded as weak and un-institutionalized. Here we argue, however, that while appearing to be feeble, sapless creatures, the political parties are actually quite rapacious and formidable. The clientilist nature of political parties indicates that the building of strong and truly democratic political parties and a concomitant party system in South Asian countries is turning out to be a much more difficult and complicated process. The ideas of liberal democracy and "good governance" lost their actual meaning in the confrontational politics of South Asia and the major political parties have deliberately or otherwise humiliated and mutilated the rules of liberal democracy in the past few years.[50]

Social and political incentives

Generally, it is agreed that donor-driven economic reforms in South Asia have not always been matched with the progress in building the institutions of political and economic governance. The degree of resistance to reforms of different kinds depends on the nature of the prevailing political cultures. Bangladesh has successfully implemented many donor-sponsored reforms that are usually considered unpopular and incompatible with local needs and demands, such as the withdrawal of agricultural and food subsidies affecting large sections of the population. Considerable progress has also been made in implementing reforms that are liable to antagonize organized militant groups who can create short-term disruptions through agitation, such as the trade unions resisting the privatization of state-owned enterprises. Successive governments have pursued more or less the same economic reform agenda, even though with varying intensities and often under the leverage of aid conditionality.[51]

The most politically challenging donor-driven reforms have been the ones aimed at dealing with a whole range of governance-related problems: willful default of bank loans, large-scale tax evasion, electricity pilferage, corruption in public procurement, deteriorating quality of public administration, poor law and order, an inadequate justice system, and the erosion of integrity of most other state institutions. These problems are largely related to the country's core governance systems as shaped by the nature of its politics. Political power has been concentrated in two major parties, which has helped to form governments with large stable majorities; this has also resulted, however, in a system in which winners in elections take all and the losers have difficulty in reconciling themselves to their loss. The result is a highly confrontational style of politics. There is little democratic practice within the major parties, which are controlled and managed by an authoritarian top elite; this is a reflection of the personalized and patron–client relationships pervading South Asian society at large.[52]

The above structure of governance provides an ideal breeding ground for corruption through the exercise of large discretionary powers with little accountability. Spoils and privileges are parceled out to different clientele groups as an essential tool of political management. On top of this, a large part of the bureaucracy is seen to be corrupt and incompetent, which further feeds this vicious circle of poor governance. Ironically, all the top elites have very good connections with the donor agency officials, helping them to secure the necessary funds, often by paying the necessary lip service to the citizens concerned.

Attempts have been made by the national elites to be accountable to the donors rather than to the people they serve; as such, the whole reform agenda does not result in ensuring homegrown pro-poor development or grassroots democracy. In spite of the failures in many cases and the adverse governance environment, there is some evidence that the government is trying to play a major developmental role. For example, the economic reforms in South Asian countries, as discussed in earlier chapters, were not implemented entirely through the leverage of aid conditionality; these have resulted to some extent from the government's own commitment to achieving higher economic growth and alleviating poverty. But, these and similar hopeful signs are largely inadequate to transform South Asian society as a whole. A clue to explaining this can be found in the preparation and presentation of the national annual budgets.

In order to have political legitimacy, budgetary measures in recent years need to be seen to conform to the broad economic objectives set by the government while at the same time the rationale of the proposed economic reforms also needs to be spelled out. This is reflected in the policy statements made by the finance ministers at the time of presenting the budgets. These statements may have to some extent a populist stance (e.g. justifiable measures for increased tax coverage are underplayed, while the not-so-justified writing-off of certain agricultural loans is highlighted), but at least they show the willingness on the part of the government to enhance its so-called "benevolent social guardian" image. In other words, any deviant political motives or compulsions have to remain hidden, only to be pursued at the time of implementing the budget.

Certain yardsticks for judging the merits of the budget proposals are now generally accepted in South Asian countries. One such yardstick is whether there is enough fiscal prudence to contain inflation and ensure economic stabilization. Raising higher revenue and containing the growth of administrative expenditures, so as to generate more domestic resources for development spending, are regarded as sound budgetary policy. Within development spending, the higher the benefits perceived to be going to the poor, the better. Moreover, finance ministers generally think it necessary to show (even with some juggling of the figures) that the allocations to education are larger than the defense budget.

Even if the delivery of public services suffers from a serious governance problem, the government has shown its commitment to improve social development indicators, such as child mortality, primary school enrollment and the adoption of modern birth control. But the budgetary allocations and other public measures to achieve these goals have been drawn up to a large extent under aid conditionality. Successive governments have found it easy to implement the macroeconomic reforms with support from the Bretton Woods institutions. Similarly, the disastrous experience with nationalization and central controls in this period was easy to dismantle because most people (except possibly the trade unions) saw the merits of doing away with a controlled economy and moving towards a private sector led development strategy.

The support for social spending and alliances with NGOs was seen as a political win-win situation since the results of these interventions were generally beneficial to the political parties. Parliamentarians could take the credit for the expansion of health and education programs in their constituencies, which were good for their vote bank, while also such spending provided business opportunities for their clients, which perpetuated patron–client relationships. It is also important to note that, by and large, South Asian countries did not see any significant reversal of reforms even as governments changed because the reforms are not home-grown but driven by the donor agencies. For example, the multi-donor-supported Health and Population Sector Project (1998–2003) stipulated that a minimum of 60 percent of the entire sector's public expenditures must go to essential healthcare, including reproductive health. However, it turned out that the government's previous patterns of health expenditures had already met this criterion. Similarly, the allocations to primary education within total public education expenditures have been high, more than 40 percent, despite the aid conditionality imposed by donors.[53] These programs are ambitious and over-designed, however, and do not provide any fruitful results for the poor.

Governments in South Asia have hesitated to reform the governance institutions and address the core governance concerns raised by the World Bank and other donors because of conflict with the fundamental interest of the party members and their leadership. They have also hesitated to take tough actions where they feared a backlash from the voters (e.g. adjustment of energy prices and the privatization of ports and public utilities). So, Bangladesh's governments only go for some cosmetic reforms. The members of parliament, instead of being concerned with lawmaking and national policies, become lobbyists for procuring projects for their respective constituencies. Much of the wastage in public resource management at the local level, such as the alleged leakage of resources in the rural works program, is the result of the above system. It also partly explains the many weaknesses in the implementation of local development projects, which have not benefited local communities.[54]

Drivers for change in South Asia

Considering the changing political economy in South Asia in terms of structural factors and current socio-economic development trends; the questions that need to be answered now are: what are the drivers that can support the steady economic development and poverty reduction trend in the middle term? How to do this? What are the drivers that can make sure that economic development will bring further human development improvements, and enhanced governance in the middle term? How to do this? However, when thinking about change in South Asia and identifying the drivers, another key analytical question should be whether support for organizational reform can actually change the informal rules of the game. And therefore, also considering the fast-approaching middle-income country (MIC) status without major governance progress, what balance should be given between support to supply-side and demand-side initiatives?

This section identifies the drivers to foster development by reducing poverty from a change perspective. That means stakeholders which can foster further economic development, inclusive growth, poverty reduction, democratic governance, human rights and overall human development in South Asia. There are, however, very few actors who have the power and capacity to drive change simultaneously in all the areas mentioned. Most of the time a driver for change can have a positive impact only on a specific sector. Moreover, the drivers for change are often characterized by high incentives and motivation, but little power and capacity. Therefore, identifying drivers for change implies automatically thinking about how they can be supported and/or empowered. Donors play a key role in supporting the drivers and help to better coordinate their actions towards holistic development.

Today in South Asia, the drivers with more potential for change are civil society organizations (CSOs),[55] but also non-state actors such as profit-oriented private business and the media. The unique position of private business in South Asian countries, especially in the ready-made garments (RMG) sector, gives it not only high power, but also many interests in and incentives for reforms in certain sectors, such as infrastructure, that can become a multiplier for development in different areas. The private sector is a potential powerful partner for donors' advocacy and leverage in the governments. Other drivers are some groups within the youth groups, CSOs; and private for-profit media, which can play a key cross-cutting role in supporting and/or pushing for the drivers' actions. Other stakeholders like women, returning migrants, religious organizations, the international community, and—under specific circumstances—the military, can act as drivers for change in specific areas or can support other drivers directly or indirectly.

The role of the government and the main political parties is controversial. Taken together they represent the most important stakeholders in terms of control over development. However, at a first glance, from a power-incentive perspective, they appear to be less interested in change. Nonetheless, to protect the status quo in the changing socio-economic scenario they will have to adapt somehow to the new reality. Therefore, even if from a self-preservation perspective, they too might have to accept certain changes. However biased this approach may be, the need for survival can be used by the drivers as an entry point for change within the government and the political parties in some specific areas.

When analysing the potential for change through the power and incentives ratio, there are no clear-cut trends or actors. It is important to acknowledge that most often the so-called drivers or agents for change, be they individuals, organizations, groups, or socio-political cultural and economic trends, are multifaceted entities/realities. It is therefore necessary to identify where and how they can play a positive role in change, but also to stress if and how, at the same time, they can represent an obstacle or be non-relevant. A booming private sector is the engine that is driving the economic development and poverty reduction process in South Asia, which should lead the region towards the achievement of the MIC status for the less-developed countries (LDCs) in South Asia. The private sector has become a key stakeholder in South Asian economic development, with high leverage capacity in the governments, and it represents a powerful driver for change. Its key role in income generation and GDP growth gives it a stronger voice than any other actor in society. And its ties with international business organizations put it at the margins of the traditional patronage scheme.

The presence of "heavyweight" external business actors significantly affects the power balance, because it introduced into the national scenario new players, less dependent on the complex web of relations that underpin the power structure within the country. The international private sector's incentives for change are different from those of the national private sector. International businesses are held accountable by a different audience, their home public's opinions. And in an increasingly globalized world where news spreads rapidly, international companies cannot outsource their production facilities without being held accountable (to a certain extent) for the working conditions in third countries. More sensible public opinion and CSOs in the rich/market countries are contributing to push private business to adopt more effective corporate social responsibility (CSR) approaches. Moreover, in order to develop its activities further, international business should look for political stability, and a rule of law which can guarantee a safe investment environment.

The alliances and links between national and international business companies in South Asian countries can therefore contribute to stronger advocacy in terms of enhanced governance and stability. The mix emerging from globalization, increasing media diffusion and growing consumers' responsibility, is creating a new space for action, where donors can play a key role in engaging with the private sector for enhanced CSR, and stronger leverage in the government for change towards more effective democratic governance. As shown by the process that led to the Labour Act Amendment, partnership with the private sector can be very effective for change, but that alone will not be sufficient. Donors should at the same time engage more with the media and support media programs, aiming at raising the awareness of public opinion, national and international, both with regard to the government's law enforcement and private business accountability. Media effects in terms of pressure on the private sector can be even more effective when they lead to mobilization in the countries of origin or markets of the companies, especially in the case of the EU and the US.

This kind of "partnership" can be replicated with other private business sectors, provided that they have enough interest in operating in the country in the middle to long term, and that media give support in terms of coverage and information outreach. The South Asian economy and the private sector need increasing FDI and better infrastructure (transport, road, energy) to keep on growing. Donors can engage with the business community in the country with a view to leveraging private sector activity and resources to deliver public goods. That could be achieved through a partnership pointing at a stronger advocacy for the Public Private Partnership Office (PPP) to manage the tendering for the much-needed infrastructure.

A new generation will soon take over leadership positions in South Asian countries in most sectors of society, ranging from politics to economy, from public administration to communications. Understanding the youth and engaging with them will therefore be fundamental to support change in these countries in the near future. It is important to stress that since the youth as a whole is such a varied population group, which would require a specific study dedicated to it, the focus should be on those youth sub-groups that appear to have more potential to drive or hinder change. In terms of change, the most interesting actors are the "independent" urban youth and young adults who are not trapped in the power structure yet. This social group, even though limited in number when compared to the overall population of the country, can be a strong driver for change in the mid-term. There is a growing number of open-minded, educated, and skilled youngsters frustrated with the high political polarization and the traditional rules of the game.

Engaging with the private sector, however, should always include the acknowledgment that its final aim is profit. Businesses' main incentive for change will be linked to whether change is convenient or not for their activities in South Asian countries. The relationship between the private sector and donors will always be based on a mutual opportunism approach, where one takes advantage of the other. That is what is happening with regard to the RMG today. But it may not always be the case. Before the growing challenges to their production, be they of image, increasing production costs or poor infrastructure, private business may simply look for new countries for their activities. Disney, for example, decided to withdraw from Bangladesh, following the Tazreen accident, most likely to protect its image, or as was stated by Bob Chapek, President of Disney Consumer Products, because "this was the most responsible way to manage the challenges associated with our supply chain."[56]

The rising power of business should not be seen as a panacea for overall development. For example, in terms of tackling corruption, the role of the private sector is less clear. While, on the one hand, private business representatives in South Asian countries, national and international, all complain about the negative impact on their activities of poor infrastructure (transport, energy, roads, ports, etc.), which they openly link to poor governance and lack of foresight, due to the rampant corruption and short-term rent-seeking. On the other hand, the impression is that as long as doing business in India and in other emerging economies in South Asia remains extremely lucrative, due to low wages and labour force availability, corruption will be informally accepted as part of the game. No business has threatened to leave the country yet because of corruption alone. The global South Asian diaspora is over 50 million strong and many of its members maintain strong social, economic and cultural connections to their countries of origin.[57] The migrant workers also engage in various causes and institutions that directly benefit their countries and people in South Asia, which has the potential to foster development if good governance is ensured in South Asian countries. Furthermore, business and politics are becoming increasingly linked.

Many politicians in South Asian countries define themselves as businessmen. The private sector will push for reform only within the limits of its interests, which are not always long-term, and most often are driven by the need for fast profits. For instance, while infrastructure development is a conditio sine qua non for further business expansion, and the private sector may be a powerful partner for the donors' advocacy in this area; the interest in promoting more transparency and fighting corruption, especially as politics and business come closer, should not be taken for granted.

Despite the many challenges and difficulties, NGOs and other CSOs will still contribute to fill the gap where public institutions perform poorly in South Asia. In a context of overpopulation, rural poverty, and limited land, CSOs play a crucial role in poverty alleviation and income generation, while promoting gender equality, health equity and access to better education. NGOs in India, Bangladesh, Sri Lanka and Nepal have shown outstanding successes in service delivery in a wide variety of areas. Moreover, they have also proved their capacity to create independently innovative and sustainable initiatives for change, like microcredit, that have contributed and still contribute to socio-economic development in the country.

CSOs become even more important as the small countries in South Asia prepare to jump from the less-developed country (LDC) to the middle-income country (MIC) status, leaving many people on the margins of positive development outcomes. CSOs will support change through supply-side initiatives where the state power does not reach, and through much-needed demand-side activities, turning the light on areas such as democratic governance and human rights that may be downsized by a strict focus on economic growth. In these areas in particular, CSOs will require the donors' backing, as the space for civil liberties in the country is shrinking. More analysis should be carried out on the role of influential think-tanks and the big social business organizations (SBOs), i.e. BRAC, Grameen Bank, with which donors might engage more through strategic partnerships for advocacy and leverage in the governments than financial support.

While continuing to support supply-side initiatives, it is the demand side that today needs the donors' special attention. Organizations working in this area play a key role in change towards enhanced democracy, human rights, rule of law, gender equality and empowerment. However, in today's South Asia, there is clear evidence of increasing pressure, harassment and attacks coming from the government. Such restrictions have been institutionalized through a series of laws and law drafts that have been approved and designed in recent years. Donors should acknowledge that the situation is worsening and strengthen their support to and engage with those organizations, while, on the other hand, they may adopt stricter conditionality with the government, should the political leadership further relax its commitment to human rights and democracy.

The changing role of women in the South Asian society is both linked to and contributing to the fast modernization process that characterizes today's South Asian countries. Women's increased participation in education and economic activities are changing the socio-cultural shape of the country. Women's employment in the growing services and industrial sectors together with women's entrepreneurship (thanks to the microfinance diffusion in the country with women being targeted by the big NGOs and SBOs), are playing a key role in poverty reduction and overall economic development. Notwithstanding the great progress and achievements, however, women as a whole are still relatively weak. Greater support for women's education, vocational training, emancipation and empowerment is needed in order to ensure more inclusive development and a sustainable process of change. All the progress made with regard to gender in the South Asian countries is still to be consolidated. The role of women as small entrepreneurs through microfinance initiatives is clearly contributing to economic growth and at the same time is fostering the change in women's roles at the household and societal level, giving women a stronger voice in family and local decision-making process.

Most of the international NGOs that operate in South Asia are active in the same areas as national CSOs and Community Building Organizations (CBOs), both in supply-side and demand-side initiatives. However, as international entities, today they are in a relatively safer position than their national counterparts. In the current trend of shrinking democratic space, that gives them more room to maneuver in terms of demand-side initiatives and engagement in sensitive issues such as corruption and political dialogue. Another area where CBOs need support to foster new SBOs is the creation of tourism and eco-tourism. CSOs are varied and numerous, ranging from small CBOs like the *sabhas* and the *salish*, which focus mostly on local dispute settling, small agribusiness and handicrafts production in remote villages, to one of the biggest NGO at global level like BRAC, which operates in many developing countries through South–South initiatives.

Conclusion

Research findings show that very few of the interviewees were optimistic about the actual outcome of the rhetorical democracy and governance programs in South Asia to reduce poverty. This process confirms that the "nature and scope" of the poverty and governance problems tend to get defined externally and in a highly "technocratic way" and that the poor are regarded as a "stock" of people, rather than a "flow." There was also criticism among the interviewees about the rhetoric of the democratic governance as well as the government's lack of participatory practice. International development agencies have sought to apply the idea of "good governance" by restructuring state bureaucracies, reforming legal systems, supporting democratic decentralization and creating accountability by enhancing civil societies. In theory, this form of governance should refer to any mode of public decision-making that is 'good' in the sense of helping to advance human welfare, however conceived. Nevertheless, because of the huge influence of aid donors, governance has come to be associated with institutions designed to support market-led development. This built-in ambiguity finds its parallel in the imprecision of the cognate terms on which has been built the "Democracy and Governance Sector," to use the term initiated by the aid business for its programmatic initiatives. Development consultants deployed to overhaul the Third World state seized, perhaps inevitably, upon two suitable ideas in particular: participation and accountability. Improving both, while not (at least openly) undermining managerial efficiency, has been the focus of intensive development agenda.[58]

The governance discourse in South Asia is geared towards enhancing policy effectiveness. The guiding motive to interfere in internal affairs in recipient countries, some would say, has been towards the establishment of new global institutional patterns of "governance" through a "discipline," in a Foucauldian[59] sense, including the governance of "self," of state and policy structures in individual countries to conform to the norms set by the global institutions. There are intriguing overlaps, though also differences, between notions of "governance" and Foucault's "governmentality."[60] However, the specific needs and potential of a particular country or its historically derived social or economic structures have not figured much as points of departure in the policy designs of South Asian countries. One of the key aims of donors in this regard has been the creation of a state and market mechanism in the context of South Asia that has the characteristics typical of the Western liberal-capitalist system.[61]

Given the apparent flaws of market-oriented governance reform programs[62] prescribed by the donors to improve macroeconomic performance of the South Asian countries in a sustainable manner, the current study poses questions about the ability of reformers, under the governance agenda, to escape the dilemma of a "poverty-laden" and "weak governance." Contrary to the claims of most mainstream analysts, this book suggests that pro-market governance reforms should be implemented in South Asian countries in a manner which can potentially stabilize the economy to meet broader development challenges by controlling inflation and addressing local needs. It is also argued that governance reforms have been misused by the political elites primarily to consolidate the power of the ruling elites.[63] Successive regimes, both military and civilian, have treated the market reform as an instrument to build and maintain political coalitions in particular with traders and industrialists.[64] In exchange for political support, they allowed business elites to use economic restructuring as the primary tool to attain their financial and economic objectives. Consequently, most of the structural adjustment, pro-market governance reforms and "good governance" programs failed in many ways to improve governance or economic performance, let alone raise the living standards for the majority by eliminating poverty in South Asia.

The donor agencies that advocate liberal democracy and good governance appear oblivious to how few of the conditions for democratic endurance exist in South Asia and what their implications for democracy might be. The legitimacy of the state, sustaining democratic politics, a secure and broad-based consensus on the rules of the political gain,[65] the existence of a rich and pluralistic social space,[66] relative social and economic equalities are all essential conditions for an enduring democratic politics as evident from previous breakdowns in the twentieth century.[67] In most of the developing countries, many of these conditions are distorted and flawed by low levels of legitimacy, consensus and elite commitment.[68] A robust and substantial middle class rarely exists, nor does a powerful working class, both of which might push for and protect democratization.

A final feature of South Asian society is that its institutions of civil society, to the extent they do exist, have been penetrated and captured by the dominant political parties and thus have been effectively transformed into their agents. Social inequalities are often grotesque, and the military or the joint force also regularly plays a significant political and coercive role in defense of the dominant interests. This in turn produces violent political cultures of terror and counter-terror.

One more problem is that the state has seldom enjoyed autonomy appropriate for decisive developmental action vis-à-vis external donors. Economic liberalization programs based on the "good governance" agenda have not addressed these problems with enough care.[69] Soaring unemployment, inflation, severe cuts in public expenditure on health, welfare and education have been the signs of this. Because of privatization and economic liberalization in the name of governance reforms, acute inequalities between the rich and poor have been amplified by the debt crisis and its adverse impacts on local economies. Yet, radical change may be precisely what is required at key points in developmental processes, and this is one of the key reasons the relationship between democracy and development is so tense. Economic liberalization and privatization in the name of the "good governance" agenda and distorted democratic politics are highly unlikely to reduce the gap between rich and poor or solve South Asia's economic problems; in fact, they can be expected to deepen them. Institution-building or improved training cannot simply produce an independent, impartial and competent administration. If local politics and the political will based on an existing local political culture cannot give rise to the kind of state that can introduce, sustain and protect an effective and independent capacity for governance, no positive developmental outcome will be possible. In the light of the contemporary scenario of South Asia, externally imported liberal democracy or a donor-driven governance agenda is unlikely to be the political form, which can generate a strong state or an improved system of governance.

Two interesting issues seem to have emerged in recent years. One is that of donor-driven conditions, i.e. conditions aimed at creating the civil society associations in South Asia that will generate social capital and stable markets and eventually strengthen and widen democracy. The other is concern about the role of the state. Within the agenda of "good governance," "civil society" is assumed to foster freedom and liberty but we have seen how this assumption may not be valid in South Asian societies marked by critical governance challenges, social divisions and confrontational politics. Individuals have to be able to associate on equal terms, and this condition can only be created by a state competent in framing and enforcing universal laws. Thus, the second issue is whether it is possible to conceive of a civil society as being detached from the state.[70] The state should not be placed vis-à-vis civil society; the latter largely weakens the state governance system and creates a legitimacy crisis, thus adding to the vicious circle of weakness and impoverishment. It follows that countries in South Asia with competent governance need to be strengthened if 'social space' is perceived to be the magic wand that brings actual good governance and democracy through a re-evaluation of the indigenous political culture and the grassroots process.

In light of the contemporary scenario of South Asia, neither electoral democracy nor a donor-driven governance agenda is likely to be the political form that will generate a strong state and/or an improved system of governance. Hence, it has not just been a managerial or "good governance" question, as one of the conditionalities of the World Bank and its literature on governance asserts, but a political one. There is a need to reconsider the governance policies of the Western donors that currently contribute to the erosion of sovereignty and autonomy of the recipient countries. For all forms and processes of development, they express crucially the central core of politics: conflict, negotiation and cooperation over the use, production and distribution of resources. This political approach will help liberate the poor from poverty and suffering and help society resist the status quo and fight the anti-developmental oligarchs who oppose empowerment and who stand in the way of development and democracy.

Without competent governance under an autonomous state, genuine development, on the basis of indigenous needs and demands and good governance, can hardly take place. Furthermore, democratic and market-friendly strategies will break on the rocks of economic inequalities and intensified poverty, escalating political strife sooner or later, especially in premature democracies in South Asia. Because of this, the Western insistence on good governance, free markets, a more prominent role for any country's civil society and liberal democracy as the keys to development is nothing but rhetorical and naïve. To harness the power of public opinion is as important as to broaden institutional, political participation, in a fruitful and synergistic connection between the state and society. The challenge to development thus lies in finding the correct way to help improve the governance system in South Asian countries. More fruitful state–society interactions, efficient public institutions and autonomous national actors based on the progressive realism and theories of Lefebvre can help promote the national interests. This is the guideline for the clarification of the role of the state and the state–society relations so that the right approach can contribute more effectively to ensure strong governance with indigenous norms of accountability in South Asian countries as in other developing countries.

Economic growth in South Asia has been modest in recent years, but the goal of ending extreme poverty by 2030 will be critical due to the many challenges facing South Asian countries. These countries must work harder on reforms to raise growth in a region where most of the world's poor live.[71] In the aftermath of the severe global economic crisis in 2008, all the countries in South Asia need to keep close tabs on the adverse economic impacts of the crisis on marginalized and poor populations. In the long term, they will need to focus on second-generation reforms including mainstreaming development, making the political process more inclusive, and ensuring proper accountability of public institutions. In these countries the management of public expectations for swift and effective development actions will also take center stage in the years to come as managing their expectations is proving to be just as important as instituting the governance reforms to reduce poverty.

Notes

1 Tocqueville, A. de, *Democracy in America* (Garden City, NY: Doubleday, 1969), pp. 1835–40.
2 Putnam, R., Leonard, R. and Nanetti, R.Y., *Making Democracy Work* (Princeton, NJ: Princeton University Press, 1993), pp. 1–52.
3 World Bank, *Sub-Saharan Africa: From crisis to sustainable growth* (Washington, DC: The World Bank, 1989), p. 3.

4 Abrahamsen, R., *Disciplining Democracy: Development discourse and good governance in Africa* (London: Zed Press, 2000), p. 51.

5 Rudolph, S.H., "Civil Society and the Realm of Freedom," *Economic and Political Weekly*, vol. 35, issue 20, (2000), pp. 1762–9.

6 Ibid.

7 *The Daily Star*, January 4, 2006, Dhaka.

8 Lofchie, M.J., "Reflections on Structural Adjustment," in *Beyond Autocracy in Africa. Inaugural Seminar of the African Governance Programme* (Atlanta, GA: The Carter Center, Emory University, 1989), pp. 121–5.

9 Weber, M., *The Theory of Social and Economic Organization* (New York: The Free Press, 1964).

10 Leftwitch, A., *Democracy and Development: Theory and practice* (Cambridge: Polity Press, 1996), pp. 14–32.

11 Cutright, P., "National Political Development: Measurement and Analysis", *American Sociological Review*, vol. 28, (1963), pp. 253–64.

12 Dahl, R.A., *Polyarchy* (New Haven, CT: Yale University Press, 1971), p. 103.

13 Tilly, C., "Reflections on the History of European States," in Tilly, C. (ed.) *The Foundation of National States in Western Europe* (Princeton, NJ: Princeton, University Press, 1975), pp. 3–83.

14 Bhagwati, J., *The Economics of Underdeveloped Countries* (London: Weidenfeld and Nicholson, 1996), p. 204.

15 Adelman, I. and Morris, C., *Society, Politics and Economic Development* (Baltimore, MD: The Johns Hopkins University Press, 1967).

16 Sirowy, L. and Inkeles, A., "The Effects of Democracy on Economic Growth and Inequality: A review," *Studies in Comparative International Development*, vol. 25, issue 1, (1990), pp. 126–57.

17 Gerschenkron, A., *Economic Backwardness in Historical Perspective* (Cambridge, MA: Harvard University Press, 1962).

18 Almond, G. and Verba, S., *The Civic Culture* (Princeton, NJ: Princeton University Press, 1963).

19 Elkins, D.J. and Simeon, R.E.B., "A Cause in Search of Its Effect, or What Does Political Culture Explain?" *Comparative Politics*, vol. 11, issue 1, (1979), pp. 127–45.

20 Pye, L.W., *Asian Power and Politics* (Cambridge, MA: Harvard University Press, 1985), pp. 7–8.

21 Huntington, S.P., "The Clash of Civilizations," *Foreign Affairs*, vol. 72, issue 3, (1993), p. 25.

22 Emmerson, D.K., "Singapore and the 'Asian Values' Debate," *Journal of Democracy*, vol. 6, issue 4, (1995), pp. 95–105.

23 Hofstede, G., *Cultures and Organization: Software of the mind* (New York: McGraw-Hill, 1991), pp. 20–43.

24 Triandis, H.C., *Culture and Social Behavior* (New York: McGraw-Hill, 1994), p. 16.

25 Abercrombie, H. (ed.) *Dictionary of Sociology* (London: Penguin Books, 1994), p. 315.

26 Mitra, S.K., "Effects of Institutional Arrangements on Political Stability in South Asia," *Annual Review of Political Science*, vol. 2, (1999), pp. 405–28.

27 Mitra, S.K., "The Rational Politics of Cultural Nationalism: Sub-national movements of South Asia in comparative perspective," *British Journal of Political Science*, vol. 25, issue 1, (1995), pp. 153–77.

28 Jalal, A., *Democracy and Authoritarianism in South Asia: A comparative and historical perspective* (Cambridge: Cambridge University Press, 1995), pp. 1–12.

29 Ibid., pp. 23–5.

30 Malkani, K.R., *The Politics of Ayodhya and Hindu-Muslim Relations* (Delhi: Har-Anand Publications, 1993), pp. 41–53.

31 Mallick, R., *Development Policy of a Communist Government: West Bengal since 1977* (Cambridge: Cambridge University Press, 1993).
32 Mizanur R.S., "Governance and Administration: Challenge of New Millennium," in Hye, A.H. (ed.) *Governance: South Asian perspectives* (Dhaka: University Press Limited, 2000), pp. 165–83.
33 Mitra, S.K., "Between Transaction and Transcendence: The state and the institutionalization of power in India," in Mitra, S.K. (ed.) *The Post-colonial State in Asia: The Dialectics of Politics and Culture* (Hemel Hempstead: Harvester Wheatsheaf, 1990).
34 Dilara, C., "Legislature and Governance in Bangladesh," in Hye, H.A. (ed.) *Governance: South Asian perspectives* (Dhaka: University Press Limited, 2000), pp. 49–69.
35 Mitra, S.K., "The Rational Politics of Cultural Nationalism: Sub-national movements of south Asia in comparative perspective," *British Journal of Political Science*, vol. 25, issue 1, (1995), pp. 153–77.
36 Gordon, W., "Democratization and Economic Reform in China," *The Australian Journal of Chinese Affairs*, vol. 31, (1994), p. 79.
37 Rehman, S. "Reprioritizing South Asia's Development Agenda: Role of governance," in Hye, H.A. (ed.) *Governance: South Asian Perspectives* (Dhaka: University Press Limited, 2000), pp. 341–67.
38 Kabor, M.H., "Governance and Economy: Bangladesh perspectives," in Hye, H.A. (ed.) *Governance: South Asian perspectives* (Dhaka: University Press Limited, 2000), pp. 393, 421.
39 Parnini, S.N., "Public Sector Reform and Good Governance: The Impact of foreign aid on Bangladesh," *Journal of Asian and African Affairs*, vol. 44, issue 5, (2009), pp. 553–75.
40 Dilara, C. (2000), op. cit., pp. 50–4.
41 Subhan, K.M., "Legislature and Good Governance," in Hye, H.A. (ed.) *Governance: South Asian perspectives* (Dhaka: University Press Limited, 2000), pp. 69–83.
42 See www.bangladeshnews.com.bd/2007/04/29/reforms-a-must-but-parties-themselves-should-decide-on-it/.
43 Rehman, S., "Governance and Local Government System," in Hye, H.A. (ed.) *Governance: South Asian perspectives* (Dhaka: University Press Limited, 2000), pp. 231–47.
44 Fritzen, S., "Institutionalizing Participation: Lessons learnt and implications for strengthening Vietnam's national programs. Final report for UNDP/UNCDF/CIDA Institutionalization of Participatory Planning Study," Hanoi: mimeo (1999).
45 Webster, N., *Panchayat Raj and the Decentralization of Development Planning in West Bengal: A case study* (Calcutta: K. P. Bagchi, 1992).
46 Raju, M.R., "Panchayat Raj in Kerala: Problems and prospects," *Kurukshetra*, April, 1998, pp.70–1.
47 David, G. (2014), "The Paradox of Patronage and the People's Sovereignty," in A. Piliavsky (ed.) *Patronage as Politics in South Asia* (Cambridge: Cambridge University Press, 2014), pp. 125–54.
48 Gunther, R. and Diamond, L., "Types and Functions of Parties," in Diamond, L. and Gunther, R. (eds) *Political Parties and Democracy* (Baltimore, MD: The Johns Hopkins University Press, 2001), pp. 12–15.
49 Huntington, S.P., *Political Order in Changing Societies* (New Haven, CT: Yale University Press, 1968).
50 Siddiqui, K., *Towards Good Governance in Bangladesh: Fifty unpleasant essays* (Dhaka: University Press Limited; 1996), pp. 11–23.
51 Obaidullah, K.A.Z.M., "Bangladesh: Governance Issues," paper prepared for the Asian Development Bank; February, 2000, Dhaka.
52 Rahman, M.H. *Models and Myths of Decentralization: The Bangladesh experience* (New Delhi: South Asian Publishers, 2001), pp. 37–51.

53 Mahmud, D. (2002), *Bangladesh Economic Survey*, Ministry of Finance (various issues), Chapter 9.
54 This is evident from the recent initiatives taken by the government to mitigate seasonal poverty, locally called *monga*, in some vulnerable areas in the north-western part of the country.
55 All non-state, not-for-profit structures, non-partisan and non–violent, through which people organize to pursue shared objectives and ideals, whether political, cultural, social or economic. They include membership-based, cause-based and service-oriented CSOs. Among them, community-based organizations, non-governmental organizations, faith-based organizations, foundations, research institutions, gender and LGBT organizations, cooperatives, professional and business associations, and the not-for-profit media. Trade unions and employers' organizations, the so-called social partners, constitute a specific category of CSOs.
56 "Disney Pulls Out of Bangladesh Factories," Emily Jane Fox, at www.money.cnn.com, May 2, 2013.
57 Tan, T.Y. and Mizanur, M.R., *Diaspora Engagement and Development in South Asia* (Basingstoke: Palgrave Macmillan, 2013), pp. 54–66.
58 Carothers, T., *Aiding Democracy Abroad: The learning curve* (Washington, DC: Carnegie Endowment for International Peace, 1999), pp. 406–11.
59 Gordon, C., "Governmental Rationality: An introduction," in Burchell, G., Gordon, C. and Miller, P. (eds) *The Foucault Effect: Studies in governmentality* (Chicago, IL: University of Chicago Press, 1991), pp. 1–5.
60 Balibar, E., "Foucault and Marx: The question of nominalism," in *Michel Foucault, Philosopher* (London: Routledge, 1992), pp. 38–56.
61 Doornbos, M., *Global Forces and State Restructuring: Dynamics of state formation and collapse* (Basingstoke: Palgrave Macmillan, 2006), pp. 93–108.
62 Burnell, P., *Foreign Aid in a Changing World* (Buckingham: Open University Press, 1997).
63 Ahmed, N., *Trade Liberalization in Bangladesh: An investigation in trends* (Dhaka: Dhaka University Press Limited, 2001), pp. 2–17.
64 Bhattacharya, D. and Rahman, M., "Experience with Implementation of WTO-ATC and Implications for Bangladesh," *CPD Policy Paper*, No. 7, September (2000), Dhaka: Centre for Policy Dialogue.
65 Linz, J.J., "The Breakdown of Democratic Regimes: Crisis, breakdown and re-equilibration," in Linz, J.J. and Stepan, A. (eds) *The Breakdown of Democratic Regimes* (Baltimore, MD: Johns Hopkins University Press, 1978), pp. 3–124; and Huntington (1993), op. cit., p. 39.
66 Lefebvre, H., *The Production of Space*, trans. D. Nicholson-Smith (Oxford: Blackwell, 1991), pp. 3–15; and Diamond, L. and Linz, J.J., "Introduction: Politics, society and democracy in Latin America," in Diamond, L. *et al.* (eds) *Democracy in Developing Countries*, vol. 4, *Latin America* (Boulder, CO: Lynne Rienner, 1989), pp. 1–58.
67 Linz (1978), op. cit., note 55.
68 Ekeh, P., "Colonialism and the Two Publics," *Comparative Studies in Society and History*, vol. 17, issue 1, (1971), pp. 91–112; and Jackson, R.H. and Rosberg, C.G., "Why Africa's Weak States Persist," in Kohli, A. (ed.) *The State and Development in the Third World* (Princeton, NJ: Princeton University Press, 1986), pp. 259–82.
69 *The Daily Star*, "The End of an Era," March 20, 2007, Dhaka.
70 Mahajan, G., "Civil Society and Its Avatars: What happened to freedom and democracy?" *Economic and Political Weekly*, vol. 34, (1999), pp. 1188–96.
71 See www.worldbank.org/en/news/press-release/2013/10/09/south-asia-economic-focus-turmoil-capital-markets-world-bank (accessed February 22, 2014).

Bibliography and further reading

Abbot, K. and Snidal, D. (1998) "Why States Act Through Formal International Organizations," *Journal of Conflict Resolution*, 42(1): 3–32.

Abrahamsen, R. (2000) *Disciplining Democracy: Development discourse and good governance in Africa*, London: Zed Press.

Abugre, C. (2000) "Still Sapping the Poor: A critique of IMF poverty reduction strategies," *ISODEC*, June.

Abul, K. (1996) *Bangladesh: Internal dynamics and external linkages*, New Delhi: Oxford University Press.

Adam, L. (2005) "The Debt of the Poorest Nations: A gold mine for development aid," *International Economic Report, Gailliot Center for Public Policy*, New York: Carnegie Mellon.

Adelman, I. and Morris, C. (1967) *Society, Politics and Economic Development*, Baltimore, MD: The Johns Hopkins University Press.

Ahluwalia, M. (2000) "Economic Performance of States in the Post Reforms Period," *Economic and Political Weekly*, May, 6: 1637–48.

Ahmed, A. and Salahuddin, F. (1994) *Bengali Nationalism and the Emergence of Bangladesh: An introductory outline*, International Centre for Bengal Studies, Dhaka: Dhaka University Press.

Ahmed, E. (1980) "Dominant Bureaucratic Elites in Bangladesh," in M.M. Khan and H. Zafarullah (eds) *Politics and Bureaucracy in a New Nation: Bangladesh*, Dhaka: Center for Administrative Studies, pp. 21–65.

Ahmed, N. (2001) *Trade Liberalization in Bangladesh: An investigation in trends*, Dhaka: University Press Limited.

Ahmed, S. (2004) "The Political Economy of Development Experience in Bangladesh," paper presented at seminar on "Accelerating Growth and Poverty Reduction in Bangladesh," organized by The World Bank and Bureau of Economic Research, University of Dhaka.

Alarcon, D. (2003) "The MDGs in National Policy Frameworks," *Development Policy Journal*, April, 3(1): 37–46.

Alberto, A. and Dollar, D. (2000) "Who Gives Foreign Aid to Whom and Why?", *Journal of Economic Growth*, 5(1): 33–63.

Alesina, A., Ozler, S., Roubini, N., and Swagel, P. (1996) "Political Instability and Economic Growth," *Journal of Economic Growth*, 1: 189–212.

Almond, G. and Verba, S. (1963) *The Civic Culture*, Princeton, NJ: Princeton University Press.

Alvin, Y. (1990) *Social Change and Development: Modernization and world system theories*, Newbury Park, CA: Sage.

Aminuzaman, S. (2000) "Institutional Framework of Poverty Alleviation: An overview of Bangladesh experiences," paper presented at the Development Studies Network Conference on Poverty, Prosperity and Progress, 17–19 November.

Anheier, H.K., Glasius, M. and Kaldor, M. (2001) "Introducing Global Civil Society," in H.K. Anheier, M. Glasius and M. Kaldor (eds) *Global Civil Society*, Oxford: Oxford University Press, pp. 3–22.

Anon (2002) "The World Bank and the PRSP: Flawed thinking and filing experiences," *Jubilee South*, Focus on the Global South, 16 November, Managua: AWEPON, Centro de Estudios Internacionales.

Appadurai, A. (1996) *Modernity at Large: Cultural dimensions of globalization*, Minneapolis, MN: University of Minnesota Press.

Asian Development Bank (2012) *Economic Review of South Asia*, June, Manila: ADB.

Babar, S. (1997) "Partners or Contractors? The Relationship between Official Agencies and NGOs, Bangladesh," Occasional Paper Series, Number 14, INTRAC, March, Oxford.

Bagchi, A.K. (1989) "Development Planning," in M. Milgate and P. Newman (eds) *The New Palgrave: A dictionary of economics*, London: John Eatwell.

Bajpai, N., Jeffrey, D.S. and Nicole, H.V. (2004) "Reaching the Millennium Development Goals in South Asia," paper prepared for the United Nations Millennium Project, Center on Globalization and Sustainable Development, Working Paper, No. 17, Columbia University, New York.

Balibar, E. (1992) "Foucault and Marx: The question of nominalism," in T.J. Armstrong (ed.) *Michel Foucault, Philosopher*, London: Routledge, pp. 38–56.

Bangladesh Bureau of Statistics (2008) *Statistical Pocket Yearbook of Bangladesh*, Foreign Aid Indicators, Dhaka: Ministry of Finance.

Bardhan, P. (1984) *The Political Economy of Development in India*, Bombay and Delhi: Oxford University Press.

Barenstein, J. (1994) *Overcoming Fuzzy Governance in Bangladesh: Policy implementation in least developing countries*, Dhaka: Dhaka University Press Limited.

Barkat, A. (2001) "How Much Foreign Aid Does Bangladesh Really Need: Political Economy of Last Three Decades," Keynote paper presented at the National Seminar titled "How Much Foreign Aid Does Bangladesh Really Need?" organized by Bangladesh Economic Association, Dhaka, 10 February.

Barnard, H. (1990) "Bourdieu and Ethnography: Reflexivity, politics and praxis," in R. Harker, C. Mahar and C. Wilkes (eds) *An Introduction to the Work of Pierre Bourdieu*, London: Macmillan, pp. 58–85.

Barro, R.J. and Lee, J.W. (1994) "Sources of Economic Growth," *Carnegie-Rochester Conference Series on Public Policy*, 40: 1–46.

Bauer, P. (1972) *Dissent on Development*, Cambridge, MA: Harvard University Press.

Bauer, P. (1991) *The Development Frontier: Essays in applied economics*, Cambridge, MA: Harvard University Press.

Beazer, Q.H. (2012) "Bureaucratic Discretion, Business Investment, and Uncertainty," *The Journal of Politics*, 74(3): 637–52.

Bela, B. (1970) "The Impact of the Industrial Countries' Tariff Structure on Their Imports of Manufacturers From Less Developed Areas: A reply," *Economica*, New Series, August, 37(147): 316–20.

Benda-Beckman, F. von (1994) "Good Governance, Law and Social Reality: Problematic relationships. knowledge and policy," *The International Journal of Knowledge Transfer and Utilization*, 7(1): 55–67.

Berg, E. (1993) *Rethinking Technical Cooperation: Reforms for capacity building in Africa*, New York: United Nations Development Program.

Bhagwati, J. (1958) "Immiserizing Growth: A geometric note," *Review of Economic Studies*, 25(3): 201–5.

Bhagwati, J. (1996) *The Economics of Underdeveloped Countries*, London: Weidenfeld and Nicholson.

Bhattacharya, D. and Mustafizur, R. (2000) "Experience with Implementation of WTO-ATC and Implications for Bangladesh," *CPD Policy Paper*, vol. 7, September, Dhaka: Centre for Policy Dialogue.

Blair, H. (2001) "Institutional Pluralism in Public Administration and Politics: Applications in Bolivia and beyond," *Public Administration and Development*, May, 21(2): 119–29.

Blair, H. (2002) *Civil Society, Advocacy, Service Delivery, Non-Governmental Organizations and USAID Assistance: A mapping exercise*, Washington, DC: Management Systems International for Office of Program and Operations Assessment, Center for Development Information and Evaluation, USAID, 5 March.

Blandine, D. (1998) *The Role of the State in Improving the Living Conditions of Workers: The case of the Shubra-El-Kheima industrial area*, Paris: CNRS URBAMA.

Blinder, A.S. (1990) "What Is New-Keynesian Economics?", *Journal of Economic Literature*, September, 28(3): 1115–71.

Bode, B. (2002) *In Pursuit of Power: Local elites and union-level governance in rural northwestern Bangladesh*, Dhaka: CARE Bangladesh.

Boone, P. (1995) "The Impact of Foreign Aid on Savings and Growth," Working Paper, London: London School of Economics and Political Science.

Boone, P. (1996) "Politics and the Effectiveness of Foreign Aid," *European Economic Review*, 40: 289–329.

Boozer, M., Gustav, R., Francis, S. and Tavnit, S. (2004) "Paths to Success: The relationship between human development and economic growth," Economic Growth Center, Discussion Paper.

Braset, J. and Higgott, R. (2003) "Building the Normative Dimensions of a Global Polity," in D. Armstrong *et al.* (eds) *Governance and Resistance in World Politics*, Cambridge: Cambridge University Press, pp. 29–55.

Brenner, N. (1997) "Global, Fragmented, Hierarchical: Henri Lefebvre's geographies of globalization," *Public Culture*, 10(1): 135 67.

Brzoska, M. (2003) "Development Donors and the Concepts of Security Sector Reform," Occasional Paper, No. 4, Geneva: Geneva Centre for the Democratic Control of Armed Forces.

Burke, A. (2001) "Caught Between National and Human Security: Knowledge and power in post-crisis Asia," *Pacifica Review*, 13(3): 215–39.

Burki, S.P.G. and Dillinger, W. (1999) *Beyond the Center: Decentralizing the state in Latin American and Caribbean studies*, Washington, DC: The World Bank.

Burnell, P. (1997) *Foreign Aid in a Changing World*, Buckingham: Open University Press.

Burnside, C. and Dollar, D. (2000) "Aid, Policies, and Growth," *American Economic Review*, September, 90(4): 847–68.

Caliari, A. (2005) "The Debt-Trade Connection in Debt Management Initiatives: Need for a change in paradigm," paper prepared for the UNCTAD Expert Meeting Debt Sustainability and Development Strategies, October, Geneva.

Carlos, J. (1981) "Dependency Theory and the Processes of Capitalism and Socialism," *Latin American Perspectives*, 8(3/4): 55–81.

Carothers, T. (1999) *Aiding Democracy Abroad: The learning curve*, Washington, DC: Carnegie Endowment for International Peace.

Cash, K. and Sanchez, D. (2003) "Reducing Poverty or Repeating Mistakes? A Civil Society Critique of Poverty Reduction Strategy Papers," Stockholm: Church of Sweden Aid, Save the Children, and the Swedish Jubilee Network.

Cassen, R. (1886) *Does Aid Work? Report to an Intergovernmental Task Force*, Oxford: Clarendon Press.

Castells, M. (1996) *The Information Age*, vol. 3, Malden, MA: Blackwell, pp. 66–150.

Centre for Policy Dialogue (n.d.) "Poverty Reduction Strategy for Bangladesh: Views of civil society," Dhaka, Bangladesh. Available at: www.cpd-bangladesh.org/work/irbd_docs/INT02–04.doc.

Chakravarti, A. (2005) *Aid, Institutions, and Development: New approaches to growth: Governance and poverty*, Cheltenham: Edward Elgar Publishing Limited.

Chambers, R., Pettit, J. and Scott, P.V. (2001) "The New Dynamics of Aid: Power, procedures and relationships," *IDS Policy Briefing*, August, pp. 31–45.

Chaudhuri, P. (1979) *India's Economy: Poverty and Development*, New York: St Martin's Press.

Chen, S. and Ravallion, M. (2008) "The Developing World is Poorer Than We Thought, But No Less Successful in the Fight Against Poverty," World Bank Policy Research Working Paper, No. 4703, Washington, DC: The World Bank.

Cheung, A.B.L. (1997) "Understanding Public Sector Reforms, Global Trends and Diverse Agendas," *International Review of Administrative Sciences*, 63: 435–57.

Chirot, D. (2000) "A Clash of Civilization or of Paradigms? Theorizing Progress and Social Change," *International Sociology*, 16: 341–60.

Chowdhury, D. (2000) "Legislature and Governance in Bangladesh," in H.A. Hye (ed.) *Governance: South Asian perspectives*, Dhaka: University Press Limited.

Christensen, T. and Laegreid, P. (2001) *New Public Management: The transformation of ideas and practices*, Aldershot: Ashgate.

Christopher, C. (1998) "Degrees of Statehood," *Review of International Studies*, 24(1): 143–57.

Clapham, C. (1996) *Africa and the International System: The politics of state survival*, Cambridge: Cambridge University Press.

Cohen, D., Jacquet, P. and Reisen, H. (2005) *"Beyond Grants vs. Loans": How to use ODA and debt for development*, Paris: Paris Press.

Cohen, J. and Arato, A. (1992) *Political Theory and Civil Society*, Cambridge, MA: MIT Press.

Collier, P. (1997) "The Failure of Conditionality," in C. Gwin and J. Nelson (eds) *Perspectives on Aid and Development*, Washington, DC: Overseas Development Council, pp. 51–77.

Collier, P. and Dehn, J. (2001) "Aid, Shocks and Growth," Policy Research Working Paper, No. 2688, Washington, DC: The World Bank.

Collingwood, V. (2000) "Good Governance and the World Bank." Available at: www.brettonwoodsproject.org (accessed 20 April 2011).

Cornwall, A.P. and Scott, P.V. (2004) *Participatory Learning Groups in an Aid Bureaucracy: Lessons for change in policy and organizations*, Paper No. 11, Brighton: Institute of Development Studies.

Cox, R. (1993) "Gramsci, Hegemony and International Relations: An essay in method," in S. Gill (ed.) *Gramsci, Historical Materialism and International Relations*, Cambridge: Cambridge University Press, pp. 162–75.

Crawford, G. (1996) "International Cooperation for Democracy and Good Governance: Moving toward a second generation?", *European Journal of Development Research*, 13(1): 154–80.

Cutright, P. (1963) "National Political Development: Measurement and analysis," *American Sociological Review*, 28: 253–64

Dahl, R.A. (1971) *Polyarchy*, New Haven, CT: Yale University Press.

Dahrendorf, R. (1997) *After 1989: Morals, revolution and civil society*, Basingstoke: Macmillan.

Danaher, K. (1994) *50 Years Is Enough: The case against the World Bank and the International Monetary Fund*, Boston, MA: South End Press.

David, G. (2014) "The Paradox of Patronage and the People's Sovereignty," in A. Piliavsky (ed.) *Patronage as Politics in South Asia*, Cambridge: Cambridge University Press, pp. 125–54.

Dean, M. (1999) *Governmentality: Power and rule in modern society*, London: Sage.

Deaton, B. (1997) *Global Social Policy: International organizations and the future of welfare*, London: Sage.

Deaton, B. (2004) "Measuring Poverty," Princeton Research Program in Development Studies, Working Paper, No. 230, Princeton University.

Deepa, N.P. and Elena, E.G. (2007) *Ending Poverty in South Asia*, Washington, DC: World Bank Publications.

Desai, V. and Potter, R.B. (2002) *The Companion to Development Studies*, London: Arnold.

DeVotta, N. (2002) "Illiberalism and Ethnic Conflict in Sri Lanka," *Journal of Democracy*, 13(1): 84–98.

Diamond, L. (1999) *Developing Democracy: Toward consolidation*, Baltimore, MD: The Johns Hopkins University Press.

Dijkstra, A.G. (2002) "The Effectiveness of Policy Conditionality: Eight country experiences," *Development and Change*, 33(2): 307–34.

Dixit, A. (1996) *The Making of Economic Policy: A transaction cost of politics approach*, Cambridge, MA: MIT Press.

Doornbos, M. (2006) *Global Forces and State Restructuring: Dynamics of state formation and collapse*, Basingstoke: Palgrave Macmillan.

Dougherty, J. and Pfaltzgraff, R. Jr. (1997) *Contending Theories of International Relations: A comprehensive survey*, New York: Longman.

Dreze, J. and Sen, A. (eds) (1998) *Indian Development: Selected regional perspectives*, Delhi: Oxford University Press.

Dushni, W. (2011) "An Uncertain Future for Policy Reforms in South Asia," *East Asia Forum*, 20 October, Canberra: ANU.

Easterly, W. (2000) "The Effect of IMF and World Bank Programmes on Poverty," Policy Research Working Paper, No. 2517, Washington, DC: The World Bank.

Easterly, W. (2002a) *The Elusive Quest for Growth: Economists: Adventures and misadventures in the topics*, Cambridge, MA: MIT Press.

Easterly, W. (2002b) "Inequality does Cause Underdevelopment: New evidence from commodity endowments, middle class share, and other determinants of per capita income," Center for Global Development: Working Paper, No. 1, January.

Easterly, W. (2006) *Multilateral Development Banks: Promoting effectiveness and fighting corruption*, Washington, DC: Senate Committee on Foreign Relations.

Eastwood, R. and Lipton, M. (2001) "Pro-Poor Growth and Poverty Reduction," paper presented at Asia and Pacific Forum on "Poverty: Reforming Policies and Institutions for Poverty Reduction," Manila: Asian Development Bank.

Eggertson, T. (1990) *Economic Behavior and Institutions*, New York: Cambridge University Press.

Eisenhardt, K.M. (1989) "Building Theories from Case Study Research," *Academy of Management Review*, 1(4): 532–50.

Ekeh, P. (1971) "Colonialism and the Two Publics," *Comparative Studies in Society and History*, 17(1): 91–112.

Elkins, D.J. and Simeon, R.E.B. (1979) "A Cause in Search of Its Effect, or What Does Political Culture Explain?" *Comparative Politics*, 11(1): 127–45.

Emmerson, D.K. (1995) "Singapore and the 'Asian Values' Debate," *Journal of Democracy*, October, 6(4): 95–105.

Erzo, F. and Luttmer, P. (2001) "Measuring Poverty Dynamics and Inequality in Transitional Economies: Disentangling real events from noisy data," Policy Research Working Paper, No. WPS 2457, 28 February, Washington, DC: The World Bank.

European Commission (2003) "Country Strategic Paper, Maldives 2003–2006," 10 October. Available at: http://eeas.europa.eu/maldives/csp/03_06.pdf (accessed 15 May 2014).

Evans, P. (1995) *Embedded Autonomy*, Princeton, NJ: Princeton University Press.

Eyben, R. (2004) *Relationships Matter for Supporting Change in Favor of Poor People: Lessons for change in policy and organizations*, No. 8, Brighton: Institute of Development Studies, pp. 21–36.

Feldman, S. (2000) "NGOs and Civil Society: (UN) Stated Contradictions," in J. Rounaq (ed.) *Bangladesh: Promise and performance*, London: Zed Books, pp. 219–46.

Ferguson, J. (2001a) "Transnational Topographies of Power: Beyond 'the state' and 'civil society' in the study of African politics," in G. Schwab, T. Vincent, and D. Nugent (eds) *The Anthropology of Politics*, New York: Blackwell.

Ferguson, J. (2001b) "Global Disconnect: Abjection and the aftermath of modernism," in R. Rosaldo and J. Xavier Inda (eds) *The Anthropology of Globalization*, Malden, MA: Blackwell, pp. 136–54.

Ferguson, N. (2004) *Empire: The rise and demise of the British world order and the lessons for global power*, New York: Basic Books.

Ferguson, N. (2009) *The Ascent of Money: A Financial History of the World*, New York: Penguin, p. 284.

Fery, B.S. and Schneider, F. (1986) "Competing Models of International Lending Activity," *Journal of Development Economics*, 20(1): 225–45.

Feyzioglu, T., Swaroop, V. and Zhu, M. (1998) "A Panel Data Analysis of the Fungibility of Foreign Aid," *World Bank Economic Review*, 74(1): 258–65.

Flyvbjerg, B. (2001) *Making Social Science Matter: Why social inquiry fails and how it can succeed again*, Cambridge: Cambridge University Press.

Fowler, J.W. (1981) *Stages of Faith: The psychology of human development and the quest for meaning*, San Francisco, CA: Harper & Row.

Fowler, J.W. (1996) *Faithful Change: The personal and public challenges of postmodern life*, Nashville, TN: Abingdon Press.

Fox, J. (1999) "The Inter-Dependence Between Citizen Participation and Institutional Accountability: Lessons from Mexico's rural municipal funds," in P. Peisterk (ed.) *Thinking Out Loud: Innovative case studies on participation instruments*, Washington, DC: The World Bank.

Frankel, F.R. (1978) *India's Political Economy, 1947–77: The gradual revolution*, Princeton, NJ: Princeton University Press.

Friedlander, F. and Brown, L.D. (1974) "Organization Development," *Annual Review of Psychology*, 25: 313–41.

Friedman, M. (1958) "Foreign Economic Aid," *Yale Review*, 47(4): 501–16.

Friedman, S. and Reitzes, M. (2001) "Funding Freedom? Synthesis Report on the Impact of Foreign Political Aid to Civil Society Organisations in South Africa," Research Report, No. 85, Johannesburg: Centre for Policy Studies.

Fritzen, S. (1999) "Institutionalizing Participation: Lessons learnt and implications for strengthening Vietnam's national programs," final report for UNDP/UNCDF/CIDA Institutionalization of Participatory Planning Study, Hanoi: mimeo.

Fukuyama, F. (1996) *Trust: The social virtues and the creation of prosperity*, New York: Free Press.

Fung, A. and Wright, E.O. (2001) *Deepening Democracy: Innovations in empowered participatory governance*, London: Verso.

Ganguly, S. (2002) "India's Multiple Revolutions," *Journal of Democracy*, 13(1): 38–51

Gary, H. (1996) "Constituencies for Reform: Strategic approaches for donor-supported civic advocacy groups," USAID Program and Operations Assessment Report, No. 12 (PN-ABS-534), Washington, DC: USAID.

Gauri, V., and Galef, J.A. (2004) "NGOs in Bangladesh: Activities, resources, and governance," *World Development*, 33(12): 2045–65.

Gedam, R. (1993) *Economic Crisis and Political Disaster*, New Delhi: Heritage Publishers.

Gellner, E. (1994) *Conditions of Liberty, Civil Society and Its Rivals*, London: Hamish Hamilton.

George, S. (1990) *A Fate Worse than Debt*, New York: Weidenfeld.

Gerschenkron, A. (1962) *Economic Backwardness in Historical Perspective*, Cambridge, MA: Harvard University Press.

Ghani, E. (ed.) (2010) *The Poor Half Billion in South Asia: What is holding back lagging regions?* Oxford: Oxford University Press.

Gilbert, C.L., Powell, A. and Vines, D. (2000) "Positioning the World Bank," in C.L. Gilbert and D. Vines (eds) *The World Bank: Structure and policies*, Cambridge: Cambridge University Press, pp. 39–72.

Gill, G. (2002) *Democracy and Post-Communism*, London: Routledge.

Gill, S. and David, L. (1989) "Global Hegemony and the Structural Power of Capital," *International Studies Quarterly*, 33(1): 475–99.

Gillin, J.K. (1965) *Social Problems*, Bombay: Bombay Publisher.

Gilpin, R. (1987) *The Political Economy of International Relations*, Princeton, NJ: Princeton: University Press.

Giri, A.K. (2004) *Reflections and Mobilizations: Dialogues with movements and voluntary organizations*, New Delhi: Sage.

Giri, A.K. (2005) "Introduction, The Modern Prince and Modern Sage: Transforming power and freedom," special issue of *Asian Journal of Social Sciences*, 33(1): 1–3.

Glasius, M. and Kaldor, M. (eds) (2001) *Global Civil Society*, New York: Oxford University Press.

Goldin, I., Rogers, H. and Nicholas, S. (2002) "The Role and Effectiveness of Development Assistance: Lessons from World Bank experience," in *A Case for Aid: Building a consensus for development assistance*, Washington, DC: The World Bank, part 3.

Goodin, R.A. (1979) "The Development Rights Trade-off: Some unwarranted economic and political assumptions," *Universal Human Rights*, 1: 31–42.

Gordon, C. (1991) "Governmental Rationality: An introduction," in G. Burchell, C. Gordon and P. Miller (eds) *The Foucault Effect: Studies in governmentality*, Chicago, IL: The University of Chicago Press, pp. 1–5.

Gordon, W. (1994) "Democratization and Economic Reform in China," *The Australian Journal of Chinese Affairs*, 31: 79–90.

Gore, C. (2003) "The International Poverty Trap," *Development Policy Journal*, 3(1): 107–26.

Gosta, E.A. (1996a) *Welfare States in Transition: National adaptation in global economies*, London: Sage.

Gosta, E.A. (1996b) "Welfare States in Transition," *The Journal of Socio-Economics*, 28(5): 647–9.

Government of Maldives (2009) "Aneh Dhivehirajje: The strategic action plan national framework for development 2009–2013," 11 November. Available at: http://planning. gov.mv/en/images/stories/publications/strategic_action_plan/SAP-EN.pdf (accessed 17 May 2014).

Government of the People's Republic of Bangladesh (2004) *A National Strategy for Economic Growth: Poverty reduction and social development*, Report of Economic Relations Division, Dhaka: Ministry of Finance.

Greenwood, R. and Hinings, C.R. (1993) "Understanding Strategic Change: The contribution of archetypes," *Academy of Management Journal*, 1(36): 1052–81.

Grindle, M.S. (2004) "Good Enough Governance: Poverty reduction and reform in developing countries," *Governance: An International Journal of Policy, Administration, and Institutions*, 17(4): 525–48.

Groves, L. and Hinton, R. (eds) (2004) *Inclusive Aid: Changing power and relationship in international development*, London: Earthscan.

Gruhn, I.V. (1983) "The Re-colonization of Africa," *Africa Today*, 30(4): 37–48.

Gunner, M. (1955) "The Political Element in the Development of Economic Theory," *Political Science Quarterly*, September, 70(3): 439–40.

Gunther, R. and Diamond, L. (2001) "Types and Functions of Parties," in R. Gunther and L. Diamond (eds) *Political Parties and Democracy*, Baltimore, MD: The Johns Hopkins University Press.

Habermas, J. (1984) *The Philosophical Discourse of Modernity*, Cambridge: Polity Press.

Haddad, L. and Hoddonott, J. (1997) *Intra-Household Resource Allocation in Developing Countries: Models, methods and policy*, London: International Food Policy Research Institute and Johns Hopkins University Press.

Hall, M. and Young, T. (1997) *Confronting Leviathan: Mozambique since independence*, London: Hurst and Co.

Hall, R. and Jones, C. (1999) "Why Do Some Countries Produce So Much More Output per Worker than Others?", *Quarterly Journal of Economics*, 114: 83–116.

Hampshire, C. and MacLean, G. (2000) "Instituting and Projecting Human Security: A Canadian perspective," *Australian Journal of International Affairs*, 54(3): 269–76.

Hann, C. (1996) "Introduction: Political Society and Civil Anthropology," in C. Hann and E. Dunn (eds) *Civil Society: Challenging western models*, London: Routledge, pp. 1–26.

Haque, M.S. (2001) "The Diminishing Public-ness of Public Service under the Current Mode of Governance," *Public Administration Review*, 61: 65–82.

Haque, M.S. (2002) "The Changing Balance of Power Between the Government and NGOs in Bangladesh," *International Political Science Review*, 23(4): 413–37.

Hardt, M. and Negri, A. (2001) *Empire*, Cambridge, MA: Harvard University Press.

Hardt, M. and Negri, A. (2004) *Multitude: War and democracy in the age of empire*, New York: Penguin.

Harrison, G. (2001) "Post-Conditionality Politics and Administrative Reform: Reflections on the cases of Uganda and Tanzania," *Development and Change*, 2(32): 657–79.

Harriss, J. (2001) "Introduction: the Missing Link and the Anti-Politics Machine," in J. Harriss (ed.) *Depoliticizing Development: The World Bank and social capital*, New Delhi: Leftword, pp. 20–5.

Hashemi, S. (1995) "NGO Accountability in Bangladesh: Beneficiaries, donors and the state," in M. Edwards and D. Hulme (eds) *Non-Governmental Organizations-Performance and Accountability: Beyond the magic bullet*, London: Earthscan, pp. 103–10.

Hearn, J. (1999) *Foreign Aid, Democratization and Civil Society in Africa: A study of South Africa, Ghana and Uganda*, Brighton: Institute of Development Studies, Discussion Paper no. 368.

Heitzman, J. and Worden, R. (1989) *Bangladesh: A country study*, Washington, DC: GPO for the Library of Congress.

Heller, P. (2001) "Moving the State: The politics of democratic decentralization in Kerala, South Africa, and Porto Alegre," *Politics and Society*, 29(1): 131–63.

Herfkens, E. (2003) "Donors and Recipients," *Development Policy Journal*, 3(1): 101–6.

Herman, B. (2004) "How Well Do Measurements of an Enabling Environment for Development Stand Up?", paper prepared for the XVIII Technical Group of the Group of 24, Geneva, March 8–9.

Herman, E.S., and Chomsky, N. (1988) *Manufacturing Consent: The political economy of the mass media*, New York: Pantheon Books.

Hewlett, S.A. (1967) "Human Rights and Economic Inequalities: Tradeoffs in historical perspectives," *Political Science Quarterly*, 94: 453–73.

Hilderbrand, M.E. and Grindle, M.S. (1997) *Building Sustainable Capacity in the Public Sector: What can be done? Getting good government: Capacity building in the public sectors of developing countries*, Boston, MA: Harvard Institute for International Development.

Hirst, P. (2000) "Democracy and Governance," in J. Pierre (ed.) *Debating Governance*, Oxford: Oxford University Press, pp. 13–35.

Hobley, M. (2003) "Power, Voice and Creating Space: Analysis of local level power relations," report prepared for the Department for International Development, British High Commission, Dhaka, January.

Hofstede, G. (1991) *Cultures and Organization: Software of the mind*, New York: McGraw-Hill.

Hood, C. (1991) "A Public Management for All Seasons?", *Public Administration*, 69(1): 3–19.

Hossain, A. (2006) "The Changing Local Rural Power Structure: The elite and NGOs in Bangladesh," *Journal of Health Management*, 8(2): 229–50.

Hossain, M. (2003) "Development Through Democratization and Decentralization: The Case of Bangladesh," *South Asia: Journal of South Asian Studies*, 26(3): 297–308.

Hoven, R.V. (2000) "Assessing Aid and Global Governance: Why poverty and redistribution objectives matter," *Employment Paper*, Geneva: International Labor Organization.

Howell, J. (2000) "Making Civil Society From Outside: Challenges for donors," *European Journal of Development Research*, 12(1): 3–32.

Howell, J. and Pearce, J. (2001) *Civil Society and Development: Exploring a complex relationship*, Boulder, CO: Lynne Rienner.

Hulme, D. (2003) "Thinking 'Small' and the Understanding of Poverty: Maymana and Mofizul's story," Working Paper, No. 22, Manchester: Chronic Poverty Research Centre.

Huntington, S.P. (1968) *Political Order in Changing Societies*, New Haven, CT: Yale University Press.

Huntington, S.P. (1993) "The Clash of Civilizations," *Foreign Affairs*, 72(3): 22–49.

Hye, M.A. (2004) *Impact of Globalization on Labor in South Asia: An explorative study*, Dhaka: BATU-SAARC Sub Regional Secretariat.

International Monetary Fund (2003) "Aligning the Poverty Reduction and Growth Facility (PRGF) and the Poverty Reduction Strategy Paper (PRSP) Approach: Issues and operations," SM/03/94, and Corr. 1. Washington, DC: IMF.

International Monetary Fund and World Bank (2001a) "Guidelines for Joint Staff Assessment of Poverty," Reduction Strategy Paper, 18 April, Washington, DC: The World Bank.

International Monetary Fund and World Bank (2001b) *Poverty Reduction Strategy Paper*, Washington, DC: The World Bank.

Jackson, R.H. (1987) "Quasi-States, Dual Regimes, and Neo-classical Theory: International jurisprudence and the third world," *International Organization*, 41(4).

Jackson, R.H. (1991) *Quasi-States: Sovereignty, international relations and the third world*, Cambridge: Cambridge University Press.

Jackson, R.H. and Rosberg, C.G. (1986) "Why Africa's Weak States Persist," in A. Kohli (ed.) *The State and Development in the Third World*, Princeton, NJ: Princeton University Press, pp. 259–82.

Jalal, A. (1995) *Democracy and Authoritarianism in South Asia: A comparative and historical perspective*, Cambridge: Cambridge University Press.

James, H. (1998) "From Grand Motherliness to Governance: The evolution of IMF conditionality," *Finance and Development*, 35(4): 21–34.

Jean, J.B. (1996) "The End of the Nation State: The rise of regional economies," *Journal of Marketing*, January, 60(1): 120–2.

Jenina, C.M. and Shalmali, G. (2002) *Structural Adjustment in the Name of the Poor: The PRSP experience in the Lao PDR, Cambodia and Vietnam*, Hanoi: Government of Viet Nam.

Jenkins, R. (1999) *Democratic Politics and Economic Reform in India*, Cambridge: Cambridge University Press.

Joan, M.N. (1996) "Promoting Policy Reforms: The Twilight of Conditionality?", *World Development*, 24(9): 1551–9.

Jolly, R. (2004) *UN Contributions to Development Thinking and Practice*, Bloomington, IN: Indiana University Press.

Julius, O.I. (1992) "Surviving at the Margins: Africa and the new global order," *Current World Leaders*, December, 35(6): 1053–72.

Kabeer, N. (2003) "Making Rights Work for the Poor: Nijera Kori and the construction of 'collective capabilities' in rural bangladesh," Working Paper, No. 200, Brighton: Institute of Development Studies, University of Sussex.

Kabor, M.H. (2000) "Governance and Economy: Bangladesh perspectives," in H.A. Hye (ed.) *Governance: South Asian perspectives*, Dhaka: University Press Limited.

Kamal, A. (2000) "Democracy and Poverty: A missing link?", AAB paper, May.

Kanbur, R. (2000) "Aid, Conditionality and Debt in Africa," in F. Tarp (ed.) *Foreign Aid and Development*, London: Routledge.

Kanbur, R., Sandler, T. and Morrison, K. (1999) "The Future of Development Assistance: Common pools and common pool dilemma," Policy Essay, No. 25, Washington, DC: Overseas Development Council, pp. 409–22.

Kapur, D. and Richard, W. (2000) "Governance-Related Conditionality of the International Financial Institutions," G-24 Discussion Paper Series 6, New York and Geneva: UNCTAD.

Kaufman, D., Kraay, A. and Pablo, Z.L. (1999) "Governance Matters," *World Bank Policy Research*, Working Paper, No. 2196, Washington, DC: The World Bank.

Keane, J (1998) *Democracy and Civil Society*, London: Verso.

Key, E.J. (2000) "Civil Society and Good Governance: Relevance for Bangladesh," in H. A. Hye, (ed.) *Governance: South Asian perspectives*, Dhaka: Dhaka University Press.

Khan, A.S. (2004) *Assessing the Labor Rights and Interventions in Some Selected Sectors in Bangladesh*, Dhaka: MRDI.

Khan, M.M. (1997) "Political and Administration Corruption: Concepts, comparative experiences and Bangladesh case," Dhaka: Transparency International, Bangladesh chapter.

Khan, M.M. (2003) "Accountability of NGOs in Bangladesh," *Public Management Review*, 5(2): 268–77.

Khan, M.M. (2011) "The Political Settlement and Its Evolution in Bangladesh," Working Paper, School of Oriental and Asian Studies, London.

Khan, M.H., Riley, T. and Wescott, C. (2012) *Public–Private Partnerships in Bangladesh's Power Sector: Risks and opportunities*, Berlin: Springer.

Khawaza, M.U. (2007) "Trade Liberalization Induces Food Price Hike," *The New Age*, 22 October.

Kibria, R. (2001) "The Political Economy of Reform: Designing, initiating, and sustaining public sector reform in developing countries," Commonwealth Advanced Seminar, Wellington, New Zealand.

Killick, T. (1996) "Principals, Agents and the Limitations of BWI Conditionality," *World Economy*, 19(2): 211–29.

Killick, T. (1997) "Principal Agents and the Failings of Conditionality," *Journal of International Development*, 9(4): 483–96.

Killick, T. (1998) *Aid and the Political Economy of Policy Change*, London: Overseas Development Institute.

Kochhar, K., Kumar, U., Rajan, R., Subramanian, A. and Tokatlidis, I. (2006) "India's Pattern of Development: What happened, what follows?" Working Paper, No. WP/06/22, Washington, DC: International Monetary Fund.

Kohli, A. (1986) "Democracy and Development," in J.P. Lewis and V. Kallab (eds) *Development Strategies Reconsidered*, New Brunswick, NJ: Transaction Books, pp. 153–82.

Kohli, A. (1990) *Democracy and Discontent: India's Growing Crisis of Governability*, Cambridge: Cambridge University Press.

Kothari, R. (1971) *The Political Economy of Development*, Bombay: Orient Longman.

Krasner, S.D. (1995) "Compromising Westphalia," *International Security*, 20(3): 115–51.

Krasner, S.D. (2001) "Rethinking the Sovereign State Model," *Review of International Studies*, 27: 17–42.

Krueger, A., Michalopoulos, C. and Ruttan, V. (1989) *Aid and Development*, Baltimore, MD: The Johns Hopkins University Press.

Kumar, K. (2001) *Revolutionary Ideas and Ideals*, Minneapolis, MN: University of Minnesota Press.

Laking, R. (2002) *Assessing the Governance-Development Relationship*, Wellington: Victoria University.

Lancaster, C. (2000) *Transforming Foreign Aid: United States assistance in the 21st century*, Washington, DC: Institute for International Economics.

Larmour, P. (2002) "Conditionality, Coercion and Other Forms of 'Power': International financial institutions in the Pacific," *Public Administration and Development*, 22(1): 249–60.

Lawrence, L. (1979) *Bangladesh: The unified revolution*, London: Zed Books.

Lefebvre, H. (1974) *La production de l'espace*, Paris: Anthropos.

Lefebvre, H. (1991) *The Production of Space*, trans. D. Nicholson-Smith, Oxford: Blackwell.

Lefebvre, H. (2001) "Comments on a New State Form," trans. V. Johnson and N. Brenner, *Antipode*, 33(5): 769–82.

Leftwitch, A. (1996) *Democracy and Development: Theory and practice*, Cambridge: Polity Press.

Lewis, D. (2004) "On the Difficulty of Studying 'Civil Society': Reflections on NGOs, state and democracy in Bangladesh," *Contributions to Indian Sociology*, 38(3): 299–322.

Lewis, D.J. (1996) "Corruption in Bangladesh: Discourse, judgments and modalities," CDS Occasional Paper, No. 5, Bath: Centre for Development Studies, University of Bath.

Linz, J.J. (1978) "The Breakdown of Democratic Regimes: Crisis, breakdown and re-equilibration," in J.J. Linz and A. Stepan (eds) *The Breakdown of Democratic Regimes*, Baltimore, MD: The Johns Hopkins University Press, pp. 3–24.

Lofchie, M.J. (1989) "Reflections on Structural Adjustment," in *Beyond Autocracy in Africa, Inaugural Seminar of the African Governance Programme*, Atlanta, GA: The Carter Centre, Emory University, pp. 121–5.

Ludden, D. (1992) "India's Development Regime," in N. Dirks (ed.) *Colonialism and Culture*, Ann Arbor, MI: University of Michigan Press, pp. 247–87.

Ludden, D. (2003) "Maps in the Mind and the Mobility of Asia," *Journal of Asian Studies*, 3 November, 62: 1057–78.

Ludden, D. (ed.) (2005) 'Preface," in D. Ludden, *Agricultural Production and South Asian History*, 2nd edn, Delhi: Oxford University Press, pp. 7–24.

Mafeje, A. (2001) "Anthropology in Post-Independence Africa: End of an era and the problem of self-redefinition," in A. Mafeje (ed.) *African Social Scientists: Reflection*, Part 1, Nairobi: Heinrich Böll Foundation, pp. 28–74.

Mahajan, G. (1999) "Civil Society and its Avatars: What happened to freedom and democracy?", *Economic and Political Weekly*, 34: 1188–96.

Mahar, C. and Wilkes. C. (eds) (n.d.) *An Introduction to the Work of Pierre Bourdieu*, Basingstoke: Macmillan.

Malaluan, G.J. and Shalmali, G. (2002) *Structural Adjustment in the Name of the Poor: The PRSP experience in the Lao PDR*, Cambodia and Vietnam, Hanoi: Government of Viet Nam.

Malkani, K.R. (1993) *The Politics of Ayodhya and Hindu-Muslim Relations*, Delhi: Har-Anand Publications.

Mallick, R. (1993) *Development Policy of a Communist Government: West Bengal since 1977*, Cambridge: Cambridge University Press.

Mamdani, M. (1996) *Citizen and Subject: Contemporary Africa and the legacy of late colonialism*, Princeton, NJ: Princeton University Press.

Mark, M. (2012) "Maldives President Resigns After Weeks of Protest," *Los Angeles Times*, 7 February.

Martin, L. and Simmons, B. (1998) "Theories and Empirical Studies of International Institutions," *International Organization*, 52(4): 729–57.

Martin, M. (2004) "Assessing the HIPC Initiative: The key policy debates," in *HIPC Debt Relief: Myths and reality*, February, The Hague: FONDAD.

Martinussen, J. (1997) *Society, State and Market: A guide to competing theories of development*, London: Zed Books.

Matin. I. and Hulme, D. (2003) "Programmes for the Poorest: Learning from the IGVGD program in Bangladesh," *World Development*, 31(3): 647–65.

Mauro, P. (1995) "Corruption and Growth," *Quarterly Journal of Economics*, 110: 628–44.

Mayntz, R. (1998) "New Challenges to Governance Theory," Jean Monet Chair Papers, No. 50, Florence: European University Institute.

McArthur, J. and Sachs, J. (2003) "A Millennium Development Strategy for Achieving Poverty Alleviation and Economic Growth," Background Paper for Taskforce 1, Millennium Development Project.

McCord, W. (1965) *The Springtime of Freedom*, New York: Oxford University Press.

McCourt, W. and Minogue, M. (2001) *The Internalization of Public Management: Reinventing the third world state*, Cheltenham: Edward Elgar.

McGillivary, M. (1989) "The Allocation of aid among Developing Countries: A multi-donor analysis using a per capita aid index," *World Development*, 17(4): 561–8.

McIlwaine, C. (1998) "Civil Society and Development Geography," *Progress in Human Geography*, 22(3): 415–24.

McIlwaine, C. and Caroline, M. (2000) *Urban Poor: Perceptions of violence and exclusion in Colombia*, Washington, DC: The World Bank.

McKinley, T. (2001) *Macroeconomic Policy, Growth and Poverty Reduction*, New York: Palgrave Macmillan.

Mearsheimer, J. (1995) "The False Promise of International Institutions," *International Security*, 19(1): 5–49.

Meier, G.M. (1995) *Leading Issues in Economic Development*, 6th edn, New York: Oxford University Press.

Meizels, A. and Nissanke, M.K. (1984) "Motivations for Aid to Developing Countries," *World Development*, 12(1): 879–900.

Meyer, C.A. (1992) "The Irony of Donor Efforts to Build Institutions: A case study from the Dominican Republic," *Journal of Institutional and Theoretical Economics*, 148: 628–44.

Michael, A. (2003) "Modernization Theory and the American Revival of the Scientific and Technological Standards of Social Achievement and Human Worth," in C.E. David, N. Gilman, H.H. Mark, and M.E. Latham (eds) *Staging Growth: Modernization, Development and the Global Cold War*, Amherst, MA: University of Massachusetts Press, pp. 25–45.

Midgley, J. (1995) *Social Development: The development perspective in social welfare*, London: Sage.

Midgley, J. (1997) *Social Welfare in a Global Context*, Thousand Oaks, CA: Sage Publications.

Midgley, J. (2003) "Social Development: The intellectual heritage," *Journal of International Development*, Part 2, 15(1): 831–44.

Miller, C. and Razavi, S. (1998) "Gender Analysis: Alternative paradigms," *Gender in Development Monograph Series*, No. 6, New York: UNDP.

Ministry of Finance (2005) *Economic Review*, Dhaka: The Government of Bangladesh.

Ministry of Finance (2007) *Economic Review*, Dhaka: The Government of Bangladesh.

Minogue, M. (2000) "Should Flawed Models of Public Management Be Exported? Issues and practices," Public Policy and Management Working Paper Series, No. 15, Manchester: Institute for Development Policy and Management, University of Manchester.

Minogue, M., Polidano, C. and Hulme, D. (1998) *Beyond the New Public Management: Changing ideas and practices in governance*, Cheltenham: Edward Elgar.

Mitchell, D. (1999) *Governmentality: Power and rule in modern society*, London: Sage, pp. 4–14.

Mitra, S.K. (1990) "Between Transaction and Transcendence: The state and the institutionalization of power in India," in S.K. Mitra (ed.) *The Post-Colonial State in Asia: The dialectics of politics and culture*, Hemel-Hempstead: Harvester, pp. 179–90.

Mitra, S.K. (1995) "The Rational Politics of Cultural Nationalism: Sub-National movements of South Asia in comparative perspective," *British Journal of Political Science*, 25(1): 153–77.

Mitra, S.K. (1999) "Effects of Institutional Arrangements on Political Stability in South Asia," *Annual Review of Political Science*, 2: 405–28.

Mokbul, M., Ahmed, M. and Nahar, L. (2000) *Donors, NGOs, the State and their Clients in Bangladesh*, Dhaka: University Press Limited.

Monem, M. (2002) "Good Governance in Bangladesh: The unheard voices," paper presented at the international conference "Towards a New Political Economy of Development: Globalization and governance," University of Sheffield, 4–6 July.

Monshipouri, M. (1997) "State Prerogatives, Civil Society and Liberalization: The paradoxes of the late twentieth-century in the third world," *Ethics and International Affairs*, 11(1): 27–42.

Montesquieu, Baron de (1900) *The Spirit of Laws*, vol. 1, trans. T. Nugent, New York: The Colonial Press.

Moore, M. (1996) "Is Democracy Rooted in Material Prosperity?" in R. Luckman and G. White (eds) *Democratization in the South: The jagged wave*, Manchester: Manchester University Press, pp. 37–68.

Moore, M. (1998) "Death Without Taxes: Democracy, state capacity and aid dependence in the fourth world," in M. Robinson and G. White (eds) *The Democratic Developmental State: Politics and institutional design*, Oxford Studies in Democratization, Oxford: Oxford University Press, pp. 1–20.

Moore, M. (2000) "Progressive Realism: Improving governance in the global south," Position Papers, October, Sussex: Institute of Development Studies.

Moore, M. (2001) "Political Underdevelopment: What causes bad governance?" *Public Management Review*, 1(3): 385–418.

Moore, M. (2003a) "Declining to Learn from the East: The World Bank on "Governance and Development'," *IDS Bulletin*, 24(1): 39–50.

Moore, M. (2003b) "How Governance Affects Poverty," in P.P. Houtzager and M. Moore (eds) *Changing Paths: International development and the new politics of inclusion*, Ann Arbor, MI: University of Michigan Press, pp. 167–204.

Morgenthau, H.J. (1946) *Scientific Man versus Power Politics*, Chicago, IL: University of Chicago Press.

Morgenthau, H.J. ([1948] 1985) *Politics Among Nations: The struggle for power and peace*, 6th edn, rev. K.W. Thompson, New York: McGraw-Hill.

Morrissey, O. and Osei, R. (2004) "Capital Flows to Developing Countries: Trends, volatility and policy implications," *IDS Bulletin*, 35.

Moser, C. (2001) "Insecurity and Social Protection: Has the World Bank got it right?", *Journal of International Development*, 13(1): 360–9.

Mosley, P. (1987) *Overseas Aid: Its defense and reform*, Brighton: Harvester Wheatsheaf.

Mosley, P., Hudson, J. and Horrel, S. (1987) "Aid, the Public Sector and the Market in Less Developed Countries," *Economic Journal*, 97: 616–41.

Mosley, P., Hudson, J. and Verschoor, A. (2004) "Aid and Poverty Reduction and the 'New Conditionality'," *Economic Journal*, 1(14): 217–43.

Mustafa, K. (2003) "The Good Governance Agenda and State Failure: A recipe for more policy failures?" paper presented to DESTIN students as part of the Friday Visiting Lecture Series, March 21.

Myrdal, G. (1944) *An American Dilemma: The negro problem and modern democracy*, New York: Harper & Row.

Myrdal, G. (1968) *Asian Drama: An enquiry into poverty of nations*, vol. 1, New York: Pantheon.

Nabi, I. and Devarajan, S. (2006) "Economic Growth in South Asia: Promising, un-equalizing, … sustainable?", *Economic and Political Weekly*, August, XLI, No. 33.

Naim, M. (1996) "From Supplicants to Shareholders: Developing countries and the World Bank," in G.K. Helleiner (ed.) *The International Monetary and Financial System*, London: Macmillan, pp. 293–323.

Nelson, P. (2000) "Whose Civil Society? Whose Governance? Decision-Making and Practice in the New Agenda at the Inter-American Development Bank and the World Bank," *Global Governance*, 6(4): 405–43.

Neumayer, E. (2003) *The Pattern of Aid Giving: The impact of good governance on development assistance*, New York: Routledge.

North, D.C. (1991) "Institutions," *Journal of Economic Perspectives*, 5(1): 97–112.

North, D.C. (1995) "The New Institutional Economics and Third World Development," in J. Harriss *et al.* (eds) *The New Institutional Economics and Third World Development*, New York: Routledge, pp. 17–26.

North, D.C., Wallis, J.J., and Weingast, B.R. (2009) *Violence and Social Orders: A conceptual framework for interpreting recorded human history*, Cambridge: Cambridge University Press.

Nunnally, J.C. and Bernstein, I.H. (2004) *Psychometric Theory*, New York: McGraw-Hill.

Nurkse, R. (1953) *The Problem of Capital Formation in Underdeveloped Countries*, Oxford: Basil Blackwell.

O'Donnell, G. (1993) "The Browning of Latin America," *New Perspectives Quarterly*, October, pp. 50–3.

Offe, C. (1984) "Thesis on Theory of the State," in C. Offe (ed.) *Contradictions of the Welfare State*, Cambridge, MA: MIT Press, pp. 119–29.

Offe, C. (1986) "The Utopia of the Zero-Option Modernity and Modernization as Normative Political Criteria," *Praxis International*, 7: 1–24.

Offe, C. (1987) "Democracy against the Welfare State? Structural Foundations of Neo-Conservative Political Opportunities," *Political Theory*, 15(4): 501–37.

Olson, G.R. (2000) "Promotion of Democracy as a Foreign Policy Instrument of Europe: Limits to international idealism," *Democratization*, 7(2): 142–67.

Olufemi, V. (1994) "The Politics of Global Marginalization," *Journal of African and Asian Studies*, 29(3): 186–204.

Ostrom, E. (1990) *Governing the Commons, The Evolution of Institutions for Collective Action*, Cambridge: Cambridge University Press.

Ostrom, E. (1997) "Investing in Capital, Institutions, and Incentives," in C. Christopher (ed.) *Institutions and Economic Development: Growth and governance in less developed and post-socialist countries*, Baltimore, MD: The Johns Hopkins University Press, pp. 153–81.

Ostrom, E. (1999) *Self-Governance and Forest Resources*, Bangor, Indonesia: Center for International Forestry Research.

Parnini, S.N. (2006) "Civil Society and Good Governance in Bangladesh," *Asian Journal of Political Science*, December, 14(2): 189–211.

Parnini, S.N. and Redzuan, M.O. (2013) "Democratic Consolidation and Credibility of Governance Institutions in Bangladesh," *Journal of Asian and African Studies*, 49(4).

Pimbert, M. (2000) *Transforming Bureaucracies: Institutional participation and people centred process in natural resource management*, London: International Institute for Environment and Development (IIED).

Poggi, G. (1978) *The Development of the Modern State: A sociological introduction*, London: Hutchison.

Pollitt, C. and Greet, B. (2000) *Public Management Reform: A comparative analysis*, Oxford: Oxford University Press.

Powell, C. (2002) "Making Sustainable Development Work: Governance, finance, and public-private cooperation," remarks at State Department Conference, Meridian.

Punit, A.E. (1982) *Profile of Poverty in India*, Delhi: B.R. Publishing Corporation.

Putnam, R.D. (2000) *Bowling Alone: The collapse and revival of American community*, New York: Simon & Schuster.

Putnam, R.D., Leonardi, R. and Nunnally, R.Y. (1993) *Making Democracy Work*, Princeton, NJ: Princeton University Press.

Pye, L.W. (1985) *Asian Power and Politics*, Cambridge, MA: Harvard University Press.

Rafi, M. and Chowdhuri, A.M.R. (2001) "Human Rights and Religious Blacklash: The experience of a Bangladesh NGOs," *Development in Practice*, 10(1): 19–30, reprinted in Deborath, E. (ed.) (2002) *Development and Advocacy: Selected essays from development in practice*, Oxford: Oxfam, pp. 47–61.

Rahman, A. and Razzaque, A. (2000) "On Reaching the Hardcore Poor: Some evidence on social exclusion in NGOs programmes," *Bangladesh Development Studies*, 26(1): 1–35.

Rahman, A., Wadood, S.N. and Mohammed, A.E. (2000) "Civil Society and Governance," in H.A. Hye (ed.) *Governance: South Asian perspectives*, Dhaka: University Press Limited, pp. 23–42.

Rahman, M.H. (1978) *Emergence of a New Nation in a Multi-Polar World: Bangladesh*, Washington, DC: University Press of America.

Rahman, M.H. (2001) *Models and Myths of Decentralization: The Bangladesh experience*, New Delhi: South Asian Publishers.

Rahman, S. (2000) "Governance and Local Government System," in H.A. Hye (ed.) *Governance: South Asian perspectives*, Dhaka: University Press Limited, pp. 231–47.

Raju, M.R. (1998) "Panchayat Raj in Kerala: Problems and prospects," *Kurukshetra*, April, Kerala: India, pp. 70–1.

Ranis, G. (2004) "The Evolution of Development Thinking: Theory and policy," paper presented at the Annual World Bank Conference on Development Economics, 3–4 May.

Ranis, G., Francis, S., and Alejandro, R. (2000) "Economic Growth and Human Development," *World Development*, 28(2): 197–219.

Ravallion, M. (2002) "Have We Already Met the Millennium Development Goals for Poverty? Surjit Bhalla's Imagine, There's No Country," *Economic and Political Weekly*, November, pp. 16–22.

Rehman, S. (1982) *The Crisis of External Dependence: The political economy of foreign aid to Bangladesh*, Dhaka: Centre for Policy Dialogue.

Rehman, S. (1990) *From Aid Dependence to Self-Reliance: Development options for Bangladesh*, Dhaka: Centre for Policy Dialogue.

Rehman, S. (2003a) *Bangladesh: Problems of governance*, Delhi: Konark Publishers Pvt. Ltd.

Rehman, S. (2003b) *Revisiting Foreign Aid: An independent review of Bangladesh's development*, Dhaka: Centre for Policy Dialogue.

Rehman, S. (2010) *Challenging the Injustice of Poverty: Agendas for inclusive development in South Asia*, London: SAGE.

Rhodes, R.A.W. (1997) *Understanding Governance: Policy networks, governance, reflexivity and accountability*, Buckingham and Philadelphia, PA: Open University Press.

Rob, C.M. (2000) *Participation in Poverty Reduction Papers*, Africa Department, Washington, DC: International Monetary Fund, August.

Robison, R. (2002) "What Sort of Democracy? Predatory and Neo-Liberal Agendas in Indonesia," in C. Kinnvall and K. Jönsson (eds) *Globalization and Democratization in Asia: The construction of identity*, London: Routledge, pp. 92–113.

Rodgers, G. (1995) "What is Special About a Social Exclusion Approach?" in G. Rodgers, C. Gore, and J.B. Figueiredo (eds) *Social Exclusion: Rhetoric, reality, responses. A contribution to the world summit for social development*, Geneva: International Institute for Labor Studies, International Labor Organization, pp. 43–55.

Rodrik, D. (2000) "Governance of Economic Globalization," in J.S. Nye and J.D. Donahue (eds) *Governance in a Globalizing World*, Washington, DC: Brookings Institution Press, pp. 347–65.

Rodrik, D. (2001) "Institutions, Integration, and Geography: In search of the deep determinants of economic growth," unpublished paper, Harvard University.

Rodrik, D. (2005) "If Rich Countries Really Cared About Development." Available at: www.ictsd.org/dlogue/2005–7-01/Docs/RODRIK-BRIDSALL_SUBRAMANIAN_what-rich-can-do_April2005.pdf.

Rooy, V.A. (2004) *Global Legitimacy Game: Civil society, globalization and protest*, New York: Palgrave Macmillan.

Rooy, V.A. and Robinson, F. (1998) "Out of the Ivory Tower: Civil society assistance and the aid system," in V.A. Rooy (ed.) *Civil Society and the Aid Industry*, London: Earthscan, pp. 253–69.

Rosenau, J. and Czempiel, E.-O. (1992) "Governance, Order and Change in World Politics," in J. Rosenau and E.-O. Czempiel (eds) *Governance Without Government: Order and change in world politics*, Cambridge: Cambridge University Press, pp. 1–29.

Rosenstein, R.P.N. (1943) "Problems of Industrialization of Eastern and Southeastern Europe," *Economic Journal*, 53: 202–11.

Royal Government of Bhutan (2007) *Organisational Development (OD): Toward excellence in the civil service*, Bhutan: Royal Civil Service Commission.

Rudolph, S.H. (2000) "Civil Society and the Realm of Freedom," *Economic and Political Weekly*, 13–19 May, 35(20): 1762–9.

Sachs, J. (2005) *Investing in Development: A practical plan to achieve the millennium development goals*, London: Earthscan.

Sachs, J. (2006) *The End of Poverty: Economic possibilities for our time*, New York: Penguin.

Sachs, J.D., McArthur, J.W., Schmidt-Traub, G., Kruk, M., Bahadur, C., Faye, M. and McCord, G. (2004) *Ending Africa's Poverty Trap*, Brookings Papers on Economic Activity 1, Washington, DC: The Brookings Institution.

Salamon, L.M. and Anheirer, H.K. (1998) "Social Origins of Civil Society: Explaining the non-profit sector cross-nationality," *Voluntas*, 9: 213–48.

Santarelli, E. and Figini, P. (2003) "Does Globalization Reduce Poverty? Some Empirical Evidence for Developing Countries," paper prepared for UNU WIDER Conference, "Inequality, Poverty and Human Well-being," Helsinki, 30–1 May.

Santiso, C. (2001) "Good Governance and Aid Effectiveness: The World Bank and conditionality," *The Georgetown Public Policy Review*, 7(1): 1–22.

SAPRIN (Structural Adjustment Participatory Review International Network) (2004) "The Policy Roots of Economic Crisis and Poverty: A multi-country participatory assessment of structural adjustment." Available at: www.saprin.org/global_rpt.html.

Sassoon, B. (1996) *One Hundred Years of Socialism: The west european left in the twentieth century*, London: I. B. Tauris Publishers.

Schearer, S.B. (1995) "The Role of Philanthropy in International Development," paper presented at the Rockefeller Foundation Bellagio Conference, "Human Centered Development: The role of foundations, FLOs, and NGOs," 16–19 October, The Synergos Institute, New York.

Schiller, H.I. (1973) *The Mind Managers*, Boston, MA: Beacon Press.

Scott, J.C.S. (1998) *Like a State: How certain schemes to improve the human condition have failed*, New Haven, CT: Yale University Press.

Scott, W. (1965) "Field Methods in the Study of Organizations," in J. March (ed.) *Handbook of Organizations*, Chicago, IL: Rand McNally, pp. 261–304.

Seckinelgin, H. (2002) "Civil Society as a Metaphor for Western Liberalism," *Global Society*, 16(4): 357–76.

Seckinelgin, H., Lewis, D. and Glasius, M. (2004) *Exploring Civil Society: Political and cultural contexts*, London: Routledge.

Sen, A. (1973) "On the Development of Basic Income Indicators to Supplement the GNP Measure," *United Nations Economic Bulletin for Asia and the Far East*, 24(66).

Sen, A. (1983) "Poor Relatively Speaking," *Oxford Economic Papers*, 35: 153–69.

Sen, A. (1999a) "Global Justice: Beyond international equity," in I. Kaul, I. Grunberg and M. Stern (eds) *Global Public Goods: International cooperation in the 21st century*, New York: Oxford University Press, pp. 116–25.

Sen, A. (1999b) *Development as Freedom*, New York: Alfred A. Knopf.

Sen, G. (1997) "Globalization, Justice and Equity: A gender perspective," *Development*, 40(2): 21–6.

Shahiduzzaman, K. (2008) "PRSP-II: Is bumpy ride ahead?" *The Financial Express*, 28 August.

Shang-Jin, W. (1993) "How Taxing Is Corruption on International Investors?", Working Paper, Cambridge, MA: National Bureau of Economic Research.

Sharma, K.S. (2007) "Development Crisis and Governance in South Asia: Some issues and suggestions: A case of India," *Samaj Vigyan Shodh Patrika*, April–September, v(1): 19–29.

Shelley, M.R. (2000) "Governance and Administration: Challenge of new millennium," in H.A. Hasnat (ed.) *Governance: South Asian perspectives*, Dhaka: University Press Limited, pp. 165–83.

Shleifer, A. and Vishny, R.W. (1993) "Corruption," *The Quarterly Journal of Economics*, 108(3): 599–617.

Shotton, R. and Boex, J. (2002) "SPPD: Promoting policy on local governance and decentralization in Bangladesh," Technical Support Mission, Mission Report, BGD/02/002, New York: United Nations Capital Development Fund.

Siddiqui, K. (1996) *Towards Good Governance in Bangladesh: Fifty unpleasant essays*, Dhaka: University Press Limited, pp. 10–20.

Siddiqi, M.S. (2001) "Who Will Bear the Torch Tomorrow? Charismatic Leadership and Second-line Leaders in Development NGOs," International Working Paper 9, London: Centre for Civil Society, London School of Economics and Political Science.

Sirowy, L. and Inkeles, A. (1990) "The Effects of Democracy on Economic Growth and Inequality: A review," *Studies in Comparative International Development*, 25(1): 126–57.

Sisson, R. and Leo, E.R. (1990) *War and Secession: Pakistan, India, and the creation of Bangladesh*, Delhi: Vistaar Publications, pp. 131–42.

Sklair, R. (1991) "Developmental Democracy," in R. Sklar and C.S. Whitaker (eds) *African Politics and Problems of Development*, Boulder, CO: Lynne Rienner, pp. 285–312.

Sklair, R. (2000) *The Transnational Capitalist Class*, Malden, MA: Blackwell.

Smith, B. (2007) *Good Governance and Development*, Basingstoke: Palgrave Macmillan.

Sobhan, R. (1998a) "How Bad Governance Impedes Poverty Alleviation in Bangladesh," Technical Paper, No. 143, Paris: OECD Development Centre.

Sobhan, R. (1998b) "Overview," in R. Sobhan (ed.) *Crisis in Governance. A Review of Bangladesh's Development 1997*, Dhaka: Centre for Policy Dialogue and University Press Ltd, pp. 539–48.

Sobhan, R. (2000) "Reprioritizing South Asia's Development Agenda: Role of governance," in H.A. Hye (ed.) *Governance: South Asian perspectives*, Dhaka: University Press Limited, pp. 341–67.

Sobhan, R. (2003a) *Aid, Governance and Policy Ownership in Bangladesh*, Dhaka: Centre for Policy Dialogue.

Sobhan, R. (2003b) *Revisiting Foreign Aid: An independent review of Bangladesh's development*, Dhaka: Centre for Policy Dialogue.

Stiglitz, J.E. (2001) *Globalization and Discontents*, New York: W.W. Norton and Company.

Stokes, S. (ed.) (2001) *Public Support for Market Reforms in New Democracies*, New York: Cambridge University Press.

Stone, D. (2004) "Transfer Agents and Global Networks in the 'Trans-Nationalization' of Policy," *Journal of European Public Policy*, 11(3): 545–66.

Straub, S. (2000) "Empirical Determinants of Good Institutions: Do we know anything?", Working Paper, No. 423, Research Department, Washington, DC: Inter-American Development Bank.

Subhan, K.M. (2000) "Legislature and Good Governance," in H.A. Hye (ed.) *Governance: South Asian perspectives*, Dhaka: University Press Limited, pp. 69–83.

Sussanne, N. (1999) "Poverty and Self-help Among Small Farmers in Chad," *Applied Geography and Development*, 54: 56–68.

Svensson, J. (2003) "Why Conditional Aid Does Not Work and What Can Be Done About It?", *Journal of Development Economics*, 70(1): 381–402.

Szirmai, A. (2005) *Dynamics of Socio-Economic Development*, Cambridge: Cambridge University Press.

Talukdar, M. (2003) *Radical Left and the Emergence of Bangladesh*, Dhaka: Mowla Brothers.

Tan, T.Y. and Mizanur, M.R. (2013) *Diaspora Engagement and Development in South Asia*, Basingstoke: Palgrave Macmillan.

Tarp, F. (2006) "Foreign Aid," in L. Blume and S. Durlauf (eds) *The New Palgrave Dictionary of Economics*, 2nd edn, Basingstoke: Palgrave Macmillan, pp. 96–103.

Thomas, C. (2000) *Global Governance, Development and Human Security: The challenge of poverty and inequality*, London: Pluto Press.

Thornbecke, E. (2000) "The Evolution of the Development Doctrine and the Role of Foreign Aid, 1950–2000," in F. Tarp (ed.) *Foreign Aid and Development: Lessons learnt and directions for the future*, London: Routledge, pp. 17–47.

Tilly, C. (1975) "Reflections on the History of European State," in C. Tilly (ed.) *The Foundation National States in Western Europe*, Princeton, NJ: Princeton University Press, pp. 3–83.

Tilly, C. (1992) *Coercion, Capital, and European States, A.D. 990–1990*, Cambridge, MA: Blackwell.

Tocqueville, A. de ([1900] 1969) *Democracy in America*, trans. H. Keane, New York: The Colonial Press.

Townsend, P. (1979) *Poverty in the United Kingdom*, Harmondsworth: Penguin.

Townsend, P. and Abel Smith, B. (1965) *The Poor and the Poorest*, London: Bell.

Toye, J. (1999) "Nationalizing the Anti-Poverty Agenda," *IDS Bulletin*, 30(2).

Triandis, H.C. (1994) *Culture and Social Behavior*, New York: McGraw-Hill.

Trumbull, W.N. and Wall, H.J. (1994) "Estimating Aid-Allocation Criteria with Panel Data," *Economic Journal*, 104: 876–82.

Ugyel, L. (2013) "Dynamics of Public Sector Reforms in Bhutan: Interaction of values within a hybrid administration," Crawford School, Working Paper, 2 January, No. 13–01, Australian National University.

UNDP (2009) *Human Development Report, 2002: Deepening democracy in an integrated world*, New York: UNDP.

United Nations (2001) *UNDP, Human Development Report*, New York: UN.

United Nations Commission on Science and Technology for Development (1997) *An Assault on Poverty*, Ottawa: International Development Research Centre, p. xi.

Uphoff, N. (1995) "Why NGOs are Not a Third Sector: A sectoral analysis with same thoughts on accountability, sustainability and evaluation," in E. Michae and D. Hulme (eds) *Non-Governmental Organizations: Performance and accountability*, London: Earthscan, pp. 23–39.

Vandemoortele, J. (2003) "Are the MDGs Feasible?", *Development Policy Journal*, 3(1): 1–22.

Vandemoortele, J. (2004) "Are the MDGs Feasible?" in R. Black and H. White (eds) *Targeting Development: Critical perspectives on the millennium development goals*, London: Routledge, pp. 124–44.

Vandemoortele, J. and Roy, R. (2005) "Making Sense of MDG Costing," in F. Cheru and C. Bradford Jr. (eds) *The Millennium Development Goals: Rising the resources to tackle world poverty*, London: Zed Books, pp. 44–5.

Vylder, D.S. (1994) "Why Deficits Grow: A critical discussion of the impact of structural adjustment lending of the external account in low income countries," paper presented at conference, Stockholm.

Waelbroeck, J. (1998) "Half a Century of Development Economics: A review based on the handbook of development economics," *World Bank Economic Review*, 12(2): 323–52.

Walter, L.A. (1980) *Hegemony and Revolution*, Berkeley, CA: University of California Press.

Walter, L.A. (1988) "Gramsci and the Politics of Civil Society," *Praxis International*, Winter 1987/88, 7: 320–9.

Weber, M. (1964) *The Theory of Social and Economic Organization*, New York: Free Press.

Webster, N. (1992) *Panchayat Raj and the Decentralization of Development Planning in West Bengal: A case study*, Calcutta: K. P. Bagchi.

Weerakoon, D. (2011) "An Uncertain Future for Policy Reforms in South Asia," *East Asia Forum*, 20 October, Canberra: ANU.

White, G., Jude, H. and Xiaoyuan, S. (1996) *In Search for Civil Society*, IDS Development Studies Series, Oxford: Clarendon Press.

Wight, M. (1966) "Why is There No International Theory" in H. Butterfield and M. Wight (eds) *Diplomatic Investigations*, London: Allen and Unwin, pp. 17–34.

World Bank (1989) *Sub-Saharan Africa: From crisis to sustainable growth*, Washington, DC: The World Bank.

World Bank (2000) *Taming Leviathan: Reforming governance in Bangladesh*, Dhaka: The World Bank.

World Bank (2002) *Costing the 7th Millennium Development Goal: Ensure environmental sustainability*, Washington, DC: The World Bank.

World Bank (2006a) *Country Assistance Strategy for Bangladesh, Nepal, Pakistan, Nepal 2006–9*, Dhaka: The World Bank.

World Bank (2006b) *External Relations Division (ERD)*, Sher-e-Bangla Nagar, Dhaka, Bangladesh.

World Bank (2006c) *Bangladesh Country Assistance Strategy 2006–9*, Dhaka: The World Bank, pp. 29–41.

World Bank (2007) "Governance Matters VI: Governance indicators for 1996–2006," Washington, DC: The World Bank. Available at: http://info.worldbank.org/governance/wgi2007/

World Bank (2012) *World Development Report 2012: Agriculture for development*, Washington, DC: The World Bank.

World Economic Forum (2011) *Global Competitiveness Index*. Available at: www3.weforum.org.

Index

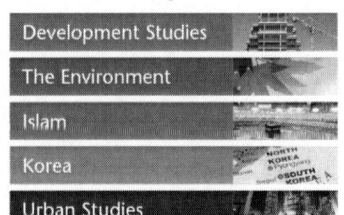